Spoken Natural Language Dialog Systems

Spoken Natural Language Dialog Systems: A Practical Approach

RONNIE W. SMITH

East Carolina University

D. RICHARD HIPP

Hipp, Wyrick and Company, Inc.

New York   Oxford

OXFORD UNIVERSITY PRESS

1994

Oxford University Press

Oxford   New York
Athens   Auckland   Bangkok   Bombay
Calcutta   Cape Town   Dar es Salaam   Delhi
Florence   Hong Kong   Istanbul   Karachi
Kuala Lumpur   Madras   Madrid   Melbourne
Mexico City   Nairobi   Paris   Singapore
Taipei   Tokyo   Toronto

and associated companies in
Berlin   Ibadan

Copyright © 1994 by Oxford University Press, Inc.

Published by Oxford University Press, Inc.,
200 Madison Avenue, New York, New York 10016

Oxford is a registered trademark of Oxford University Press

Library of Congress Cataloging-in-Publication Data
Smith, Ronnie W.
Spoken natural language dialog systems: a practical approach /
Ronnie W. Smith, D. Richard Hipp.
p.   cm.   Includes bibliographical references and index.
ISBN 0-19-509187-6
1. Speech processing systems.
2. Natural language processing (Computer science).
I. Hipp, D. Richard.   II. Title.
TK7895.S65S62 1994 006.4'54—dc20   94-17053

9 8 7 6 5 4 3 2 1

Printed in the United States of America
on acid-free paper

Acknowledgments

This book is based on research conducted primarily while the authors were graduate students at Duke University. Our deepest thanks goes to our dissertation advisor and good friend, Dr. Alan Biermann, who provided the vision, encouragement, and constructive questions and suggestions that made this research and book possible. Another project collaborator, Dr. Robert Rodman of North Carolina State University, provided many helpful comments about the directions this research should undertake. The scope of the experimental results obtained would not have been possible without the assistance of Dr. Ruth Day of Duke University who provided us with innumerable suggestions and comments concerning the experimental design.

We are also thankful to several fellow students for help. Most notably, Dania Egedi implemented a key portion of the system for resolving domain ambiguities and assisted in carrying out the experiment. Robin Gambill implemented the computer's utterance generator. We also had productive discussions about this research with Barry Koster, Al Nigrin, and Curry Guinn. We are also thankful to the volunteers who helped us test system prototypes at various times. These include Michael Brown, Dave Reed, Dania Egedi, Boyce Byerly, Curry Guinn, Wendy Heine, and Anna Harwell.

Development of the final manuscript has benefited greatly from the support and suggestions of our editor Don Jackson and from the tireless efforts of our copy-editor, Virginia Holman. Special thanks go to the Department of Computer Science at Duke University for its continued support of our work and to the Department of Mathematics at East Carolina University. We would also like to thank Dr. Steve Gordon, Curry Guinn, and Dr. Alan Biermann, who have provided useful suggestions about the book's content. Our appreciation also goes to the anonymous reviewers whose comments assisted us greatly in our final revisions. Any remaining errors are, of course, the sole responsibility of the authors.

Financial support for this work has come from National Science Foundation grants IRI-88-03802 and IRI-92-21842, Dr. Charles Putman of Duke University, and the Research and Creative Activity Committee of East Carolina University. Any opinions, findings, and conclusions or recommendations expressed in this material are those of the authors and do not necessarily reflect the views of the National Science Foundation.

Contents

Spoken Natural Language Dialog Systems

Chapter 1

Achieving Spoken Communication with Computers

The most sophisticated and efficient means of communication between humans is spoken *natural language* (NL). It is a rare circumstance when two people choose to communicate via another means when spoken natural language is possible. Ochsman and Chapanis [OC74] conducted a study involving two person teams solving various problems using restricted means of communication such as typewriting and video, typewriting only, handwriting and video, voice and video, voice only, etc. Their conclusion included the following statement.

> The single most important decision in the design of a telecommunications link should center around the inclusion of a voice channel. In the solution of factual real-world problems, little else seems to make a demonstrable difference.

Thus, it would seem desirable to develop computer systems that can also communicate with humans via spoken natural language dialog. Furthermore, recent reports from the research community in speech recognition [Adv93] indicate that accuracy levels in speaker-independent continuous speech recognition have reached a threshold where practical applications of spoken natural language are viable.

This book addresses the dialog issues that must be resolved in building effective spoken natural language dialog systems—systems where both the human and computer interact via spoken natural language.[1] We present an architecture for dialog processing for which an implementation in the equipment repair domain has been constructed that exhibits a number of behaviors required for efficient human-machine dialog. These behaviors include the following.

- Problem solving to achieve a target goal.

- The ability to carry out subdialogs to achieve appropriate subgoals and to pass control arbitrarily from one subdialog to another.

- The use of a user model to enable useful verbal exchanges and to inhibit unnecessary ones.

- The ability to use context dependent expectations to correct speech recognition and track user movement to new subdialogs.

- The ability to vary the task/dialog initiative from strongly computer controlled to strongly user controlled or somewhere in between.

---

[1] We do not preclude typewritten interaction, but we focus on phenomena of spoken interaction.

The ability to vary initiative is called *variable initiative* dialog, and represents a major advance in the utility of natural language systems. With such capability, a natural language system can effectively communicate with both task novices and experts as well as users with intermediate levels of expertise. Task novices require a computer-controlled dialog to lead them through the details. Task experts need occasional advice while pursuing their own task strategies. Users with intermediate expertise may be capable of carrying out portions of the task with little assistance, but they may also need detailed help during unfamiliar stages. A variable initiative dialog system is required for effective interaction in all these situations.

The following sample dialogs recorded on the videotape [HS91] illustrate the flexibility of a variable initiative dialog system. These dialogs were obtained from usage of the implemented system by an experimental subject that had no special knowledge about the implemented system or circuit repair. In the first dialog, the computer controls the dialog while in the second dialog, the system operates in such a way as to allow an experienced user to take the initiative and to control the dialog. The words in parenthesis beside or below a user utterance represent the actual sequence of words that the speech recognizer sent to the dialog system for analysis.

Dialog 1: Computer Controlled—elapsed time 4 minutes 35 seconds

computer: This is the circuit fix it shop. How may I help you?
user: I want to fix this circuit. (power a six a circuit)
Due to speech recognition errors, the system understood the meaning of this utterance as "There is a wire on connector six nine." This could not be understood in any active context.
computer: I do not understand. Please repeat what you said.
user: I want to fix this circuit. (i want a fix a circuit)
computer: What is the ID of the circuit?
user: RS111. (rs111)
computer: I am familiar with that circuit. The LED is supposed to be displaying alternately flashing one and seven.
user: The LED is displaying nothing. (be led a displaying nothing)
The computer must now supply context in order to get the user to make the desired observation.
computer: What is the switch at when the LED is off?
user: The switch is down. (the switch yes down)
computer: Put the switch up.
user: Done. (done)
computer: Put the knob to one zero.
user: Which knob? (which knob)
There are two knobs on the circuit board.
computer: Near the top boundary and in the center is a green region. Now, in the middle right of this green region is the control knob.
user: The knob is at one zero. (the knob and add one zero)
computer: What is the LED displaying?
user: The LED is displaying a one and seven at the same time.
(be led a displaying one an seven at the same time)

computer:	Put the knob to zero.
user:	Done. (done)
computer:	What is the LED displaying?
user:	The same thing. (the same same)

Due to a speech recognition error, the computer was uncertain about what the user said, and therefore verifies that it understood correctly. Notice how the machine fills in an elliptic portion of the user's meaning: "the LED is displaying."

computer:	Did you mean to say the LED is displaying the same thing?
user:	Yes. (yes)
computer:	Is there a wire between connector six eight and connector eight seven?
user:	Yes. (yes)
computer:	Is there a wire between connector three zero and connector seven zero?
user:	No. (know)

There is no (know?) phonetic difference between "know" and "no." Dialog context must be used to determine the correct interpretation.

computer:	Add a wire between connector three zero and connector seven zero.
user:	Done. (done)
computer:	Put the knob to one zero.
user:	Done. (done)
computer:	What is the LED displaying?
user:	The LED is displaying an alternately flashing one and seven. (be led it displaying alternately flashing one and seven)
computer:	Is the one on the LED displaying for a longer period of time?
user:	No. (know)
computer:	Is the seven on the LED displaying for a longer period of time?
user:	No. (know)
computer:	Put the knob to zero.
user:	Done. (done)
computer:	What is the LED displaying?
user:	The one is flashing for a longer period of time. (one is flashing forth longer in a time)

The word "period" is not in the vocabulary of the speech recognizer. As a result, the output of the speech recognizer was badly mangled. The parser was only able to make sense of the three words "one is flashing" and took its meaning from them.

computer:	Did you mean to say the LED is flashing a one?
user:	The LED is flashing a one and seven. (be led it flashing one and seven)
computer:	Is the one on the LED displaying for a longer period of time?
user:	Yes. (yes)
computer:	Put the switch down.
user:	Done. (done)
computer:	What is the LED displaying?
user:	The LED is displaying nothing. (be led a displaying nothing)
computer:	The circuit is working correctly. Good-bye.

In the second dialog the user now has the initiative. Notice the two places where the user makes an abrupt shift of context, which the computer tracks correctly.

Dialog 2: User Controlled—elapsed time 1 minute 28 seconds

computer: This is the circuit fix it shop. How may I help you?

user: I want to fix this rs111. (i want fix this rs111)

computer: I am familiar with that circuit. The LED is supposed to be displaying alternately flashing one and seven.

user: The LED is displaying an alternately flashing one and the top corner of a seven.
(be led it displaying alternately flashing one in top corner a seven)
With the user in control the computer does not ask about the switch position as in the previous dialog, but instead bases its response on the perceived user focus.

computer: There is supposed to be a wire between connector nine nine and connector one zero zero.

user: It is there. (it in there)

computer: There is supposed to be a wire between connector nine eight and connector one zero two.

user: There is no wire on connector one zero four.
(stays know wire i connector one zero for)
While checking for the wire between 98 and 102, the user notices that there is no wire on the nearby connector 104. She makes a change in context to alert the machine to this fact, which she now suspects is the cause of the problem.

computer: There is supposed to be a wire between connector one zero four and connector one zero two.

user: The circuit is working. (the circuit is working)
After finding that the wire between 102 and 104 is missing, the user is able to finish repairing the circuit on her own. She makes another context shift to notify the machine.

computer: Glad to have been of assistance. Good-bye.

Obtaining such robust and efficient behavior from a spoken natural language dialog system requires integrating methods for achieving each of the target behaviors previously mentioned into a single self-consistent mechanism. While the individual behaviors have been well studied, it is the development of the mechanism for integration that is the major research contribution presented in this book. In addition, we present results on system effectiveness, usability, and human performance based on a formal experiment involving usage of the system by eight different subjects in 141 dialogs.

1.1   Problem Solving Environment: Task-Oriented Dialogs

Task-oriented dialogs are dialogs about the performance of a task that occurs as the task is being performed. The associated problem solving environment studied in this research is characterized by the following.

- The user is a person with the ability to carry out all the required sensory and mechanical operations to solve the problem, but with insufficient knowledge to solve the problem without assistance.

- The computer has complete knowledge about the task and its purpose. This means that the computer has sufficient knowledge to perform the task if it can perform the required sensory and mechanical actions and that the assistance to be provided is based on knowing the purpose of the underlying task. Consequently, the role of the dialog is to ensure that the necessary data is obtained and the proper actions performed. This contrasts with isolated fact retrieval or database query systems whose cooperativeness can extend beyond simple question-answering only to consideration of presuppositions (see Kaplan [Kap82] for example).

- The computer will communicate with the user via natural language. The requirement for sufficient cooperativeness necessitates such an interface to allow for all the functions of human communication as described by Sowa [Sow84]. Among other things, the user may wish to select between a possible set of descriptions, express a relationship that provides a description, issue a command to the computer to perform some action, ask a question about some information, or explain the motivations for performing some action. To allow the user and computer to communicate in all these necessary ways requires the use of natural language.

In such an environment, the human and computer must cooperate to solve the problem. Furthermore, this cooperation requires the use of natural language dialog in order to succeed. For these dialogs Grosz [Gro78] notes that *the structure of a dialog mirrors the structure of the underlying task*. Since tasks normally follow a well-structured set of operations, dialogs about tasks should also be well-structured. It will be seen that exploitation of the close relationship between dialog and task structure is crucial for obtaining the efficiency in human-computer dialog that is ubiquitous in human-human dialog.

1.2 Integrating Dialog with Task Assistance: The Target Behaviors

The purpose of the architecture is to deliver to users in real time the previously listed behaviors that are needed for efficient human-machine dialog. The difficulty in developing the architecture is that the phenomena associated with task assistance are independent of the method of communication. Successful task assistance (i.e. domain problem solving) can be accomplished without any natural language interaction. However, as noted at the beginning of the chapter, natural language interaction is likely to be the most efficient form of communication between domain problem solver and human user. Furthermore, coherent natural language dialog requires consideration of the dialog's context. Consequently, a connection must be made between the task assistance context and the dialog processing architecture. As illustrated in figure 1.1 and to be shown in chapters 3 and 4, the Missing Axiom Theory for language use offers a connection between task assistance and dialog.

1.2.1   Problem Solving to Achieve a Goal

Efficient dialog requires that each participant understand the purpose of the interaction and be able to cooperate in its achievement. This is captured by the *intentional structure* of Grosz and Sidner [GS86], the description of the underlying goal-oriented purposes for engaging in the overall dialog, and the needed subdialogs. Required facilities include: (1) a domain problem solver that can suggest the necessary actions; and (2) a mechanism for determining when these actions are completed.

Developing a computational model that generalizes over task-oriented dialogs requires a general notion of task processing. The framework adopted here uses standard artificial intelligence (AI) planning terminology (see Nilsson [Nil80] for example) in saying that *actions* change the world state where the world state can be described by physical and/or mental state descriptions. During the course of a task, both the user and computer will have various *goals* to accomplish different actions or achieve different states. The task is accomplished by carrying out a sequence of actions that result in an appropriate world state as defined by the task.

Because variable initiative dialogs are allowed, the sequence of actions that occurs during the task may vary significantly during different executions of the task. This is especially true in repair tasks, where differences in the error source may require various diagnostic and corrective actions. When the computer has more initiative, the computer may require that specific actions be performed. Conversely, when the user has more initiative, the computer may merely offer recommendations or provide other relevant data.

Regardless of the lofty goals of a general abstract theory for task processing, a working system must contain domain-specific knowledge. How can a general theory be combined with a concrete implementation? As shown in chapter 3, a separation is required between the dialog processing component of the system and the domain specific task processing component. The general theory must provide a standardized method for communication between the two that facilitates successful task assistance.

1.2.2   Subdialogs and Effective Movement Between Them

An alternative title for this section could be, "Why Do We Say Anything?" Efficient human dialog is usually segmented into utterance sequences, *subdialogs*, that are aimed at achieving individual subgoals. These are called "segments" by Grosz and Sidner [GS86] and constitute the *linguistic structure* defined in their paper. The global goal is approached by a series of attempts at subgoals. Each attempt involves a set of interactions that constitutes a subdialog. We adopt the view that when an action is being attempted, the primary role of language is assistance in completing the action. To provide a well established computational framework, action completion will be defined by theorems, and determination of action completion will be accomplished by carrying out a proof of the appropriate theorem. With this viewpoint, the role of language

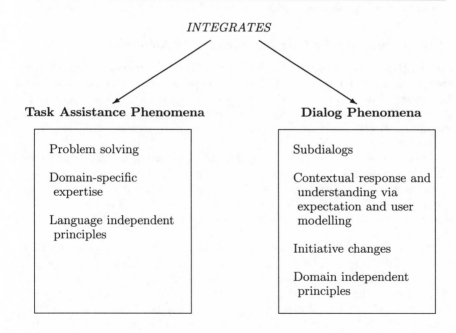

MISSING AXIOM THEORY FOR LANGUAGE USE

- Completion of subgoals achieves task assistance
- Theorem proving determines subgoal completion
- Missing axioms of proof require dialog
- Separate subdialogs discuss separate subgoals
- Goal completion proofs exploit user model axioms
- Specific subgoals expect specific user response
- Dialog and task initiative reflect relative priority of participants' goals

INTEGRATES

Task Assistance Phenomena

Problem solving

Domain-specific expertise

Language independent principles

Dialog Phenomena

Subdialogs

Contextual response and understanding via expectation and user modelling

Initiative changes

Domain independent principles

Figure 1.1
Integrated Processing Overview

is to supply missing axioms for completing the proof, and the utterances associated with a particular theorem constitute a subdialog. Consequently, the theorem prover must be able to suspend itself when it encounters a missing axiom to request its acquisition from an outside source (i.e. dialog). This view summarizes our *Missing Axiom Theory* for language use. As will be seen throughout the book, this theory is the key to achieving integrated dialog processing.

An aggressive strategy for successful task completion is to choose the subgoals judged most likely to lead to success and carry out their associated subdialogs. As the system proceeds on a given subdialog, it should always be ready to abruptly change to another subdialog if it suddenly seems more appropriate. This leads to the fragmented style that so commonly appears in efficient human communication. A subdialog is opened which leads to another, then another, then a jump to a previously opened subdialog, etc., in an unpredictable order until all necessary subgoals have been completed. Thus, the theorem prover must be capable of arbitrarily suspending the proof of one theorem to resume proving another as directed by the overall dialog processing mechanism. Furthermore, the theorem prover must be able to alter the structure of proofs that are being attempted to allow arbitrary clarification subdialogs.

1.2.3 Accounting for User Knowledge and Abilities

Cooperative problem solving involves maintaining a dynamic profile of user knowledge, termed a *user model*. The user model specifies information needed for efficient interaction with the conversational partner. Its purpose is to indicate what needs to be said to the user to enable the user to function effectively. It also indicates what should be omitted because of existing user knowledge.

Because considerable information is exchanged during the dialog, the user model changes continuously. Mentioned facts are stored in the model as known to the user and are not repeated. Previously unmentioned information may be assumed to be unknown and may be explained as needed. Questions from the user may indicate lack of knowledge and result in the removal of items from the user model.

To integrate the user model with the Missing Axiom Theory, the user model must also be represented as axioms. In this case, the axioms are about a particular user, what the user knows or believes, what the user can do, etc. Consequently, the user model can be utilized in a natural fashion in proving completion of actions. Where the user model indicates the user knowledge is adequate, no language interaction is needed. Where it is inadequate, the missing axiom indicates the need for dialog.

1.2.4 Expectation of User Input

Since all interactions occur in the context of a current subdialog, the user's input is far more predictable than would be indicated by a general grammar for English. In fact, the current subdialog specifies the *focus* of the interaction; the set of all objects and actions that are locally appropriate. This is the *attentional structure* described by Grosz and Sidner [GS86], and its most important function is to predict the content of user utterances. For example, if the user is asked to measure a voltage, the user's response may refer to the voltmeter, leads, voltage range, locations of measurement points, or the resulting measurement.

Therefore, based on the relevant missing axiom, the subdialog structure provides a set of expected utterances at each point in the dialog, and these have two important roles.

- The expected utterances provide strong guidance for the speech recognition system so that error correction can be enhanced. Where ambiguity arises, recognition can be biased in the direction of meaningful statements in the current context. In conjunction with the theory of parsing spoken natural language presented in chapter 5, this mechanism enabled the implemented system to understand correctly 81% of 2840 utterances spoken by experimental subjects although only 50% of the utterances were recognized correctly word for word.

- The expected utterances from subdialogs other than the current one can indicate that a shift from the current subdialog is occurring. Thus, expectations are one of the primary mechanisms needed for tracking the dialog when subdialog movement occurs. This is known elsewhere as the *plan recognition* problem, and it has received much attention in recent years.[2]

1.2.5 Variable Initiative

A real possibility in a cooperative interaction is that the user's problem solving ability, either on a given subgoal or on the global task, may exceed that of the machine. When this occurs, an efficient interaction requires that the machine yield control so that the more competent partner can lead the way to the fastest possible solution. Thus, the machine must not only be able to carry out its own problem solving process and direct the user toward task completion, but also be able to yield to the user's control and respond cooperatively as needed. This is a variable initiative dialog. As a pragmatic issue, we have found that at least four dialog initiative *modes* are useful.

---

[2]Carberry [Car90] describes recent work in plan recognition and also provides an extensive bibliography and review that includes a summary description of important work by Allen and Perrault [AP80] and Litman and Allen [LA87].

- *Directive*—The computer has complete dialog control. It recommends a subgoal for completion and will use whatever dialog is necessary to obtain the needed item of knowledge related to the subgoal.

- *Suggestive*—The computer still has dialog control, but not as strongly. The computer will suggest which subgoal to perform next, but it is also willing to change the direction of the dialog according to stated user preferences.

- *Declarative*—The user has dialog control, but the computer is free to mention relevant, though not required, facts as a response to the user's statements.

- *Passive*—The user has complete dialog control. The computer responds directly to user questions and passively acknowledges user statements without recommending a subgoal as the next course of action.

Referring to the sample dialogs at the beginning of the chapter, Dialog 1 was carried out in directive mode while Dialog 2 was carried out in declarative mode.[3] The computer verbally guided the user through every step in Dialog 1. On the other hand, in Dialog 2 the computer did not try to verbally verify many subgoals in order to provide cooperative utterances based on its perceptions of the user's focus during the problem solving process. Thus, variable initiative dialog complicates dialog processing for the subproblems of: (1) choosing the subgoals for completing the task, (2) moving between subdialogs, and (3) producing the expectations for user responses.

1.2.6 Integrated Behavior Via the Missing Axiom Theory

As will be seen in the next chapter, there has been a significant amount of important research on each target behavior. However, most of the work is based on an isolated study of an individual behavior, and there is a limited amount of work on integrating in one overall controlling process the mechanisms for obtaining each behavior. The Missing Axiom Theory mentioned in section 1.2.2 provides the linchpin for an integrated model. As illustrated in figure 1.1 and seen from the discussion in chapters 3 and 4, it does so in the following ways.

- Task and dialog are related via this theory through the theorems that define completion of task actions. Each theorem constitutes a subdialog, and the detection of a missing axiom in a proof attempt initiates the dialog interaction.

---

[3]While variable initiative behavior implies the ability to vary the initiative both between and within dialogs, our work emphasizes varying initiative between dialogs. A discussion of the difficulty in coherently varying initiative within a dialog is given in section 4.7.3.

- Within the above framework, maintenance of the user model as axioms provides a seamless interface for user model usage. This is done by determining the status of user knowledge as part of the action completion proofs. Missing user knowledge is detected as a missing axiom and may trigger a computer utterance to provide this knowledge.

- Expectations are produced according to the current dialog focus. This focus is provided by the action associated with the missing axiom that is triggering the language interaction. A record of these expectations for all active and previously active subdialogs can be used to determine when subdialog movement is occurring as well as assist in speech recognition.

- Finally, variable initiative behavior is enabled by augmenting the processing model to take into account the conflicting priorities of diverse user and computer goals and subdialog focus. Processing must vary as a function of the current dialog initiative mode.

1.3   Preliminary Study

Early in the development of the dialog processing model, many dialogs were collected and analyzed. The vast majority of these came from a study by Moody [Moo88] on the effects of restricted vocabulary size on discourse structure in spoken natural language dialog. Her results showed that human subjects could successfully adapt to a restricted vocabulary size. Furthermore, with increased expertise due to practice, subjects could become almost as efficient in completing the task as when subjects had an unrestricted vocabulary.

Moody's dialogs were collected using the "Wizard of Oz" paradigm, wherein a person simulates the computer in providing the needed expertise to human users for completing the circuit repair task. Because of the use of subjects in repeated trials, the simulations were conducted in such a way as to allow the human user to have control of the dialog at various times as their added experience permitted. Consequently, the dialogs were invaluable in validating many aspects of the dialog processing model, especially the work on variable initiative dialog, before it received the ultimate validation via testing the implemented system in experimental trials.

1.4   An Outline of the Book

Chapter 2 examines previous work on various problems in dialog processing. Chapter 3 presents the general dialog processing theory while chapter 4 gives the details of the computational model. Chapter 5 presents a theory of parsing spoken natural language that in conjunction with available dialog knowledge about possible user responses, enables a system to behave robustly in the presence of speech recognition errors. Chapter 6 describes the implemented system while chapters 7 and 8 present performance results based on experiments with the implemented system. Chapter 9 discusses an enhancement of the dialog processing model for verifying uncertain inputs. This enhancement was developed after the initial implementation was completed and the experiments were conducted. Finally, chapter 10 offers a concluding summary and critique of this research, highlighting ongoing and future areas of exploration.

Chapter 2

Foundational Work in Integrated Dialog Processing

Building a working spoken natural language dialog system is a complex challenge. It requires the integration of solutions to many of the important sub-problems of natural language processing. This chapter discusses the foundations for a theory of integrated dialog processing, highlighting previous research efforts.

2.1 Problem Solving in an Interactive Environment

The traditional approach in AI for problem solving has been the planning of a complete solution. We claim that the interactive environment, especially one with variable initiative, renders such a strategy inadequate. A user with the initiative may not perform the task steps in the same order as those planned by the computer. They may even perform a different set of steps. Furthermore, there is always the possibility of miscommunication. Regardless of the source of complexity, the previously developed solution plan may be rendered unusable and must be redeveloped. This is noted by Korf [Kor87]:

> Ideally, the term planning applies to problem solving in a real-world environment where the agent may not have complete information about the world or cannot completely predict the effects of its actions. In that case, the agent goes through several iterations of planning a solution, executing the plan, and then replanning based on the perceived result of the solution.
>
> Most of the literature on planning, however, deals with problem solving with perfect information and prediction.

Wilkins [Wil84] also acknowledges this problem:

> In real-world domains, things do not always proceed as planned. Therefore, it is desirable to develop better execution-monitoring techniques and better capabilities to replan when things do not go as expected. This may involve planning for tests to verify that things are indeed going as expected.... The problem of replanning is also critical. In complex domains it becomes increasingly important to use as much as possible of the old plan, rather than to start all over when things go wrong.

Consequently, Wilkins adopts the strategy of producing a complete plan and revising it rather than reasoning in an incremental fashion. This may be satisfactory in some cases, but in a sufficiently dynamic environment, developing a complete plan is often a waste of resources because the conditions under which the plan was developed may later be discovered to be inaccurate. This is particularly true in an interactive environment such as voice dialog where miscommunication can occur.

Recently there has been an interest in studying reasoning in dynamic environments where the conditions may change as the plan is being developed. Pollack and Ringuette [PR90] have constructed a system called Tileworld that consists of a simulated robot agent and a simulated environment that is dynamic and unpredictable. Their purpose is to experimentally evaluate the adequacy of various meta-level reasoning strategies in managing the explicit action planning that occurs during task performance.

Boddy and Dean [BD89] use a simulated world called *gridworld* that consists of a rectangular subset of the integer plane on which a robot courier must be scheduled to make as many pickups and deliveries as possible in a given amount of time. Since planning an optimal tour is in general a computationally expensive problem, they are interested in testing strategies that consider both the time for the robot to move from place to place as well as the planning time required for determining an optimal tour. Consequently, the optimal tour must minimize the sum of the traversal time together with the planning time required to construct the tour.

Although these two approaches do not consider an integration of such reasoning with NL dialog, they are consistent with our proposal for incrementally selecting the next task action to be performed without planning all the necessary remaining steps.

2.2   Language Use in a Problem-Solving Environment

2.2.1   The Missing Axiom Theory

Integrating dialog with the problem solving required for task completion necessitates a specification for the computational role of language. We propose the Missing Axiom Theory (section 1.2.2) that says language is used to acquire missing axioms needed for proving completion of actions. This view provides a practical computational paradigm for simulating human performance in a dialog. It seems clear that a human expert would focus responses on those parts of the task that the client is having difficulty with. Thus, although the Missing Axiom Theory may not be an accurate cognitive model of a person's thinking, it does lead to similar and effective surface behavior.

Quilici et al. [QDF88] use a similar approach in providing explanations for user misconceptions. User misconceptions are detected when the advisory system proves that it does not share a user's belief. Based on this proof, the system's explanation about the misconception must include a description of why it does not share the user's belief. Theorem-proving is also used in the process for computing an explanation for the user's erroneous belief. Thus, the missing user beliefs correspond to missing axioms that motivate the system's explanation.

Cohen and Jones [CJ89] also use a similar approach in selecting concepts to be discussed in responding to a user's query. Their domain is educational diagnosis. In this domain, the system is trying to assist a user in diagnosing the learning difficulties of a student. Such assistance involves developing a hypothesis about the cause of a student's learning difficulties along with suggesting a diagnostic procedure for verifying the hypothesis. The system's explanation takes into account missing user knowledge about the domain and/or the student.

Gerlach and Horacek [GH89] define rules for the use of language for a consultation system. The rules embody meta-knowledge about knowing facts and wanting goals as well as knowledge about the domain of discourse. Language is used when the system needs to inform the user that either: (1) a goal has been accomplished; or (2) a significant difference in the beliefs of the user and the system has been detected.

2.2.2 Speech Act Theory

In general, many researchers have proposed theories about the role or purpose of language. The origin of much of this research, including the Missing Axiom Theory, is *speech act* theory. As summarized in Allen [All87], speech act theory was developed based on the realization that statements can do more than just make assertions about the world. Statements can serve other functions. For example, when a minister says, "I now pronounce you husband and wife," at a wedding ceremony, the words act to change the state of the world. Another perspective is provided by Sadock [Sad90]:

> Speech act theory is concerned with providing an account of the fact that the use of expressions of natural language in context invariably involves the accomplishment of certain actions beyond the mere uttering (or writing, or telegraphing) itself. The context and the form of the utterance both enter into the equation. Holding the context constant and varying the utterance changes the accomplishments, and likewise holding the utterance constant and varying the context generally has profound effects on the actions that are performed.

Speech act theory, originally proposed by Austin [Aus62], is a development in the philosophy of language designed to explain the purpose of language in terms of the actions that speakers intend to perform by virtue of making an utterance. These types of actions are known as *illocutionary* acts. *Locutionary* acts are the actions associated with the physical production of the utterance. *Perlocutionary* acts are the effects that the utterance has on the hearer, independent of the effects the speaker intends. For example, if a police officer knocks on a door and asks the people inside if they have seen a certain criminal, the illocutionary act is to request information. However, if the criminal is hiding nearby, the utterance will also have the effect of warning and scaring the criminal although these were not the effects intended by the speaker. These are perlocutionary effects. The theories on the role of language that are of present concern involve the illocutionary acts of language.

An area of particular interest has been the production of *indirect speech acts*. For example, "Can you pass the salt?", is on the surface, an act to find out if someone is capable of passing the salt. However, it is most commonly intended as a request to actually pass the salt. Searle [Sea75] gives a philosophical discussion of the problem of indirect speech acts.

Grice [Gri75] introduces the notion of conversational implicature to describe implications or inferences that can be made from utterances. He also introduces the idea of the Cooperative Principle: "Make your conversational contribution such as is required, at the stage at which it occurs by the accepted purpose or direction of the talk exchange in which you are engaged." In addition, he proposes maxims of Quantity, Quality, Relation, and Manner as associated principles regarding the appropriateness of utterances in conversation. Consider the following exchange between speakers A and B.

```
A:   I have a flat tire.
B:   There is a tire store down the street.
```

B's response would violate the Relation maxim of, "Be relevant," if the tire store was in fact closed. Grice introduces the notion of "flouting a maxim" as a means for introducing conversational implicatures and figures of speech into language. Although non-computational, Grice's and Searle's work provided a rich description of ideas and theories concerning language phenomena that have been explored by other researchers.

2.2.3   Computational Speech Act Theory: Analyzing Intentions

In developing computational approaches to speech act theory, a key idea has been that of *intention*. Simply stated, speakers intend to achieve certain goals, and these intentions influence what they say. Power [Pow79] presents one of the earliest attempts at developing a computational model for connecting language to goals. However, the model does not address issues of discourse structure, user model, or linguistic realization of utterances. Cohen and Perrault [CP79] describe a computational theory of speech acts by modeling them in a planning system. The speech acts are defined as operations on the speaker's and hearer's beliefs and goals. This work also does not extend to the linguistic realization of the speech acts.

In subsequent work on intention, Allen and Perrault [AP80] develop a model of cooperative behavior that tries to infer the intentions behind a speaker's question. Their model involves the inferring of a speaker's plan and the idea of "obstacle detection" as a means for determining the most cooperative response. An obstacle is defined as any goal specification that is not initially true or achieved within the plan. If obstacles are found other than those specifically mentioned, a response can be formed that provides more information than specifically requested. For example, if a speaker asks, "When does the train from Montreal arrive?", the response might be "2:45 at gate 7." Although the location of the arrival is not specifically questioned, it is inferred as another possible obstacle and information pertaining to it is included in the response. Obstacle detection in question-answer dialogs can be seen as a precursor to the Missing Axiom Theory.

More recently, in the collection edited by Cohen, Morgan, and Pollack [CMP90], several researchers report on issues concerning the purposes or intentions of communication and consequently concerning the purpose or role of language. These researchers have studied the problem from various philosophical, linguistic, and computational viewpoints as seen from the discussion in the remainder of this section.

In extending the previous work of Allen on the recognition of speaker intentions, Pollack [Pol90] extends the notion of cooperative responses to situations where a conversant's plans may be invalid. She does this by representing and reasoning about the mental states needed to produce the plan being inferred from the speaker's utterance. She defines what it means for an agent A to have a plan to carry out some global action B in the following manner.

1. A believes that he can execute each action in the plan.

2. A believes that executing the actions in the plan will entail the performance of B.

3. A believes that each action in the plan plays a role in the plan.

4. A intends to execute each action in the plan.

5. A intends to carry out the plan as a way to do B.

6. A intends each action in the plan to have a role in the plan.

Pollack formalizes this definition for a subset of plans called *simple plans*, plans where the agent believes that all the acts in the plan serve to accomplish another act (e.g. by saying to a friend "Do you know the phone number of the high school?", an agent has done the action of asking the friend to tell the agent the phone number). Based on the formal definition it can be concluded that an agent has an invalid simple plan when one or more of the beliefs underlying the plan is incorrect with the consequence that one or more of the intentions is unrealizable. A cooperative response in such a situation must address these incorrect beliefs. We have made no attempt to represent such sophisticated plan inference in our model, but such a capability is clearly desirable.

Perrault [Per90] applies "default logic" (see Reiter [Rei80]) in a formalization of speech act theory. He makes the key observation that, "the mental state of the speaker and hearer after an utterance is strongly dependent on their mental state before." He assumes what he calls a *persistence theory of belief*: "that old beliefs persist and that new ones are adopted as a result of observing external facts, provided that they do not conflict with old ones. In particular, I assume that an agent will adopt the beliefs he believes another agent has, as long as those do not contradict his existing beliefs." Perrault uses default logic to formally represent the persistence theory and shows it can account for the changes (or lack thereof) in speaker and hearer beliefs for sincere assertions, successful and unsuccessful lies, and irony. Cohen and Levesque [CL90] hold a similar viewpoint: "we treat utterances as instances of other events that change the state of the world; utterance events per se change the mental states of speakers and hearers." Their work is based on the idea that, "just as there are grammatical, processing, and sociocultural constraints on language use, so may there be constraints imposed by the rational balance that agents maintain among their beliefs, intentions, commitments, and actions." Consequently, Cohen and Levesque treat illocutionary acts as complex actions that view language use in a very cognitive fashion, but it is also a much more complex method than the Missing Axiom Theory. This is illustrated in the following description of assumptions formalized by Cohen and Levesque for describing the conditions under which an utterance event of an imperative sentence would constitute the performance of a request from a speaker to a hearer to carry out a set of desired actions.

- Speaker wants Hearer to do the actions.

- Speaker believes Hearer does not already want to do the actions.

- Speaker believes Hearer does not already think it is mutually believed that Hearer will do the actions.

- Speaker wants it to be the case that after uttering the imperative that the Hearer should be helpful to Speaker and not want not to do the actions.

- Speaker knows that after uttering the imperative sentence, Hearer thinks it is mutually believed that Speaker wants Hearer to be helpful.

Relative to this description, the Missing Axiom Theory would say, "there is no axiom stating that the hearer wants to do the actions," therefore, language should be used to get Hearer to want to do the actions. The other assumptions implicitly underlie the Missing Axiom Theory without any explicit representation in our model.

Thomason [Tho90] gives a general discussion of the required features for a theory of pragmatics, the use and understanding of utterances within context. Thomason introduced the notion of "accommodation" that is analogous to Allen's notion of "obstacle elimination." Thomason argues strongly for the implementability of pragmatics theories:

> Examining the performance of a program is a powerful way of relating theories to linguistic evidence, and certainly is very different from either the introspective methods that are common in syntax

or the more sociological methods that are used in discourse analysis. Moreover, this demand forces theories to be explicit, which is an extremely valuable constraint in pragmatics; and it imposes efficiency requirements as well.

Litman and Allen's highly influential implemented theory will be discussed next.

2.2.4 Differing Subdialog Purposes: The Plan-Based Theory of Litman and Allen

Litman and Allen [LA90] present a plan recognition model of discourse understanding for task-oriented dialogs. They use a general notion of the task-oriented dialog that also considers dialogs about tasks not being executed concurrently with the dialog. Their key contribution is to distinguish between *domain plans* and *discourse plans*. Domain plans are plans to accomplish goals in the given domain whereas discourse plans are plans about using language in conjunction with the domain plans. Litman and Allen note that "previous plan-based models have not clearly distinguished between what one says in a discourse about a task and the actual knowledge about the domain task itself." Their notion of the discourse plan makes that distinction. They present the following discourse plans.

1. TRACK-PLAN: discuss the execution of a non-linguistic task action (e.g. "I have turned the switch up.").

2. IDENTIFY-PARAMETER: supply a piece of information needed to complete a task action (e.g. "The switch is in the lower left portion of the circuit board," when uttered in response to "Where is the switch?", when an individual is trying to execute the task action of determining the switch position.).

3. CORRECT-PLAN: Specify correction of a plan after unexpected events occur (e.g. "Loosen the screw," when uttered in response to "The switch is stuck," which is uttered when an unforeseen problem is encountered in an individual's plan for moving the switch into the up position.).

4. INTRODUCE-PLAN: Introducing a new plan for discussion that is not part of the previous topic of conversation. This corresponds to initiating a new subdialog.

5. MODIFY-PLAN: Introducing a new plan by performing a modification on a previous plan (e.g. "Bypass the switch by connecting a wire between 111 and 110," when uttered in response to "The switch is stuck," which is uttered when the user was trying to activate the power in a circuit by moving the switch into the up position.).

These plans can be subdivided into three classes: (1) expected continuation of a plan (TRACK-PLAN), (2) clarify or correct a plan (IDENTIFY-PARAMETER and CORRECT-PLAN), and (3) introduction of new plans (INTRODUCE-PLAN and MODIFY-PLAN). These classes of discourse plans allow Litman and Allen to connect the purpose for using language, which they call the *discourse intention*, with the underlying domain task. This is illustrated in the following dialog excerpt from their paper.

(11)   Person: Where do I get the CAN-AM train?
(12)   Clerk: It's not until six.
(13)   They're meeting at cubicle C.
(14)   Person: Where's that?

The initial domain plan of Person is GOTO-TRAIN. When the person realizes that this plan cannot be executed because the train's location is not known, Person executes an IDENTIFY-PARAMETER discourse plan to carry out the discourse intention that "Person intends that Clerk intends that Clerk clarify Person's plan to take a trip." Because response (13) of Clerk still does not provide enough information to execute the original domain plan, GOTO-TRAIN, Person will have the intention that the Clerk intends that Clerk identify a parameter of the IDENTIFY-PARAMETER discourse plan intended to provide the location parameter for the train in the GOTO-TRAIN domain plan (the discourse plan that led to response (13)).

Litman and Allen propose a formal model for plan recognition in this environment, but have not extended the work to actual participation in dialogs by parsing utterances and planning and generating natural language responses. What their model illustrates is the importance of separating general task-oriented discourse knowledge, the discourse plans, from the specific required domain knowledge, the domain plans. It also describes a model of language use based on acquiring and supplying needed knowledge, an approach closely akin to the Missing Axiom Theory.

2.2.5 Collective Intentions

A final area of related work in communicative intention is that of *collective intentions*. As claimed by Searle [Sea90], "collective intentional behavior is a primitive phenomenon that cannot be analyzed as just the summation of individual intentional behavior." This claim makes sense when an assumption of "cooperative behavior" is applied as is the case in our research.

Grosz and Sidner [GS90] extend Pollack's [Pol90] notion of the simple plan for a single agent (see section 2.2.3) to that of a "shared plan" between two agents. Their extension requires that there be mutual beliefs about the relations among actions, and that different agents may perform different actions as part of the overall task that execution of the plan is intended to achieve. They illustrate how their notion of the shared plan can describe the following phenomena of collaborative behavior.

1. Simultaneous actions by the two agents.

2. Conjoined actions by the two agents (i.e. the combined actions of the two agents, though not necessarily occurring simultaneously, achieve the desired result).

3. Sequence of actions together generate the desired action.

4. Actions performed only by one agent.

The motivation for this work is to provide a theoretical understanding of collaborative behavior so that an actual discourse processing model based on their tripartite model of discourse (to be discussed in section 2.6.3) can be constructed. At this point they do not provide a concrete plan recognition process or implementation. Initial work on the required plan recognition algorithm is described in Lochbaum [Loc91]. However, as will be outlined at the end of section 2.6.3 and discussed in detail in chapters 3 and 4, our dialog processing model based on the Missing Axiom Theory yields a constructive model for dynamically producing a representation of their tripartite discourse structure for the class of task-oriented dialogs that have been the focus of this research, dialogs about a task that occur as the task is being performed.

Finally, Clark and Wilkes-Gibbs [CWG90] provide results from a study undertaken to see how people collaborate and coordinate in providing definite references. They propose the following principle of behavior.

> The participants in a conversation try to establish, roughly by the initiation of each new contribution, the mutual belief that the listeners have understood what the speaker meant in the last utterance to a criterion sufficient for current purposes.

When a computer is one of the participants, modeling the role of language as a means for supplying missing axioms to theorems, the Missing Axiom Theory, provides an efficient and effective approach to satisfying this behavioral principle.

2.3 User Model

Integrating user modeling into a global dialog processing model requires the consideration of three issues: (1) architecture—how the user modeling component fits into the dialog processing system architecture; (2) usage—how will user model information be utilized; and (3) acquisition—how is the user model information acquired. The Missing Axiom Theory provides for exploitation of user model information via representing the user model as axioms acquired from user utterances. The axioms can then be utilized by the theorem prover during determination of action completion. Consequently, flexibility in the usage of user model information is achieved via the theorem specifications for goal completion. A more or less detailed theory of user model usage can be tested by adjusting the theorem specifications accordingly.

Researchers who have concentrated on the development of user modeling facilities have explored many details in greater depth than was possible in our research. The collections [KW88] and [KW89] provide several fine examples of user modeling research with the article by Kass and Finin [KF88] providing a good overview of the general issues in user modeling. This section examines the user modeling research most influential on our decisions for handling the issues of architecture, usage, and acquisition for user models.

2.3.1   General User Modeling Architecture

Our architectural view of the user model is very similar to that proposed by Finin [Fin89]. Finin describes a general architecture for a domain independent system for building and maintaining long term models of individual users. He lists five important features for user models.

- *Separate Knowledge Base*—The user model is kept in a separate module.

- *Explicit Representation*—User model knowledge is encoded in some type of representation language that allows inferences so that knowledge can be implicit, but automatically inferred when needed.

- *Declarative Knowledge*—User model knowledge should be encoded in a declarative rather than procedural manner.

- *Support for Abstraction*—The user modeling system should be able to describe the general properties of classes of users as well as describe the properties of individuals.

- *Multiple Use*—User model knowledge should be represented in such a way as to allow it to be reasoned about (e.g. to classify a user as having a certain general level of competence) as well as reasoned with (e.g. to decide what to say to a person during a dialog).

Finin presents a General User Modeling Shell (GUMS) that provides user models that have these features. GUMS is maintained as a separate module. It communicates with the application program with which the user interacts. Thus, it is the responsibility of the application program to inform GUMS of any new information to be stored in the user model. GUMS takes this new information and updates the user model. As a result of this update, any of the following could occur.

- GUMS may detect an inconsistency and notify the application program.

- GUMS may infer a new fact about the user.

- GUMS may need to update some previously inferred default information about the user.

GUMS knowledge about users consists of two parts: (1) a collection of *stereotypes*; and (2) a collection of individual models. A stereotype consists of a set of facts and rules that apply to any person who is seen as belonging to that stereotype. For example, the individuals belonging to the *UnixExpert* stereotype might be assumed to know about all the commands involving copying, renaming, and printing files for the UNIX[1] operating system. The facts and rules of a stereotype may be *definite* or *default*. Definite information must be true about a person in order for that person to belong to the stereotype. Default information is assumed to be true in the absence of contradictory information. Such contradictory information could be part of the individual user model. Returning to the UnixExpert stereotype, the knowledge of the previously mentioned file operations might be definite information while information about the *awk* utility might be considered default information. Thus, a clause of the form understands(how_to_use,awk,false) in the individual user model would override the default. Stereotypes are organized into a hierarchy such that more general stereotypes are at the top of the hierarchy. When it is ascertained that an item of information about the user contradicts with the definite knowledge of the current stereotype into which a user is classified, GUMS will reclassify the user into a more general stereotype where there is no contradiction. As more specific information is acquired about a user, and contradictions found with the user's current stereotype model, the user will be classified into more and more general stereotypes. As time goes by, the system will rely more on specific information about the user and less on the stereotype, an intuitively plausible action.

As a result of this distinction between definite and default knowledge, there is also a distinction between truth or falsity by default and truth or falsity by logical implication. Consequently, GUMS uses a four-valued logic of belief about user information. The four values follow.

- **True**—Definitely true according to the current knowledge base.

- **Assume(true)**—True by assumption/default.

- **Assume(false)**—False by assumption.

- **False**—Definitely not true according to the current knowledge base.

The four value logic allows GUMS to distinguish between conclusions made from purely logical information and conclusions dependent on default information.

Relative to Finin's description of the five features of user models that are supported by GUMS, our architecture supports the first three—separate knowledge base, explicit representation, and declarative knowledge. Our architecture can easily support abstraction of stereotypes by pre-specifying axioms,

---

[1]UNIX is a trademark of Bell Laboratories.

but no attempt at the creation of stereotypes has been made. To summarize, Finin's general user modeling module and logical view of user model reasoning and usage integrates easily into the Missing Axiom Theory for integrated dialog processing.

2.3.2   Using User Model Information in Generation

Missing user model axioms can lead to the generation of computer responses whose intention is to provide the user with necessary knowledge. The TAILOR system (Paris [Par88]), produces descriptions of devices according to whether the user is a novice or expert in various areas of knowledge about the device. Descriptions for experts focus on subparts of the device and their properties while descriptions for novices focus on general process information. The general format of these descriptions can be characterized by the use of *schemas* (McKeown [McK85]). Schemas are general patterns for organizing information in multisentential responses. The user model information can be used to produce individualized tests for users with intermediate levels of expertise by mixing the expert and novice strategies. For example, a user may have local expertise about a car radiator without having expertise about the complete engine. The general process strategy can be used to discuss the overall engine while the subpart strategy can be used when specifically focusing on the radiator. Such usages of user models allow computer systems to be more cooperative.

McCoy [McC88] proposes the notion of a "highlighted" user model as being useful in responding to user misconceptions. User misconceptions may involve associating properties with one object that actually belong to a different, but similar object. An example is the belief that whales have gills, which is a property of fish, when in fact whales are mammals and have lungs. Since the dialog context provides information about the user's perspective on the similarity of objects, a highlighted user model that contains information on how a user views the similarity of objects can be obtained by dynamically determining similarity as a function of the current dialog context. The highlighted user model can then facilitate more helpful responses to user misconceptions.

Sarner and Carberry [SC88] describe how to use user model information to influence the production of definitions in advice-giving dialogs. They note that the production of definitions during a dialog by an information-provider for an information-seeker must take into consideration (1) the goals of the information-seeker, (2) the specific domain knowledge of the information seeker, and (3) the response of the information-seeker to the definition provided to see if elaboration is necessary. They hypothesize that, "beliefs about the appropriate content of a definition should guide selection of a rhetorical strategy, instead of the choice of a rhetorical strategy determining content." Consequently, they propose the use of this user model and dialog information in the process of selecting the content of a definition. For example, consider the following responses to the question, "What is Numerical Analysis?"

```
R1:   It is a computer science course. . . .
R2:   It is a mathematics course. . . .
```

The choice of the answer depends on whether the user model indicates that the user is trying to satisfy the computer science requirements or the mathematics requirements. Besides identification of the entity as shown above, there are several other rhetorical strategies that can be used depending on what the user model indicates should be contained in the content of the response. Two other possible strategies are naming characteristics of the entity or describing how something works. The final selection of the content is based on a heuristic weighting of the relevance of a piece of knowledge with its familiarity to the user to obtain an overall significance metric. User model knowledge plays a crucial role throughout the selection process.

2.3.3   Acquiring User Model Information

Due to our focus on dialog processing, our emphasis has been on the acquisition of user-specific information during the ongoing dialog. Section 3.4.2 lists the inferences about user knowledge that we make from user inputs during the course of a dialog. These inferences deal with user knowledge about actions and objects. The inferences are based on a study of the transcripts obtained in the preliminary study described in section 1.3.

Kass and Finin [KF87] conducted a detailed analysis of transcripts of a large number of interactions between advice-seekers and a human expert in order to identify several rules for acquiring user model information. These rules are listed below.

1. If the user says P, the user modeling module can assume that the user believes that P, in its entirety, is used in reasoning about the current goal or goals of the interaction.

2. If the user omits a relevant piece of information from a statement, then either the user does not know of that piece of information, does not know whether that information is relevant to his current goal or goals, or does not know the value for the piece of information.

3. If the user makes a statement that the system finds ambiguous in the current context, then the user lacks knowledge of one or more of the alternative meanings for his statement.

4. If the user model includes the belief that a user knows an action, then the user modeling module can attribute to the user knowledge of the preconditions and postconditions of that action.

5. If the user believes a fact that is a possible consequence of a small set of actions, then the user believes that one or more of these actions has occurred.

6. If the user model indicates that the user knows several concepts that are specializations of a common, more general concept in the domain model, the user modeling module may conclude that the user knows the more general concept, and the subsumption relationship between the more general concept and the more specialized concepts as well.

7. If the user is the agent of an action, then the user modeling module can attribute to the user knowledge about the action, the substeps of the action, and the factual information related to the action.

8. If the system is able to evaluate actions taken by the user given a certain situation, and those actions do not conform to the actions the system would have taken, then the user modeling module can identify portions of the reasoning done by the system that the user does not know about.

The first three rules are termed *communicative rules* as they are activated by user statements. These rules are based on Grice's maxims for cooperative communication (see section 2.2.2). The first rule deals with the relevance of the user statement. The second rule deals with the sufficiency or completeness of the user statement. The third rule is concerned with the ambiguity of the user statement. Rules 4 through 6 are called *model-based rules* as they utilize information already contained in the user model and domain model to extend the system's knowledge about the user. The last two rules are called *human behavior rules* as they are based on general principles of human behavior. One can observe some overlap between these rules and the ones listed in section 3.4.2. In the interest of minimizing system complexity, only the rules believed to be most useful in the domain application were implemented.

Lehman and Carbonell [LC89] offer a particularly innovative view of user model acquisition that is especially relevant in spoken natural language dialog, although they studied natural language interaction using typewritten input. They emphasize the acquisition of "individualized grammar rules" to assist in the processing of ungrammatical inputs. They acknowledge the certainty of ungrammatical inputs in natural language interfaces and propose a method called "least-deviant parsing" that attempts to determine the deviations from the grammar that can account for the ungrammatical utterance. Other than misspellings, the possible deviations are deletions, insertions, substitutions, and transpositions of words and/or sentence constituents. Once the deviations are determined, a generalization is placed in the user's individual grammar rules so that the ungrammatical utterance is now added to the grammar. Besides demonstrating another useful type of knowledge that can be acquired during an ongoing dialog, Lehman and Carbonell also highlight the importance of dealing with ungrammatical inputs in a natural language interface, a problem exacerbated by speech input as will be discussed in chapter 5. Resource limitations prohibited our exploration of such user model knowledge in our project. In general, our research proposes a theory of user model that permits acquisition of user model information during dialog and provides a general paradigm for user model usage that allows the testing of arbitrary theories of usage by incorporating the appropriate descriptions in the theorem specifications for goal completion.

2.4 Expectation Usage

We use expectations for the meaning of a user utterance to assist in error correction by the system when parsing spoken input (chapter 5) as well as to assist in the contextual interpretation of inputs, including detection of subdialog shifts (section 3.5). As described in section 3.5, these expectations are derived from domain-specific knowledge as well as general principles of task-oriented dialogs. Previous work on these issues has come from researchers in speech recognition and plan recognition. This section mentions influential work from both of these fields.

2.4.1 Speech Recognition

Most of the research interest in expectation has been studies performed by groups interested in speech recognition. Erman et al. [EHRLR80] and Walker [Wal78] use word-based expectations as provided in their sentence grammars to predict the next words to occur in utterances. These expectations help constrain the search process for identifying words within the fuzzy acoustic signal of the spoken input. Fink and Biermann [FB86] use historical information about a set of past dialogs to infer a general dialog structure. This general structure is used to predict the meaning of utterances in the current dialog. At any given point in a dialog, only a subset of all possible meanings are expected (the subset that has been observed at this point in previous dialogs). Based on these predictions, recognition and error correction are performed. Mudler and Paulus [MP88] interleave the generation and verification of expectations at a lexical level. Thus, once a partial recognition of a sentence has occurred, for example the recognition of a phrase, subsequent expectations based on this partial recognition are generated and used in recognizing the next portion of the utterance. Carbonell and Pierrel [CP88] propose an architecture that uses dialog sources for assisting in voice communication, but they do not integrate this with actual linguistic components or attempt to generalize their expectations.

The utility of high-level dialog sources in assisting with speech recognition was first demonstrated in the MINDS system by Young et al. [YHW+89]. The VODIS system of Young and Proctor [YP89] also uses expectations in a similar fashion. These systems will be discussed in more detail in section 2.7.4.

2.4.2 Plan Recognition

Identifying the underlying purposes and goals of users based on their utterances is termed plan recognition. Researchers who have worked on this problem include Allen and Perrault [AP80], Allen [All83], Carberry [Car90], Lambert and Carberry [LC91], Litman and Allen [LA87], Nagao [Nag93], Pollack

[Pol86], Ramshaw [Ram89] and [Ram91], and Sidner and Israel [SI81]. The following general model for plan recognition comes from Carberry [Car90].

1. From the semantic content of the speaker's utterance, determine the speaker's immediate goal (IG).

2. Apply a set of plan identification heuristics that relate IG to the set of possible domain-dependent goals and plans the speaker might have to produce a set of *candidate focused goals* and associated *candidate focused plans*.

3. Relate the speaker's utterance to the overall plan the user is believed to be constructing. Focusing heuristics are used to determine which hypothesized subplan proposed in step 2 is most expected given the speaker's current focus of attention. Call this subplan SP.

4. Insert SP into the *context model*, a tree structure that represents the system's beliefs about the speaker's underlying task plan. SP becomes the new current focus of attention, and the context model is expanded to include the new subplan.

This processing is equivalent to the system asking itself: (1) What task-related subplans might the speaker be addressing in the new utterance? and (2) Based on the preceding dialog, which of these subplans is most likely to be the speaker's current focus, and what is its relationship to the speaker's overall plan that is under construction? Carberry presents domain-independent plan identification heuristics and focusing heuristics that utilize domain-dependent knowledge of domain goals to assist in plan recognition during information-seeking dialogs. These are dialogs where the user is seeking information in order to construct a plan for carrying out a task at some later time.

Whether a system is engaged in a task-oriented dialog or an information-seeking dialog, plan recognition is extremely useful in identifying the relevant subdialog of an utterance, a crucial step in dialog processing. In developing a practical integrated dialog processing model for spoken natural language, we have also considered the following issues.

- Using the expectations to constrain the search for a basic interpretation of the utterance at the time of speech recognition as was done by Young et al. [YHW+89].

- Exploiting the existing dialog context and not just the set of possible speaker plans in identifying the relevant subdialog. More recent plan recognition work such as Carberry [Car90] has also addressed this.

- Engaging in variable initiative dialog, not just the stereotypical user controlled query dialogs normally addressed in plan recognition models.

- Obtaining real-time response. Plan recognition techniques tend to be computationally expensive (see Allen [All87]).

2.5 Variable Initiative Theory

Although researchers have noted the need for variable initiative interaction in natural language dialog, it has been difficult to develop a testable theory about it. McCann et al. [MTT88] note in the discussion of their system (ISIS):

> The *control* of intelligent dialogue is another key aspect, having to do with the amount of initiative that is available to the dialogue partners. Traditionally, computer systems have been designed for trained users, who, by virtue of knowing their goals and the system's capabilities, can control the execution of those goals from the interface. As systems like the proposed ISIS will be used more for iterative problem-solving and decision support by relatively untrained users, the computer must have the ability to direct the dialogue, perhaps toward aspects of the problem that the user has not considered.

In this section we describe the work of other researchers who have tackled this difficult problem.

2.5.1 Defining Initiative

Whittaker and Stenton [WS88] propose a definition for dialog control based on the utterance type of the speaker (question, assertion, command, or prompt) as follows.

- **Question**—the speaker has control unless the question directly followed a question or command by the other conversant.

- **Assertion**— the speaker has control unless it was a response to a question.

- **Command**—the speaker has control.

- **Prompt**—the listener has control because the speaker is abdicating control.

In their study of control shifts, they list the following main sources of shifts (1) prompts, (2) repetitions/summaries, and (3) interruptions. They further note that there is a close relationship between topic shift and control shift. Consequently, they believe dialog control is useful in identifying the discourse structure. No study of the potential relationship between task control and dialog control or of the effect of utterance content is mentioned.

2.5.2   Discourse Structure in Variable Initiative Dialogs

Walker and Whittaker [WW90] apply the dialog control rules mentioned above
to analyze how initiative affects discourse structure. Their analysis distinguishes between advisory dialogs and task-oriented dialogs, but they do not
allow for the possibility that the novice in a task-oriented dialog can gain
knowledge over time and want more control of the dialog. Their key observations include the following.

- Transfer of control is often a collaborative phenomenon. Since
  a noncontrolling participant has the option of seizing control at
  any moment, then the controlling participant must have control
  because the noncontroller allows it.

- Anaphoric references are more likely to cross discourse segment
  boundaries when the control change is due to an interrupt, a situation where the listener seizes control. With summaries and abdi-
  cations, the speaker is explicitly signaling for a change of control.
  With an interrupt, however, the interrupted speaker may not have
  been ready to change the topic, resulting in anaphoric references
  to the interrupted topic.

- The expert retains more control in the task-oriented dialogs, but
  there are still occasional control changes when the novice has to
  describe problems that are occurring while completing the task.

- Summaries are more frequent in advisory dialogs due to the need
  for both participants to verify they share the mutual beliefs needed
  to develop the necessary plan.

The issue of developing a computational model for participating in a variable initiative dialog is left unresolved.

2.5.3   Plan Recognition for Variable Initiative Dialog

Kitano and Van Ess-Dykema [KVED91] extend the plan recognition model
of Litman and Allen [LA87] to consider variable initiative dialog. Their key
insight is the observation that the two participants may have different domain
plans that can be activated at any point in the dialog. Thus, there are speaker-
specific plans instead of simply joint plans as in the Litman and Allen model.
This separation of plans permits greater flexibility in the plan recognition
process. Furthermore, they extend the initiative control rules proposed by
Whittaker and Stenton to consider the utterance content by observing that a
speaker has control when the speaker makes an utterance relevant to his or her
speaker-specific domain plan. Although they do not consider a computational
model for participating in variable initiative dialogs, their observation that
there are speaker-specific plans or goals is crucial to developing the model in
section 3.6.

2.6   Integrated Dialog Processing Theory

The previous sections have described work on individual subproblems of dialog processing. There remains the crucial issue of a theoretical model that combines solutions to these subproblems into a coherent integrated dialog processing theory. In chapter 3 we describe how the Missing Axiom Theory for language use leads to such an integrated theory. This section presents three significant alternative theories: (1) conversational moves, (2) conversation acts, and (3) a tripartite model of discourse structure.

2.6.1   Subdialog Switching: Reichman's Conversational Moves

An influential work in identifying and tracking subdialog movement is that of Reichman [Rei85]. Based on a detailed analysis of human-human dialogs, she constructs a computational model of both the conversational flow and the underlying model of understanding performed by each conversant as a conversation progresses.

At the heart of Reichman's theory is the notion of the *conversational move*, which refers to the underlying purpose of a subdialog. The different categories of conversational moves are: (1) Support, (2) Restatement and/or conclusion of point being supported, (3) Interruption, (4) Return to previously interrupted context space, (5) Indirect challenge, (6) Direct challenge, (7) Subargument concession, (8) Prior logical abstraction, and (9) Further development. In determining when a particular conversational move is being introduced, Reichman emphasizes the role of *clue words*. For instance, "By the way" signals the Interruption conversational move. She does not address issues concerning the relationship of an ongoing task to the dialog associated with it. Her emphasis is on the rhetorical purposes of subdialogs.

The notion of subdialog, the fundamental unit of discourse processing, is captured by Reichman's *context space*. In addition to its purpose (a conversational move), a context space is defined by the specific set of utterances relevant to its conversational move as well as by a marker denoting the influence of the context space in interpreting utterances at the current point in the discourse. A context space is deemed *active* if it is currently under development; it is said to be *controlling* if the active context space is a part of it. Reichman's restatement of the Relevance maxim of Grice [Gri75] indicates how these context spaces determine the appropriateness of an utterance.

> To be relevant means either to embellish the active context space by stating a succeeding utterance that continues the current conversational move or to shift to a different context space (new or old) via the development of a distinct conversational move, whose relationship to some preceding context space is clear. If all preceding topics have been fully developed (all criteria for the development of particular conversational moves satisfied), then the new move may begin an entirely new topic. If, on the other hand, there are

uncompleted conversational moves in the discourse, the new move
either will constitute a temporary interruption or will have to signal
clearly to which portion of the preceding discourse it is related.

The *discourse grammar* defines the conventional relations between the different types of context spaces. The grammar is based on the Augmented Transition Network (ATN) grammars of Woods [Woo70]. One of the key features of such grammars is the ability to test the value in one or more special memory registers that can be updated as part of the actions in transitioning to a new state. One particularly important register is used for holding the *discourse expectations*. These expectations derive from the realization that the current context space constrains the type of utterances that can occur next in a coherent discourse. Reichman's concept of discourse expectations is seen in her restatement of Grice's Quantity maxim.

In the development of a context space, only specify those aspects of
the referent being discussed that are needed for the accomplishment
of the one specific conversational move served by this context space.

The discourse expectations serve to constrain the quantity of material presented in the utterance.

Reichman's computer program simulates the high-level changes in a discourse, but does not address the production of actual natural language dialog. This is reflected in her notion of the conversational move, which is very much based on rhetorical purposes of subdialogs. Nevertheless, her work is influential due to its:

- attempt to apply Grice's maxims computationally;

- recognition of the hierarchical structure of general discourse;

- attempt to deal with suspension and resumption of subdialogs;

- recognition of the utility of discourse expectations.

Jönsson [J91] extends the work of Reichman by constructing a dialog controller (based on the Reichman approach) that uses more than clue words to determine the movement to new subdialogs. Jönsson identifies *initiative-response units* (IR-units) as the fundamental unit of dialog. These units are combinations of conversational moves such as Question (Q), Answer (A), Assertion (AS), and Directive (D). Each move can be associated with a particular *topic* that describes the appropriate knowledge source to consult: task (T), dialog (DG), or the background system (S). When associating a move with its topic, the topic is placed in the subscript position. In describing the possible IR-units, the following notation is used. Q_T refers to a question about the task. Typical IR-units in a database query environment include: Q_T/A_T for a question-answer about the task, Q_S/A_S for a user clarification request,

Q_T/AS_S when the requested information is not in the database, and Q_{DG}/A_{DG} for questions about the ongoing dialog.

A dialog tree is constructed for maintaining the dialog structure. It shows the relationship between IR-units. For example, a clarification IR-unit will be a child node of the IR-unit that led to the clarification. Associated with each IR-unit is an action plan. These plans are stored on a stack so that as the level of clarification increases, the action plan associated with the deepest level of clarification is the first to be executed. Such a mechanism works well in a database query environment, but it may run into difficulty in a task-assistance environment where some IR-units may be left implicitly incomplete (i.e. while in the depths of clarification about performing some action, the user may suddenly determine how to carry out the action and take care of all the remaining clarification steps without mentioning them).

2.6.2 Beyond Speech Acts: Conversation Acts of Traum and Hinkelman

Spoken natural language often requires the participants to verify a mutual understanding of the conversational content under discussion. Traum and Hinkelman [TH92] propose a theory of *Conversation Acts* for modeling the methods by which such mutual understanding is obtained. Conversation act theory distinguishes between four levels of action that are necessary for maintaining dialog coherence: (1) Turn-taking acts, (2) Grounding acts, (3) Core speech acts, and (4) Argumentation acts.

The turn-taking acts are those parts of an utterance that are used to signal when a speaker is claiming the right to speak (**take-turn**), claiming a need to continue to speak (**keep-turn**), and yielding the right to speak (**release-turn**). The core speech acts are simply the traditional speech acts while the argumentation acts are higher level discourse acts composed of combinations of core speech acts. The argumentation acts provide the connection to the domain task structure. In their sample planning domain there are three types of argumentation acts: (1) specify goal, (2) construct plan, and (3) verify plan. The argumentation acts also include lower level actions that are independent of the domain, such as asking and answering questions, and convincing another agent of some fact.

A grounding act defines the purpose of an utterance within its associated subdialog.[2] Some of the possible grounding acts include: (1) Initiate, (2) Continue, (3) Acknowledge, (4) Repair, (5) Request Repair, (6) Request Acknowledgement, and (7) Cancel. It is important to realize that in this model, an utterance can be considered as part of multiple subdialogs, and consequently have a different grounding act in each subdialog of which it is a part. Consider the following excerpt[3] from their sample human-computer interaction where

---

[2]Traum and Hinkelman use the term *discourse unit* rather than subdialog.

[3]The utterance numbering sequence has significance within the context of the full paper, but is used here only as a convenient reference. M denotes the human manager is speaking

the computer system is to be a helpful assistant in planning the usage of trains.

```
5.1 M: so we need an engine to move the boxcar
5.2  : right?
6.1 S: right
7.1 M: so there's an engine at Avon
7.2  : right?
```

Utterance 5.1 initiates a new subdialog concerning the need for an engine to move a boxcar while utterance 5.2 is a request for explicit acknowledgement of 5.1. Consequently 6.1 is an acknowledgement, but it also initiates the next subdialog whose purpose is to verify the correctness of the information just presented. Similarly, utterance 7.1 is part of two subdialogs: It acknowledges the verification given in 6.1, but it also initiates a new subdialog concerning the proposition that there is an engine located at Avon.

Traum and Hinkelman propose a model for recognizing conversation acts during an ensuing dialog. The most concrete portion of this model is the recognition of subdialogs and the grounding acts associated with each utterance. In agreement with the dialog behavior principle of Clark and Wilkes-Gibbs mentioned at the end of section 2.2.5, a subdialog is deemed to be complete when the intent of the initiating participant of the subdialog is mutually understood. The model provides a finite automaton for tracking the state of a subdialog that describes the preferred and possible grounding acts for each state. The recognition of a grounding act is based on the utterance's content relative to the current model of mutual understanding as well as the content of any uncompleted subdialog.

The model of Traum and Hinkelman provides an integrated view of spoken discourse, (1) from the sub-utterance level turn-taking acts, (2) to the grounding acts of utterances within subdialogs, (3) to the speech acts being performed in a subdialog, and (4) to the argumentation acts that motivate the role of each utterance in the overall task-related purpose of the dialog. The model offers a detailed analysis based on many simulated human-computer interactions, and it considers the possibility of multiple utterances in a turn as well as the important role of speech factors like intonation and pitch in performing the interpretation. It does not explicitly address issues of dialog initiative. Work continues on implementing the model as part of an overall participating computer system.

2.6.3   Integrated Discourse Structure: The Tripartite Model of Grosz and Sidner

Seminal work that integrates research about focusing in discourse (Grosz [Gro81]) and work on intention recognition in discourse (Allen [All83]) is the tripartite model of Grosz and Sidner [GS86]. Their main idea is that discourse structure is composed of three distinct but interacting components: linguistic

---

while S denotes the system is speaking.

structure, intentional structure, and attentional state. Linguistic structure is the grouping of the utterances into the various subdialogs[4] that constitute a dialog along with information about the relationship of the subdialogs to each other. Intentional structure describes the underlying purposes for engaging in subdialogs and their structural relationships to each other. The primary intention of a subdialog is called the *discourse segment purpose* (DSP). Consider the following subdialog[5]

1. C: You need to measure the voltage between connectors 24 and 83.
2. U: Where do I connect this red wire?
3. C: To connector 24.
4. U: Where is it?
5. C: To the right of the switch.
6. U: I have made the connection.

The overall DSP (DSP1) is to perform a voltage measurement. The DSP of utterances 2 through 6 (DSP2) is to get the red wire properly connected. Satisfaction of this intention is a requirement for satisfaction of the overall intention. Examining the relationships of the associated purposes represented in the intentional structure helps determine if one subdialog is part of another. Grosz and Sidner do not attempt to place a limit on the possible purposes of a subdialog as did Reichman. Instead, they argue that the important fact concerning intention is the potential structural relationships between intentions. They identify two relationships: *dominate* and *satisfaction-precedes*. In the above example, DSP1 is said to *dominate* DSP2 since satisfying DSP2 is part of satisfying DSP1. The *satisfaction-precedes* relation defines the ordering in which the DSP's can be satisfied. This is not necessarily a total ordering.

The attentional state represents the conversational participants' focus of attention. It is a dynamic structure that records the objects, properties, and relations that are salient at each point in the discourse. It is modeled by a set of *focus spaces*. There is a focus space associated with each subdialog. It contains those entities that are salient because they have been explicitly mentioned in the subdialog or because they became salient in the process of producing or comprehending the utterances in the subdialog (as in Grosz [Gro78]). An example of this second type of saliency is the ability to use "the red wire" in utterance 2 of the sample subdialog. It became salient due to its association with the voltmeter that became salient as a result of the discussion in utterance 1 about performing a voltage measurement. Furthermore, the attentional state can be used to constrain the search for the relevant subdialog of an utterance as well as the search for determining referents of noun phrases. This avoids the computational overhead of exhaustive search and allows the

---

[4]Grosz and Sidner use the term *segments* rather than subdialogs.

[5]Here and throughout the sample dialogs in the remainder of the book, C denotes utterances spoken by the computer while U denotes utterances spoken by the human user.

possibility of real-time processing.

In general, the tripartite discourse structure model contributes to a theory of integrated dialog processing by:

- extending the notion of purposeful dialog beyond task-oriented dialogs;

- providing an explanation for the behavior of such discourse phenomena as clue words, referring expressions, and interrupts;

- asserting that a subdialog's purpose is more than a rhetorical relation;

- separating distinct components of the discourse structure that were previously intertwined, thus eliminating task dependencies in the structure and consequently providing a general model.

In their conclusion, the authors note that "Although admittedly still incomplete, the theory does provide a solid basis for investigating both the structure and meaning of discourse, as well as for constructing discourse-processing systems." Our dialog processing model supports this claim since the Missing Axiom Theory yields a constructive model for dynamically producing a representation of the tripartite discourse structure while the dialog occurs. A subdialog's intention is reflected in the theorem goal to be proven. The linguistic structure is based on the relationship of user utterances to the active missing axioms. This relationship is determined through the use of expectations for user responses when attempting to acquire missing axioms. Thus, these expectations model the attentional state. The Grosz and Sidner discourse structure model can provide the framework for an efficient and effective integrated dialog processing model.

2.7   Dialog Systems

Tables 2.1 and 2.2 summarize various dialog systems according to their basic functionality and mechanisms for achieving the target behaviors outlined in the first chapter. Table 2.1 gives a description of the basic system characteristics. In addition to describing how the systems deal with the various target behaviors, table 2.2 summarizes how the implementations were evaluated. The criteria for comparison of the various systems follow.

1. Application Domain—application area of the implemented system.

2. Input Modality—allowed forms of input to the implemented system.

3. Output Modality—forms of output produced by the implemented system.

4. Error Correction—types of erroneous inputs for which the implementation had a correction mechanism.

5. Subdialog Mechanism—the means by which the implementation represents and manipulates subdialogs.

6. User Model Mechanism—the means by which a system maintains a user model.

7. Expectation Usage—the types of processing for which the system uses predictions of user responses.

8. Initiative Level—participant who has the task/dialog initiative while the system is running.

9. Performance Evaluation—the means by which the functionality of the system was tested.

These tables are based on the cited references. While some of the entries may be controversial due to conflicting terminology, an attempt was made to faithfully represent each system's features as derived from the cited publications. Our system is presented first for comparison.

In the remainder of this section, we provide a further discussion of the listed systems. The emphasis will be on the ones whose breadth of coverage of the target behaviors is closest to ours.

2.7.1 Requirements

Hayes and Reddy [HR83] provide a description of a number of skills that are necessary in order for a computer to achieve "graceful interaction" with a human via dialog. Some of the skills they outline which have been studied in our research include: the ability to handle clarification subdialogs, keeping track of the focus of attention, contextual interpretation and response, and performing problem solving reasoning. They did not construct a dialog system but instead provided an analysis of some of the features required.

Similarly, Nielsen [Nie90] describes a set of "usability principles" to be followed by all user interfaces. These apply to all interfaces and not just NL interfaces. Some of these principles to which our research adheres by virtue of the use of natural language include: (1) natural dialog, (2) speaking the user's language, (3) consistency, and (4) access to shortcuts. These principles indicate the need for NL dialog systems.

2.7.2 Portable Systems

It is clear that practical NL dialog systems require large amounts of domain knowledge. However, there is a natural desire to separate general language processing capabilities from the domain-specific knowledge to maximize the utility of the NL system. In our research this has been done by generalizing the approach to task-oriented domains rather than a specific domain. The expectation-driven approach to NL dialog processing does assume a strong coupling between task and dialog, but does not assume a specific task. Other

System	Application Domain	Input Modality	Output Modality	Error Correction
Circuit Fix-It Shop Smith et al. [SHB92]	circuit repair	speech (125 words) or keyboard	speech or text	ungrammatical utterances
TEAM Grosz et al. [GAMP87]	database query portability	keyboard	text	none
Datalog Hafner and Godden [HG85]	database query portability	keyboard	text	none
HAM-ANS Hoeppner et al. [HCM+83]	portable interface	keyboard	text	spelling correction
IREPS Carberry [Car88]	information seeking	keyboard	text	ill-formed queries
PSLI3 Frederking [Fre88]	medical database	keyboard	text/graphics	spelling correction input interpretation
LADDER Hendrix et al. [HSSS78]	database query naval info	keyboard	text	spelling correction
DIALOG Bolc et al. [BKKS85]	medical database	keyboard	text	spelling correction
CO-OP Kaplan [Kap82]	database query portability	keyboard	text	invalid presuppositions
PRAGMA Levine [Lev90]	database query portability	keyboard	text	invalid user plans
UC Wilensky et al. [WCL+88]	UNIX help	keyboard	text	user misconceptions
MINDS Young et al. [YHW+89]	database query naval info	speech (1000 words) keyboard, and touch	multimedia	ungrammatical utterances
VODIS Young and Proctor [YP89]	train timetable database	speech	speech	ungrammatical utterances
SUNDIAL Peckham [Pec91]	portable voice interface	speech (1000-2000 words)	speech	none
TINA Seneff [Sen92]	database query portability	speech or keyboard	text	none
Trost et al. [TBD89]	circuit repair expert system interface	highly restricted speech	speech	none
Discourse System Allen et al. [AGH+89]	advisory dialog interpretation	keyboard	text	none
ARGOT Allen et al. [AFL82]	computer operator	keyboard	text	spelling correction
ESTEAM-316 Jullien and Marty [JM89]	financial advisor	keyboard	text	none
GUS Bobrow et al. [BKK+77]	travel agent	keyboard	text	none
XCALIBUR Carbonell et al. [CBM83]	expert system interface	keyboard	text	spelling correction

Table 2.1

Dialog Systems Comparison — Part 1

System	Subdialog Mechanism	User Model Mechanism	Expectation Usage	Initiative Level	Performance Evaluation
Circuit Fix-It Shop	Missing Axiom Theory	input inferences as axioms	predict utterance meanings	variable	8 users/141 dialogs 2840 utterances
TEAM	none	none	none	user	sample interactions multiple domains
Datalog	none	none	none	user	sample queries multiple domains
HAM-ANS	domain scripts	semantic network	none	user	ported to 3 domains
IREPS	plan structure	context model for user plan	predict user goals	user	?
PSLI3	none	none	ellipsis resolution	user	sample interactions
LADDER	none	none	elliptical queries of previous utterance	user	sample interactions
DIALOG	none	none	none	user	sample interactions
CO-OP	none	presuppositions	none	user	sample interactions two domains
PRAGMA	none	recognize user goals	predict user goals	user	sample interactions
UC	none	input inferences	predict user expertise level	user	sample interactions
MINDS	goal trees	hand-coded domain knowledge	predict utterance meanings	user	10 speakers 200 sentences
VODIS	object frames	none	predict utterance meanings	computer	32 subjects 96 dialogs
SUNDIAL	task-structured history	belief model	predict utterance meanings	user	preliminary prototypes
TINA	none	none	utterance word predictions	user	two domains 200 and 560 utterances
Trost et al.	none	updated stereotypes	none	computer	?
Discourse System	discourse segments	none	contextual interpretation	non participatory	?
ARGOT	dialog grammar	recognize user goals	plan recognition	user	?
ESTEAM-316	dialog plans	none	plan recognition	variable (limited)	?
GUS	frame tree	none	understand sentence fragments	computer	sample interactions
XCALIBUR	case frames	none	error recovery ellipsis resolution	user	?

Table 2.2

Dialog Systems Comparison — Part 2

researchers who have worked on the problem of portability in NL dialog systems include Grosz et al. [GAMP87], Hafner and Godden [HG85] and Hoeppner et al. [HCM+83]. The research of Hafner and Godden, and Grosz et al. are similar to each other in that they do not deal with variable initiative interaction but are focused on database query systems. Hoeppner et al. describe a dialog system that functions in various domains including database query and hotel reservations, but does not deal with variable initiative dialog or make use of expectations.

2.7.3 Question-Answer Systems: Keyboard Input

Many dialog systems have been developed for question-answer domains where it seems natural that the computer could function as a source for knowledge in the particular domain of interest. Usually these systems are developed to study specific research problems. Carberry [Car88] and [Car90] is primarily interested in plan recognition and user model usage. Frederking [Fre88] is interested in handling elliptical utterances, but does not deal with context changes or top-down expectations. In addition, there is no task model in the Frederking system. Hendrix et al. [HSSS78] is very interested in issues of ellipsis and paraphrase. Bolc et al. [BKKS85] describes the deduction process for answering natural language queries. Kaplan [Kap82] discusses issues of "cooperativeness" in question-answering based on an analysis of presuppositions behind user questions. Levine [Lev90] extends the work of Kaplan by including considerations of domain and discourse plans as proposed by Litman and Allen [LA87]. Levine's system is also notable for its use of a bidirectional grammar as well as bidirectional knowledge sources for plan recognition and response planning.

One of the most ambitious question-answer systems is the UNIX consultant (UC) of Wilensky et al. [WCL+88], a system for answering questions about how to carry out operations with the UNIX operating system. In addition to questions, UC allows statements that can be interpreted as specifying user goals. In determining a response the system goes through the following stages: (1) parsing, (2) contextual interpretation, (3) recognizing user plans and goals, (4) determining its own goals, (5) planning to determine an appropriate response, (6) determining utterance content, and (7) producing the actual utterance. In addition, the system maintains a model of the user's knowledge of UNIX. Significantly, all parts of the system make use of knowledge represented in a single knowledge representation system called KODIAK, for which a description is also given. As with the other systems described in this section, the dialog is user controlled.

2.7.4 Spoken Input Systems

Systems that use spoken natural language input must develop strategies for robust input understanding. The MINDS system of Young et al. [YHW+89] was the first spoken natural language system to exploit high level dialog information to assist with the speech recognition process. They use a knowledge base of domain concepts together with hierarchical AND-OR goal trees to represent the possible goals that a user may have. In conjunction with a user model that represents what the user knows about the domain concepts and the relations between them, these knowledge sources can be used to predict the likelihood that the user's next utterance will refer to a set of concepts about a particular goal. These predictions are dynamically expanded into a semantic grammar that is used to constrain the search during the speech recognition process for the next user utterance. Furthermore, MINDS produces several layers of predictions, ranging from very specific to very general according to the hypothesized set of active goals. These layers provide for robust behavior when user utterances fail to be recognized using the more specific predictions. The resulting system demonstrates dramatic improvements over performance levels that have been observed without such predictive capabilities, improving word recognition accuracy from 82.1% to 97.0% in one test. MINDS illustrates the power of high level expectations with a domain-specific dialog environment of user-controlled database query.

The VODIS system of Young and Proctor [YP89] uses expectation in a similar fashion. In their application domain of obtaining information from a train timetable database they use frames to represent the constituents of a complete query (e.g. destination, departure location, day, time, etc.). Based on these frames, their system outputs a question requesting the user supply some item of information required for completing the query. This question leads to specific expectations for the user response that constrain the grammatical choices in interpreting the user input. They also talk about variable initiative dialog, but their view of initiative is somewhat limiting. Their notion of initiative pertains to the amount of information that can be supplied in an utterance and has nothing to do with the task initiative, which remains with the computer. Nevertheless, VODIS also illustrates the power of high level expectations, in this case within a computer-controlled database query environment.

The SUNDIAL project [Pec91] is an attempt to develop a portable spoken natural language interface for telephone usage in four different languages (English, French, German, and Italian). A uniform underlying semantic representation has been developed that is usable with any of the four languages. Their system architecture for managing a dialog is very similar to ours. It involves different modules that contain information on the dialog history, the task information, a belief module, a belief knowledge base, and a linguistic input interface. These modules communicate via message passing. A typical dialog processing cycle is initiated by the task module, which makes a request to the dialog module for task information. The dialog module uses its information on the dialog history to propose the next action of the computer system and to send to the linguistic module a set of expectations of what the user may do. The linguistic module then uses the expectations to constrain the parsing process for the user's response. Once a user input is processed, the semantic description of the utterance is passed to the belief module. This module updates its status and performs the necessary contextual interpretation, before sending the information back to the task module. The emphasis in the SUNDIAL project is on information queries over the telephone, but they may be queries that require several clarifying utterances before the query formulation is complete. The current implementations are in the prototype stage. Further details about their dialog model can be found in Bilange [Bil91].

The TINA system described in Seneff [Sen92] also provides a portable spoken natural language interface to database query systems. This system uses probabilistic networks to parse token sequences provided by the SUMMIT speech recognition system of Zue et al. [ZGG+90]. The probabilistic networks are created dynamically from context-free grammar rules augmented with feature specifications for enforcing syntactic and semantic constraints. The probabilities are derived from frequency counts on the rules generated in parsing a set of training sentences selected by the system designer. The networks serve to provide expectations on the occurrence of words during parsing. Consequently, the expectations are primarily syntax-based. The semantics is built directly into the parse trees which are translated into SQL for access to a database.

Finally, Trost et al. [TBD89] describes a dialog system that provides task assistance for electronic circuit repair within a computer-driven dialog. Their usage for user model is restricted to stereotypical user models that do not take into account specific facts about the user that may be acquired during the dialog.

2.7.5   A Discourse System

In analyzing the lack of integrated dialog processing systems, Allen et al. [AGH+89] astutely observe that, "there is a fundamental problem that is preventing the construction of a full discourse system, namely, that no one knows how to fit all the pieces together." Using the tripartite discourse structure model of Grosz and Sidner as a basis, Allen et al. describe an architecture called the Discourse System for maintaining information about the subdialogs in an ongoing dialog. They use a blackboard architecture whereby each subdialog is allocated its own partition where the relevant information about the subdialog is maintained. This information is available as needed to all the different processing modules corresponding to the various "pieces" in dialog processing. There are subroutines to handle processing at the lexical, syntactic, and semantic levels as well as modules for determining: (1) the objects referred to in expressions, (2) the speech acts underlying an utterance, and (3) the temporal relationship of the events discussed in the subdialogs. This last module is strongly influenced by the work of Webber [Web88] and Moens and Steedman [MS88]. One of its most important uses is in assisting to determine the relevant subdialog of an utterance. It does so by noting for which of the candidate subdialogs that the utterance cannot be a constituent due to temporal constraints. A typical task for the system is to properly parse and analyze a given dialog without actually being a participant.

The Discourse System follows previous work on the ARGOT dialog system described in Allen et al. [AFL82]. This system uses plan recognition to translate between task goals and communicative goals, but does not address the wide scope of issues handled in the Discourse System.

2.7.6 Variable Initiative Systems

Clancey [Cla79] describes a tutorial system, GUIDON, which bases dialog initiative on task initiative as proposed here. However, as noted by the author, "GUIDON is not intended to be a complex natural language converser, such as GUS" (the Bobrow [BKK+77] system, see below). "[We] have avoided the problem of recognizing new dialogue situations in free text." Users interact with the system via a keyword-based system with artificial system labels used for reference to previous contexts. "DISCUSS" and "STOP" are the main commands available to a user for taking initiative by changing the topic of discussion. A directed tutorial does not allow a user to maintain control of the dialog throughout.

Jullien and Marty [JM89] describe a dialog system for managing an interaction between a novice user and an expert system for providing financial advice. They focus on the subdialog for discussing the user's investment problem. Because it is dealing with novice users, the dialog is essentially computer-directed, but it has a limited capability for variable initiative due to a design decision to allow users to change topic within the plan formulation process. Even with the topic change, the user is still under the direction of the computer to provide all the information the computer demands. In addition, their mechanism for clarification subdialogs is similar to ours—inserting a subplan into the overall plan for the subdialog being clarified.

Bobrow et al. [BKK+77] discuss the GUS system for which they claim variable initiative behavior. However, they define initiative with respect to the extent to which one participant always responds to the direct expectations of the other participant. Using this notion, a clarification subdialog would be a cause for a change in initiative. In our research, the conversational initiative is related to the task initiative. From this viewpoint, Bobrow's system does not engage in variable initiative dialog because the task initiative remains constant with the computer. They use a collection of frames to represent the subdialog structure (i.e. there is a dialog frame, a trip specification frame that is a filler for a slot in the dialog frame, a trip leg frame that is a filler for a slot in the trip specification frame, etc.). GUS directs the user through the dialog, filling in values for vacant frame slots until all needed values have been supplied.

Carbonell et al. [CBM83] claim variable initiative behavior for their dialog system, but they do not define what they consider variable initiative behavior to be. It appears that the user has control of the task throughout, and that the variable initiative capability is encompassed in the ability of the system to initiate a clarification subdialog when it needs more information. It does not appear that they relate conversational initiative to task initiative.

2.8   Summary

One cannot expect to construct a dialog processing theory that integrates solutions to several subproblems of dialog processing unless there are concrete theories proposing solutions to these subproblems. Sections 2.1 through 2.5 described a variety of research efforts directed at these individual subproblems. Section 2.6 presented three alternatives for achieving integrated dialog processing, none of which address all of the subproblems. In particular, none of these theories deal with variable initiative dialogs. Finally, the implemented systems presented in section 2.7 serve the important role of providing benchmarks in determining the extent to which our theories are truly computational and the extent to which our theories enable realistic natural language behavior when interacting with a human in a specific context.

In our research we have tried to establish a new benchmark for the status of dialog processing theory by proposing a theory that integrates solutions to *all* of the subproblems discussed *and* enables a practical working system based on the theory to be constructed and evaluated in formal user trials. The results of this research effort are presented in the following chapters.

Chapter 3

Dialog Processing Theory

Consider the following dialog situation. The computer is providing a human user with assistance in fixing an electronic circuit that causes a Light Emitting Diode (LED) to display in a certain way. The current focus of the task and dialog is to determine the status of a wire between labeled connectors 84 and 99, a wire needed for the circuit that is absent. Figures 3.1 and 3.2 show two possible dialog interactions that could occur at this point. In figure 3.1, the computer has total dialog control, and a total of 29 utterances are needed to guide the user through the rest of the dialog. In figure 3.2, the human user has overall dialog control, but the computer is allowed to provide direct assistance as needed (i.e. in helping add the wire). Only 11 utterances are needed for the experienced user to complete the dialog.

These samples are from interactions with a working spoken natural language dialog system. To engage in such dialog interactions, a system must exhibit the behaviors mentioned at the beginning of chapter 1: (1) problem solving for providing task assistance, (2) conducting subdialogs to achieve appropriate subgoals, (3) exploiting user model to enable useful interactions, (4) exploiting context dependent expectations when interpreting user inputs, and (5) engaging in variable initiative dialogs.

Achieving these behaviors while facilitating the measurement of system performance via experimental interaction requires a theory of dialog processing that integrates the following subtheories.

- An abstract model of interactive task processing.

- A theory about the purpose of language within the interactive task processing environment.

- A theory of user model usage.

- A theory of contextual interpretation.

- A theory of variable initiative dialog.

This chapter presents such a theory of dialog processing. Frequent reference to the dialog examples in figures 3.1 and 3.2 will guide the discussion. The first section discusses the overall system architecture that facilitates integrated dialog processing. The remainder of the chapter addresses each subtheory in turn, emphasizing how each fits into the overall architecture. The chapter concludes with a summary description of the integrated model.

3.1 System Architecture

The overall system architecture shown in figure 3.3 provides the overall framework into which the subtheories are integrated. The major modules of the

NOTE: In the actual system, numbers were spoken using the digit
        form. Thus, 84 was uttered as "eight four" by both the
        computer and human user.

Computer Controlled Sample

1. C: Is there a wire between connector 84 and connector 99?
2. U: It is not there.
3. C: Add a wire between connector 84 and connector 99.
4. U: I need help.
5. C: Obtain a wire.
6. U: Okay.
7. C: Connect metal of one free end of the wire to connector 84.
8. U: How?
9. C: Bend back connector 84.

(At this point the user realizes how to add the wire. In
so doing the user notices an additional wire that connects
connectors 84 and 30 and is unsure about that wire. It in
fact, is also needed.)

10. U: There is a wire from 84 to 30.
11. C: Add a wire between connector 84 and connector 99.
12. U: The wire is connecting.
13. C: What is the LED displaying?

(16 additional utterances required to complete the dialog
by verifying that the added wire causes the circuit to
function correctly.)

Figure 3.1
Example System Dialog Interaction: Computer Controlled

architecture are shown along with a brief description of what each module
contains. A further description of each module is given next.

- *Dialog controller*—It is the overall supervisor of the dialog processing system. It determines the role that the computer plays in the
  dialog by determining how user inputs relate to the already established dialog as well as determining the type of response to be
  given. It also maintains all dialog information shared by the other
  modules and controls their activation. Its control algorithm *is* the
  dialog processing algorithm.

                    User Controlled Sample

1. C: There is supposed to be a wire between connector 84 and
      connector 99.
2. U: How do I add it?
3. C: Obtain a wire.
4. U: Okay.
5. C: Connect metal of one free end of the wire to connector 84.
6. U: How?
7. C: Bend back connector 84.

      (As in the previous sample, the user now realizes how to add
      the wire. In so doing the user notices an additional wire
      that connects connectors 84 and 30 and is unsure about that
      wire. It in fact, is also needed.)

8. U: There is a wire from 84 to 30.
9. C: There is supposed to be a wire between connector 84 and 30.

      (After adding the wire between 84 and 99, the user carries out
      all tests to verify the circuit is working without further
      assistance from the computer.)

10. U: The circuit is working.
11. C: Glad to have been of assistance. Good-bye.

Figure 3.2
Example System Dialog Interaction: User Controlled

- *Domain processor*—It is the application dependent portion of the
  system. It contains all the information about the application domain. As shown in section 3.2.3, its interface with the dialog controller must allow it to recommend needed actions, provide expectations about responses to performing these actions, and update
  its view of the task based on domain inputs provided by the dialog controller. In our implemented system the domain processor
  assists in electronic circuit repair.

- *General reasoning*—It is the domain-independent reasoning facility. Its realization is an interruptible theorem prover that can be
  controlled externally, permitting outside interaction (such as dialog) for obtaining missing axioms. Its interface with the dialog
  controller must allow the controller to also be able to dynamically
  alter and/or suspend and resume proofs. The theorem prover will
  be introduced in section 3.3.

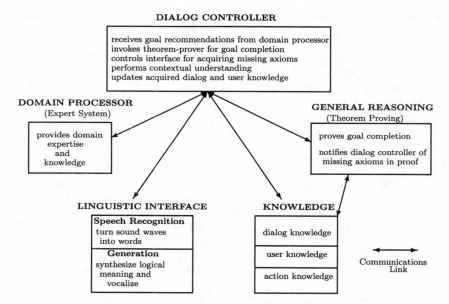

Figure 3.3
System Architecture

- *Knowledge*—It is the repository of information about task-oriented dialogs. This includes the following general knowledge about the performance of actions and goals.

    1. Knowledge about the decompositions of generic actions into substeps.

    2. Knowledge about theorems for proving completion of goals.

    3. Knowledge about the expectations for responses when performing an action.

    General dialog knowledge includes knowledge about the linguistic realizations of task expectations as well as discourse structure information. Finally, there is also knowledge about the user that is acquired during the course of the dialog. This knowledge is in the form of axioms available to any theorem-proving process that might be used. Note that *the predefined information of this module is easily modified without requiring changes to the dialog controller*.

- *Linguistic interface*—It consists of the generation and recognition modules. They use information on context and expectation as provided by the dialog controller.

This architecture evolved during the course of the research as each of the various subtheories was addressed. Presenting it first gives the reader a global context from which to understand the proposals for the various subtheories that are discussed in the following sections.

3.2   Modeling Interactive Task Processing

This section presents an abstract model of interactive task processing suitable for an integrated theory of dialog processing. It discusses (1) the assumptions made concerning the prerequisite knowledge and skills of the person and computer, (2) a suitable notation for representing the major concepts of task processing, (3) a robust method for selecting task steps in the presence of user digressions, and (4) a computational method for determining when a selected task step is completed.

3.2.1   Computer and User Prerequisites

For an individual to be able to accomplish a task requires that the individual has (1) all necessary knowledge about the task, (2) the required sensory abilities to observe the world, and (3) the required mechanical abilities to perform the actions. The necessary knowledge includes knowledge about the changes in the world state as a result of each action as well as the ability to select an appropriate action at each point during the task. There is usually no fixed set of actions that can be performed in the same order each time the task is to be accomplished.

In the environment of human-computer interaction for task accomplishment the following situation is assumed. The computer has the knowledge but does not have the required sensory and mechanical abilities to perform the task. The human has some limited knowledge about the task, but does not know everything required to carry out the task. The amount of knowledge the human has is a function of the individual. However, the individual does have the ability (it is assumed) to perform the required sensory and mechanical operations. Thus, the computer and human depend on each other for successful completion of the task.

To provide the problem solving assistance demonstrated in the sample dialog segments, the computer must have:

1. A representation of the goals, actions, and states that model the task in order to reason about the appropriate steps needed to complete the task.

2. A robust algorithm for selecting the next recommended task step, accounting for user digressions to task steps other than the one of current interest to the computer.

3. A computationally effective method for determining when a task step is completed.

The first and third requirements are essential for any type of problem solving/task planning process the computer may undertake. The second requirement comes from the need for variable initiative behavior where the computer may not always have control. For example, compare the computer's response in the different segments of figures 3.1 and 3.2 to the user utterance, "There is a wire from 84 to 30" (utterance 10 in figure 3.1, and utterance 8 of figure 3.2). With the computer in control, it continues to focus on the original task step of connecting a wire between connectors 84 and 99. With the user in control, the computer directly addresses the user's concern about the wire between connectors 84 and 30. One observes that the computer's response varies according to who has control of the dialog. Thus, a robust response mechanism is required to take into account the possibilities of variable initiative behavior. The remainder of this section presents the key ideas for modeling interactive task processing that meet these requirements.

3.2.2 A Domain-Independent Language for Describing Goals, Actions, and States

The first step was to define a notation, independent of any domain, that could be used to define the major entities of task processing—goals, actions, and states. The Goal and Action Description Language (GADL) is a notation for representing goals that may be accomplished as part of accomplishing a task. A detailed description is provided in appendix A. A representative description for a goal, an action, and a state are given next.

- *goal(computer,obs(phys_state(prop(wire(84,99),exist,X),TS))).*

- *learn(ext_know(phys_state(prop(wire(84,99),exist,present),true))).*

- *phys_state(prop(wire(84,99),exist,absent),true).*

The first description is the computer goal for the performance of an observation concerning the existence of a wire between connectors 84 and 99 (note utterance 1 of the computer controlled dialog segment). The values X and TS represent uninstantiated variables. The second description is the action of learning that there should be a wire between connectors 84 and 99 (note utterance 1 of the user controlled dialog segment). The final description is the physical state that no wire exists between connectors 84 and 99. Comparing this to the *phys_state* component of the first description, it is observed that the value for X is now instantiated with the term *absent* while the value for TS is instantiated with the term *true*. An abbreviated notation is sufficient for the discussion in the text. The key points to be observed about the notation are the following.

1. It can represent either physical or mental states. The types of physical states are:

   - Properties—qualitative information (e.g. "the switch is up").

- Measures—quantitative information (e.g. "the voltage is 10").
- Behaviors—conditional properties and measures (e.g. "the LED is on when the switch is up").

While the types of mental states are:

- Extensional belief—belief in the existence of a physical or mental state (e.g. "the user knows there is a wire between connector 84 and 30").
- Intensional belief—belief in being able to determine the existence of a physical or mental state; or belief about an action (about knowledge on how to do the action or on the action's effects on the world state) (e.g. "the user knows how to locate connector 84").

2. It can represent physical or mental actions. The types of physical/sensory actions are:

- "Sense" a physical state (e.g. see the state, hear the state, etc.).
- Manually achieve a physical state.
- Perform a specific physical or sensory action (affects states as a side-effect).

While the types of mental actions are:

- Learn about a physical or mental state (extensional or intensional belief).
- Learn information about physical actions.

3. Actions may be composed of action hierarchies that define an action in terms of substeps or subactions. Actions with no subactions are deemed *primitive actions*. The primitive actions will be specific physical or sensory actions that accomplish the required state effects as consequences of the action. When a primitive action cannot be performed, its ancestor actions cannot be performed either.

4. The notation can be augmented as needed for a more sophisticated world model. For example, GADL state descriptions can be integrated with a representation that maintains time information if desired. A theory on the representation and semantics of time information has not been considered in this research. As another example, all states are associated with a level of certainty for which belief about the state's existence is held. The only certainty levels currently implemented are *true* and *false*, but there could be intermediate levels if desired.

These characteristics of GADL are necessary for any notation that is used to represent goals, actions, and states within an interactive task processing environment.

3.2.3   Robust Selection of Task Steps

As previously noted, variable initiative behavior prohibits the computer from planning the required sequence of task steps from start to finish. A more robust system is needed to compensate for digressions and possible mistakes and misunderstandings. For example, the utterance from the sample dialog segments, "There is a wire from 84 to 30," digresses from the computer's current task step (bending back connector 84). Another possibility is that a user may report erroneous information or perform actions incorrectly. It is assumed that the human user is cooperative. Nevertheless, people are fallible. Mistakes may be made or misunderstandings may occur. The system may assume that the user is always reporting correct information and correctly performing actions, but if it does, it will fail in situations where errors occur. Since any complete system plan for the task may be rendered unusable, a better approach is for the computer to recommend the next task step or goal to be pursued based on the current state of the task without planning all the steps required to complete the task.

In the interactive environment, the nature of dialog can influence the way in which the task is performed. To separate the dialog processing model from specific task application domains, there must be separate modules for dialog processing (the *dialog controller*) and task processing (*domain processor*). However, robust selection of task steps requires frequent communication between the domain processor and the dialog controller. The domain processor recommends necessary domain task steps while the dialog controller handles the necessary communication with the user for obtaining required information. This information allows the domain processor to update its world model upon which it bases its next task step selection.

To maintain independence between the domain processor and the dialog controller, they are considered as separate components that communicate via a standardized interface to allow the dialog controller to be usable with all types of domain processors. This is illustrated in figure 3.4. In this system, the dialog controller will send messages to the domain processor. The messages will consist of any necessary input and a code to signify the appropriate reasoning operation to be performed. The domain processor will perform the requested reasoning operation and return an appropriate response. To facilitate domain independence, GADL is used for representing both the inputs and responses. The only restriction on the domain processor is that it must be capable of performing these reasoning operations. How they are performed is a function of the individual domain processor. This list of reasoning operations is given next.

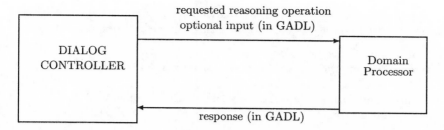

Figure 3.4
Interface between Dialog Controller and Domain Processor

1. Determine the next recommended task step according to internally computed goals.

2. Revise internal goals based on a state description provided by the dialog controller and then determine next recommended task step.

3. Assimilate user input (a state description) into domain processor knowledge about the world state.

4. Provide a helpful item of information to assist with the user goals. The underlying goals of the user are reflected in the state information supplied by the dialog controller. This information is given priority even when it conflicts with the domain processor's task goals.

5. Provide expectations for inputs that result in continuation of the current goals (i.e. provide a list of state descriptions that are relevant to the recommended task step).

6. Provide answers to questions about state information or the relevance of proposed task steps.

3.2.4   Determining Task Step Completion

At any given moment during a task, some task step is being attempted. However, a particular task step may be quite complicated, requiring several subactions or substeps to be completed. In the computer controlled sample dialog, adding the wire between connectors 84 and 99 requires the following substeps to be carried out.

```
1. Locate connector 84.
2. Locate connector 99.
3. Obtain an extra wire.
4. Connect one end of the wire to connector 84.
5. Connect the other end of the wire to connector 99.
```

Furthermore, these steps can be subdivided. For example, connecting one end of the wire to connector 84, a metal spring, can be broken down as follows.

```
4a. Bend back connector 84.
4b. Insert the wire end into connector 84.
4c. Release connector 84.
4d. Check that the wire end is securely connected to
    connector 84.
```

In an interactive environment, many substeps may take place without any dialog, or there can be extended interaction about some or all of the substeps. Nevertheless, the domain processor is only interested in the completion of the task step regardless of the amount of dialog that occurs. Given the complications that may occur in completion of the task step, how can task steps be represented in a computational system so that determination of completion is clear? The solution proposed in this research is to use the paradigm of theorem-proving, for which computational approaches are well established. Nilsson [Nil80] provides a discussion of theorem-proving for first order predicate calculus that is sufficient to understand the usage of theorem-proving in this research. A relevant summary of this discussion is provided in the following paragraphs.

In a typical theorem-proving problem there are a set of statements expressed in a formal language (in this case predicate calculus), from which a goal statement (also expressed in the formal language) is to be derived. A theorem-proving system will use *axioms* and *rules* to try to derive the goal statement. The axioms are simply the set of statements given to be true. The rules tell how to derive new statements from other statements already shown to be true, either by virtue of being an axiom, or by derivation from another rule. As an example, consider the following system:

axioms

$father(mary, john)$ $male(john)$
$parent(john, bill)$ $male(bill)$

rules

$male(Y) \wedge parent(X, Y) \Rightarrow father(X, Y)$

where

$father(X, Y)$ denotes Y is the father of X
$male(X)$ denotes X is male
$parent(X, Y)$ denotes Y is a parent of X

In this system a goal of the form $father(A, B)$ may be proven in one of two ways.

1. By finding an axiom of the form $father(A, B)$ (e.g. $father(mary, john)$)

2. By using the rule that $father(A, B)$ is true if B is a male ($male(B)$) and

B is a parent of A ($parent(A, B)$) (e.g. $father(john, bill)$ can be proven this way)

Research into automatic theorem-proving has progressed to the point where there now exists at least one practical programming language, Prolog (see Clocksin and Mellish [CM87] for an introduction to the language), based on the theorem-proving paradigm. In fact, Prolog has been used extensively in implementing the system developed in this research. Consequently, logical rules can be given that state how a task step may be completed (part of the information provided in the *knowledge* module of the system), and a theorem-proving process can be invoked to determine if a task step has been completed. This process is performed by the *general reasoning* module of the architecture.

3.2.5 What About Dialog?

This section has developed a model of interactive task processing whereby the system can exhibit robust behavior in providing recommendations about necessary task steps during a dynamic task-oriented dialog as well as determine when a task step is completed via theorem-proving. However, in listing the substeps of adding a wire between connectors 84 and 99, one can observe that some substeps are mentioned in the dialog (i.e. substeps 3, 4, and 4a), while others are not. This leads to consideration of the next major question in the overall dialog processing model, *"what is the purpose of language within the interactive task processing environment?"* Why are some task steps and substeps discussed while others are not mentioned? These concerns are the topic of the next section.

3.3 Integrating Task Processing with Dialog: The Missing Axiom Theory

This section presents a model for the role of language in assisting with completion of a task. This model is based on the premise of Grosz [Gro78] that for task-oriented dialogs the dialog structure mirrors the task structure. In this model the fundamental unit of task structure will be called a *task step*. Completion of a task step implies that a new state description has been obtained that can be used by the domain processor. What qualifies as a task step varies from task domain to task domain, but the common bond is that when a task step is completed, a new state description for the domain processor is obtained. By considering task step completion as a theorem to be proven, the role of language becomes the acquisition of missing but needed axioms for proving completion of task steps.

This section discusses this approach to determining task completion and the associated role of language this entails. Also discussed is the major question about this approach, "What happens when the missing axiom is not supplied by the dialog?" The Interruptible Prolog SIMulator (IPSIM) is introduced as a means for allowing the appropriate control of the theorem-proving paradigm for task step completion within a dialog environment.

3.3.1 The Role of Language: Supplying Missing Axioms

Using the theorem-proving paradigm for determining task step completion, we consider specifying completion of a possible task step, learning about the existence of a wire between connectors 84 and 99. In GADL this is represented as

$$goal(computer, learn(ext\_know(phys\_state(prop(wire(84, 99), exist, X), true)))).$$

X denotes the unknown value for the existence of the wire. Furthermore, it is assumed that known axioms will be represented as $axiom(Axiom)$ where $Axiom$ represents the known information. For example,

$$axiom(phys\_state(prop(wire(84, 99), exist, present), true))$$

denotes that the wire is present while

$$axiom(phys\_state(prop(wire(84, 99), exist, absent), true))$$

denotes the wire is absent. Thus, a possible first step in proving the theorem for learning about the existence of the wire might be to look in the knowledge base for the appropriate axiom which gives the wire's status. What if no such axiom exists? Perhaps the computer can get the user to look for the wire and report the information to the computer. The computer must use language to attempt to have the user perform the desired action. Thus, the role of language for the computer is the acquisition of missing axioms needed for proof of task step completion. This is the working definition for the role of language that has been used throughout the course of this research.

3.3.2 Interruptible Theorem Proving Required ⇒ IPSIM

Consider utterance 3 of the computer controlled dialog, "add a wire between connector 84 and connector 99." This is uttered in the hope of obtaining the missing axiom that the wire is now present. However, the user response, "I need help" does not satisfy the missing axiom. In the conventional theorem-proving paradigm, this would cause backtracking to find another rule that could be used for the proof. This would require explicitly listing theorem descriptions for each possible response that provides an axiom other than the one needed, a very non-practical approach. This type of clarification subdialog is very common to general dialog, especially task-oriented dialogs, and requires the general solution outlined below.

1. Dynamically modify the original theorem to insert completion of the substep for which clarification is needed. In this case, the substep is "learn how to do the substeps of adding a wire between connectors 84 and 99."

2. Resume the theorem-proving process by first trying to complete the substep.

In order for this solution to be viable, there is a need for the theorem-proving process to be under the guidance of the overall controlling process for the dialog processor, the dialog controller. The dialog controller must decide when theorem-proving is to be activated, when language can be used to acquire missing axioms, and when theorems must be dynamically modified. This has led to the development of the Interruptible Prolog SIMulator (IPSIM), a Prolog-like theorem-prover which is controlled by the dialog controller via a standard set of commands. A description of IPSIM is provided in appendix B. Section 3.4.3 shows how IPSIM facilitates integration of task processing with dialog processing after first considering the following question: *how can the computer exploit what it knows about the user?* The integration of user modeling into the dialog processing theory is discussed next.

3.4 Exploiting Dialog Context: User Model

3.4.1 Accounting for User Knowledge and Abilities

Cooperative problem solving involves maintaining a dynamic profile of user knowledge, termed a *user model*. This concept is described in the collections [KW88] and [KW89], as well as in [Chi89], [CJ89], [Fin89], [LC89], [Mor89], and [Par88]. The user model contains information about specific properties of users in order to have a system that is sufficiently flexible for a variety of users. Its purpose is to indicate what needs to be said to the user to enable the user to function effectively. It also indicates what should be omitted because of existing user knowledge. User model information is maintained in the knowledge module of the architecture, available for whatever reasoning processes that need knowledge about the user.

Because considerable information is exchanged during the dialog, the user model changes continuously. Consequently, a theory of user model must provide for its update throughout the course of the dialog. Consider again the computer-controlled dialog from figure 3.1. Utterance 4, "I need help," indicates that the user needs to be led through the substeps for adding the wire. These substeps were previously listed and are reproduced below.

1. `Locate connector 84.`
2. `Locate connector 99.`
3. `Obtain an extra wire.`
4. `Connect one end of the wire to connector 84.`
5. `Connect the other end of the wire to connector 99.`

Notice that the computer resumes with a request for obtaining a wire, the third substep. The first two substeps about locating connectors 84 and 99 are not mentioned. Why? From utterances 1 and 2, the computer was able to infer that the user already knew how to locate the connectors. How were these inferences made, and how did they affect the course of the dialog? This is discussed in the following section.

3.4.2   Computing Inferences from User Input

This is the mechanism by which additional axioms are asserted about the user. Once a user input is received, the dialog controller invokes an inferencing procedure whereby some possible inferences about user knowledge are attempted. Some possible inferences are given below.

1. If the axiom meaning is that the user has a goal to learn some information, then conclude that the user does not know about the information. An example is: *if the user has the goal to learn how to add a wire, then infer that the user does not know how to add the wire.*

2. If the axiom meaning is that an action (to achieve or observe a physical state) was completed, then conclude that the user knows how to perform the action. An example is: *if the user has added a wire, then infer that the user knows how to add a wire.*

3. If the axiom meaning describes some physical state, then conclude that the user knows how to observe this physical state. In addition, if the physical state is a property, then infer that the user knows how to locate the object that has the property. An example is: *if the axiom is that a wire exists, then infer that the user knows how to observe that the wire exists and infer that the user knows how to locate the wire.*

4. If the axiom meaning is that the user has or has not performed some primitive action, then make the appropriate inference about the user's knowledge about how to perform this action. An example is: *if the user has located the wire, then infer that the user knows how to locate the wire.*

5. If the user has completed an action by completing each substep, then conclude that the user knows how to do the action. An example is: *if the user has completed adding a wire by explicitly performing each substep, then infer that the user knows how to add a wire.*

These inferences are represented in GADL, and thus the inferences are based on the abstract representation of an action, with the specific details based on the specific values for the given action. Note that these inferences are based on intuitive notions about their usefulness without pursuing any careful theoretical study. It could be a separate research project on user modeling to formalize a theory of what constitutes appropriate inferences (see section 2.3.3 for a description of one such study). Here the main focus is on a theory for exploiting the user model, including any reasonable inferences such as the ones described above. A theory of usage is described next.

3.4.3   User Model Usage: Integrating Task Processing with Dialog

The user model is used when the theorem prover tries to prove completion of a goal. The user model axioms are available to the theorem prover just

1. C: Is there a wire between connector 84 and connector 99?
2. U: It is not there.
3. C: Add a wire between connector 84 and connector 99.
4. U: I need help.
5. C: Obtain a wire.
6. U: Okay.
7. C: Connect metal of one free end of the wire to connector 84.
8. U: How?
9. C: Bend back connector 84.
10. U: Done.
11. C: Insert free end of wire into connector 84.
12. U: The wire is connecting.
13. C: What is the LED displaying?

Figure 3.5
Sample dialog for illustrating relationship of theorem-proving and dialog

like any other axioms that may be defined or inferred. Thus, user model usage is a function of the theorem specifications for proving completion of goals. This research has not been concerned with developing a theory of the optimal way to utilize the user model in the theorem specifications. Rather, this research presents a theory on the organization of user model information that permits usage within the framework of a dialog system. The viability of this theory is demonstrated in the example dialog segment of figure 3.5, which also shows how the Missing Axiom Theory integrates task processing and dialog processing. This segment is identical to the computer-controlled sample except for utterances 10 and 11.

The proof trees of figure 3.6 illustrate the relationship between the theorem-proving process and the subdialogs. After determining that a wire between connectors 84 and 99 is missing (MAIN TASK STEP 1), the computer initiates a subdialog to have this wire added (MAIN TASK STEP 2). Utterance 4 initiates a clarification subdialog for this main task step. Consequently, the dialog controller instructs IPSIM to insert into the active theorem specification the substep on learning how to accomplish the main task step (the "learn to do add" substep). The insertion occurs immediately before the theorem step of finding or acquiring the needed axiom about adding the wire.

Resumption of theorem proving leads to an expansion of the substep on learning how to add the wire. This expansion requires leading the user through each substep of the main task step. The first two substeps are to locate connectors 84 and 99. These are satisfied trivially by the theorem prover without the use of language. The user model axioms indicating that the user knows how to locate these connectors were inferred by the dialog controller

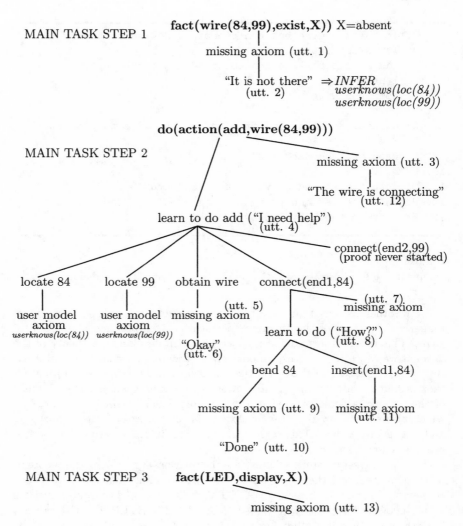

Figure 3.6
Theorem-proving/dialog relationship

from the user statement, "It is not there."

The next substep requires language to acquire the missing axiom (utterances 5 and 6). The substep introduced by utterance 7 (connect(end1,84)) requires the dialog controller to initiate a second clarification subdialog for learning how to do its substeps as a result of utterance 8. After completing the first two of these substeps, utterance 12 indicates the wire has been obtained. The system searches through the possibilities for missing axioms for the unsatisfied task steps introduced at utterances 11, 7, and 3 to determine that this supplies the missing axiom for the main task step, adding the wire. Consequently, proofs of the substeps are discontinued (note also that the proof of the substep "connect(end2,99)" does not even need to be started), and the dialog continues with the next main task step (MAIN TASK STEP 3).

Thus, the Missing Axiom Theory not only integrates task and dialog processing, but it also facilitates exploiting user model knowledge as a natural part of the dialog interaction. The next section discusses another important feature of dialog context, expectation of user inputs.

3.5 Exploiting Dialog Context: Input Expectations

3.5.1 Foundations of Expectation-Driven Processing

It is common knowledge among researchers in natural language processing that contextual information must be used in order to properly understand and respond to utterances in a dialog (see Allen [All87] for a general discussion). This is true for all types of dialogs including task-oriented dialogs, the object of study in this research. Consider again the first part of the computer controlled dialog sample.

```
1. C: Is there a wire between connector 84 and connector 99?
2. U: It is not there.
3. C: Add a wire between connector 84 and connector 99.
4. U: I need help.
5. C: Obtain a wire.
6. U: Okay.
```

The system must use the established dialog context in order to properly interpret every user utterance as follows.

- Utterance 2: to determine what "it" refers to (i.e. the wire from 84 to 99).

- Utterance 4: to determine what the user needs help with (i.e. adding the wire).

- Utterance 6: to determine whether "okay" denotes confirmation or comprehension (i.e. confirmation that the wire has been obtained).

This section discusses how a specific contextual feature, expectation, can be used to facilitate the proper understanding of utterances in dialog. The foundation for this model of expectation-driven processing comes from the notion of attentional state proposed in [GS86] by Grosz and Sidner. In their theory of discourse structure attentional state is one of three distinct but interacting components that integrates research about focusing in discourse (Grosz [Gro81]) with work on intention recognition in discourse (Allen [All83]). The overall theory is described in section 2.6.3.

As previously noted in the description of the overall theory of Grosz and Sidner, the attentional state represents the conversational participants' focus of attention. For current purposes, the key factor to note is that the attentional state enables certain processing decisions to be made locally. This avoids the computational overhead of exhaustive search and allows the possibility of real-time processing. In the following section we present details on how Grosz and Sidner's model of attentional state can be cast in a framework based on expectation and used to make local processing decisions essential to proper understanding of utterances produced within the context of a dialog.

3.5.2   Using Expectation-Driven Processing

The Role of Language and Attentional State

Since expectation-driven processing is to be used in understanding utterances, it is useful to briefly review the purpose of these utterances. The Missing Axiom Theory says that language is used to obtain missing axioms needed to prove completion of task steps. As a result, at any point in the dialog there is a specific task step under discussion for which there is a missing axiom. Consequently, there are specific expectations based on the task step being discussed. For example, after the computer produces an utterance that is an attempt to have a specific task step S performed, where S and another task step T must be completed as part of performing task step R, there are expectations for any of the following types of responses.

1. A statement about missing or uncertain background knowledge necessary for the accomplishment of S (e.g. "How do I do substep S_1?").

2. A statement about a subgoal of S (e.g. "I have completed substep S_1.").

3. A statement about the underlying purpose for S (e.g. "Why does S need to be done?").

4. A statement about ancestor task steps of which accomplishment of S is a part (e.g. "I have completed R.").

5. A statement about another task step which, along with S, is needed to accomplish some ancestor task step (e.g. "How do I do T?").

6. A statement indicating accomplishment of S (e.g. "S is done.").

Expectations for a specific task step denote a focus space, and the collection of all the expectations models the attentional state.

Sources of expectation

The two sources of expectation in a dialog system are the dialog controller and the domain processor. As the overall control mechanism for the dialog system, the dialog controller has knowledge about the general nature of task-oriented dialogs, independent of the particular task being performed. The dialog controller's knowledge about expectations is stored within the knowledge module of the architecture (figure 3.3). In contrast, the domain processor is the task-specific component of the dialog system and consequently has the knowledge about the specific details of the actions applicable within the domain. The knowledge sources for these modules provide information for different categories of expectation as shown below.

Categories of expectation

Our primary emphasis has been to categorize *semantic* expectations. These expectations are based on the current dialog topic independent of the linguistic form used to initiate the dialog topic. *In task-oriented dialogs, the dialog topic is about the completion of a task step.* We have identified the following four categories of expectation.

> **Situation Specific Expectations (SSE)**—These are computed by the domain processor whenever the content for the current topic comes from the domain processor. These expectations are based on the situation specific content of the topic. For example, if the topic is, "What is the LED displaying?", then the SSE for this topic consist of the possible descriptions for the LED display.

> **Situation Related Expectations (SRE)**—These are also computed by the domain processor. These expectations are also based on the situation content of the topic, but describe expectations related to the situation rather than specifically about it. For the above topic, the SRE consist of other possible circuit observations that could be reported instead of the LED display. For example, alternative observations could include the presence or absence of wires, the position of the power switch, and the presence or absence of a battery.

> **Task Specific Expectations (TSE)**—These are computed by the dialog controller. These expectations are based on the specific content of the topic, but are based on considering the topic as an instantiation of an abstractly defined action. For example, "What is the LED displaying?" is an instantiation of the abstract action, *"observe* the *value* for a *property* of an *object*," where *property* is instantiated to *display,* and *object* is instantiated to *LED.*[1] In general, TSE for observing the *property* value of an *object* include questions on the location of the *object*, on the definition of the *property*, and on how to perform the observation. In addition, the TSE include responses that can be interpreted as state descriptions

---

[1] The GADL representation would be *obs(phys_state(prop(LED,display,X),TS)),* where X and TS are uninstantiated values (see section 3.2.2).

User Response Type	Expectation Category			
	SSE	SRE	TSE	TRE
(1) (about uncertain background knowledge)			X	
(2) (about a subgoal)			X	
(3) (about the purpose)				X
(4) (about ancestor task steps)				X
(5) (about another task step)		X		X
(6) (indicating accomplishment)	X		X	

Note: SSE and SRE are computed by the domain processor. The TSE and TRE are computed by the dialog controller.

Table 3.1
Relationship between expectation categories and response types

of the relevant *property*. In general, the TSE include potential questions and statements about substeps of the current action.

Task Related Expectations (TRE)—These are also computed by the dialog controller. These expectations are very broad and based on general principles about the performance of actions. Example TRE include general requests for help or questions about the purpose of an action. Another important constituent of the TRE are the expectations for topics which are ancestors of the current topic.[2] For example, the current topic could be the location of a connector, which could be a subtopic of connecting a voltmeter wire, which could be a subtopic of performing a voltage measurement. The TRE for the location of this connector includes all the expectations, partitioned into the different categories, for the topics of connecting a voltmeter wire and performing a voltage measurement.

Table 3.1 shows the relationship between these four categories of expectation and the list of response types given previously. An X denotes that the given statement type is considered a part of the given expectation category. There may be multiple entries in a row because the dialog controller may produce expectations also computed by the domain processor.

Now that we have overviewed the process by which expectations are obtained, we will show how they are used to handle some important problems of dialog processing.

---

[2] A topic's ancestors are determined from the structure of the theorem proof containing the topic's associated task step.

Expectation Usage

After the semantic expectations are computed, they are used by the language understanding process of the dialog controller to assist in the understanding of utterances. The understanding process takes each expectation in turn and attempts to find an interpretation of the utterance that matches the expectation. In order for this to be successful, the expectations must be ordered from most expected to least expected. The ordering of groups is SSE, TSE, SRE, and TRE. The expectations within the SSE, TSE, and SRE are arbitrarily ordered while the TRE expectations are ordered according to their hierarchical distance from the current topic. By using expectations in this way, they can assist in resolving several problems in natural language understanding pertaining to contextual interpretation as shown below.

1. The referent of pronouns (in the implemented system the only pronoun is "it")—The initial interpretation will leave the slot for the referent of "it" unspecified. If this interpretation of the utterance can be matched to the expectation, the value for "it" will be filled with the value provided by the expectation. Consider the following example from the beginning of the section:

   ```
   1. C: Is there a wire between connector 84 and connector 99?
   2. U: It is not there.
   ```

   In computing the SSE as well as TSE for the user utterance, one expectation in each category will be for a statement asserting a fact about the wire's existence or absence. When the understanding system interprets the user statement, it will interpret it as a statement asserting that some unspecified object is absent.[3] The dialog expectation will provide the value of the unspecified object.

2. The meaning of short answers (in the implemented system these include such responses as "yes," "no," and "okay")—The idea for each of these is similar. These utterances have a restricted meaning of one or two alternatives. The proper choice will be determined by the expectations produced based on the situation. In the following example from the beginning of the section,

   ```
   5. C: Obtain a wire.
   6. U: Okay.
   ```

   it is likely that okay denotes confirming completion of the goal to obtain a wire. It is less likely that it denotes comprehension of the request. To properly resolve the meaning of okay, intonation and pitch would be required when speech is used (Barry Koster, personal communication). In

---

[3] In GADL, this would be $phys\_state(prop(\_, exist, absent), true)$.

any case, after the computer's statement the SSE includes an expectation for an utterance confirming completion, and this will consequently
be the interpretation given to okay.

However, in the following,

```
5.  C:  Obtain a wire.
6a. U:  What color?
6b. C:  The color is irrelevant.
6c. U:  Okay.
```

the more likely interpretation is that okay denotes comprehension of
utterance 6b rather than denoting confirmation that the original goal
has been accomplished. In this case, after utterance 6b, an attempt at
completing a *learn* goal to learn the required wire color, there is a TSE
for a comprehension utterance to acknowledge learning, and this will be
the interpretation okay receives.

3. Maintain dialog coherence when dealing with clarification subdialogs—
   consider figure 3.7, a segment of computer controlled dialog that differs
   from that of figure 3.1 only at utterances 10 and 11. When the final utterance is spoken there are three active goals: (1) adding the wire (from
   utterance 3), (2) the subgoal of connecting the metal on one end of the
   wire to connector 84 (from utterance 7), and (3) the deeper subgoal of
   inserting the wire end into connector 84 (from utterance 11). The user
   response does not satisfy the missing axiom for completing either subgoal. However, it does satisfy the missing axiom for completing the main
   goal. The dialog controller uses the expectations for these active goals
   in determining the active goal to which the statement is relevant before
   checking if the utterance satisfies a missing axiom. There is greater expectation for utterances about the subgoals, but this utterance is not
   one of them. It is expected as an utterance about the main goal. Expectations remain active until terminating pursuit of the goal for which
   the expectations were computed. Thus, expectations play a key role in
   handling subdialog movement.

This section has shown how expectation-driven processing is used to facilitate contextual understanding of utterances. In chapter 5 it will be shown
how expectations assist in parsing ungrammatical inputs that are inherent
with spoken language. Next we address the problem of integrating variable
initiative dialog into the theory.

3.6   A Theory of Variable Initiative Dialog

3.6.1   Defining Variable Initiative and Dialog Mode

"Variable initiative dialog" is dialog where: (1) either dialog participant can
have control of the dialog, (2) control can vary between participants during

3. C: Add a wire between connector 84 and connector 99.
4. U: I need help.
5. C: Obtain a wire.
6. U: Okay.
7. C: Connect metal of one free end of the wire to
      connector 84.
8. U: How?
9. C: Bend back connector 84.
10. U: Done.
11. C: Insert free end of wire into connector 84.
12. U: The wire is connecting.

Figure 3.7
Example System Dialog Interaction: Clarification

the dialog, and (3) intermediate levels of control are allowed.

A variable initiative dialog system contrasts with other NL dialog systems such as those described in section 2.7 for which the dialog is either purely user controlled or purely computer controlled. In user controlled dialog systems the computer acts as a passive agent responding to user queries. The main type of dialog system that has been built, the question-answer system, is an example of a user controlled dialog system. In computer controlled dialog systems the user is totally dependent on the computer for accomplishment of the task. However, in general task assistance, it is inappropriate for the computer to control the entire dialog when the user can accomplish large portions of the task without guidance.

The need for variable initiative dialog arises because at some points the user has sufficient knowledge to take control of the dialog and accomplish several goals without much computer assistance while at other times, the user needs detailed assistance. In other words, user initiative is characterized by giving priority to the user's goals of carrying out steps uninterrupted, while computer initiative is characterized by giving priority to the specific goals of the computer. If dialog is the medium of interaction, then dialog must be used to indicate who has current control of the task (i.e. whose goals currently have priority). Thus, for human-computer variable initiative task-oriented dialog the key idea is that *the level of initiative in the dialog should mirror the level of initiative in the task.* This principle is analogous to the principle noted by Grosz [Gro78] for task-oriented dialogs—*the structure of a dialog mirrors the structure of the underlying task.*

Consider again the computer controlled and user controlled dialog samples. In particular, note the differing response to the user utterance, "There is a wire from 84 to 30." In the computer controlled sample the computer's goal is still its unproven goal of adding a wire between connectors 84 and 99. Conversely, in the user controlled sample, the computer directly responds to the user's assertion. In the first sample the computer's goal has priority while in the second sample the user's goal has priority. In general, we have observed that the level of initiative that the computer has in the dialog is primarily reflected in the degree to which the computer allows the user to interrupt the current subdialog in order to discuss another topic. When the user has control the interrupt is allowed, but when the computer has control it is not.

However, initiative is not an all or nothing prospect. Either the user or computer may have the initiative without having complete control of the dialog. In the user controlled sample the computer is still able to provide direct assistance about adding the wire while the user is ultimately able to complete the verification of the circuit's proper behavior without explicitly discussing each of the computer's specific goals for verifying circuit behavior. Based on these observations four dialog *modes* have been identified that characterize the level of initiative that the computer can have in a dialog. These are described below.

1. *Directive*—The computer has complete dialog control. It recommends a task goal for completion and will use whatever dialog is necessary to complete this goal. No interruptions to other subdialogs are allowed.

2. *Suggestive*—The computer still has dialog control, but not as strongly. The computer will recommend a task goal for completion, but will allow minor interruptions to closely related subdialogs.

3. *Declarative*—The user has dialog control and can interrupt to any desired subdialog at any time. However, the computer is free to mention relevant facts as a response to the user's statements.

4. *Passive*—The user has complete dialog control. Consequently, the computer will passively acknowledge user statements. It will provide information only as a direct response to a user question.

3.6.2 Response Formulation in Variable Initiative Dialog

From the description of each mode, one observes that the degree of interruptibility allowed by the computer increases from directive to passive mode. Thus, the dialog mode has a critical effect on the computer's choice of response. Response topic selection by the dialog controller can be viewed as shown in figure 3.8. It is a function of the computer's goal, the user focus, and the dialog mode. When the user focus differs from the computer's goal (i.e. an interrupt situation), the dialog mode becomes the decisive factor in the selection process as described next.

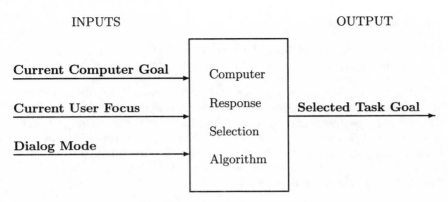

INPUTS   OUTPUT

Current Computer Goal

Current User Focus

Dialog Mode

Computer Response Selection Algorithm

Selected Task Goal

Figure 3.8
Flow Diagram of Computer Response Selection Process

1. **Mode = directive**

   • Select the computer goal without any regard for the user's focus.

2. **Mode = suggestive**

   • Try to find a common relationship between the computer goal and the user focus and select this as the next goal.[4]

   • If no common relationship is found, then select the computer's original goal as it still has the initiative.

3. **Mode = declarative**

   • Try to find a common relationship between the computer goal and the user focus as in the suggestive mode case. If a common relationship is found, convert the goal into an item of knowledge that may be useful to the user, effectively making the selected goal a "learn" goal rather than some explicit domain action.

   • If no common relationship was found, find an uncommunicated fact relevant to the user focus and select the learning of that fact as the next task goal.

---

[4]This search for a common relationship is a search through the domain knowledge hierarchy. For example, in our implemented domain of circuit repair, the circuit is decomposed into subcircuits where each subcircuit is decomposed into electronic components such as switches, resistors, transistors, wires, and lights, and each of these subcircuits and components has a set of specifications about how they should function. A common relationship is found when the user focus and computer goal share a sufficiently close common ancestor in the knowledge hierarchy.

4. **Mode = passive**

- Select as a goal that the user learn that the computer has processed the user's last utterance.

The mechanics of the response selection algorithm will be illustrated via the following situation: suppose that the user initially states, "the light is off," and suppose the computer knows that in order for the light to be lit, the switch must be turned up to activate the power (i.e. **state(switch,up)** $\Rightarrow$ **state(power,on)**). Consequently, the computer goal of highest priority is to put the switch up, while the user focus is on the light.[5] The selection process as a function of mode would be as follows:

1. Directive—User focus is ignored with no interrupts permitted. The selected goal is to put the switch up.

2. Suggestive—User focus is seen to be related to the computer goal via the domain fact relating the switch and the light. The selected goal is to "observe the switch position when the light is off."

3. Declarative—User now has control. Consequently, the selected goal must be a relevant fact. The previous goal is converted to "user learn that the power is on when the switch is up."

4. Passive—User has complete control. Computer must content itself to acknowledge processing the last user utterance.

As another example, the differing computer response to the user utterance, "There is a wire from 84 to 30," in the two sample dialog segments is a result of the differing dialog mode between the two segments. The mode is directive in the computer controlled segment. Consequently, the computer's selected response topic is its goal about adding the wire between connectors 84 and 99. In contrast, the mode is declarative in the user controlled segment. Consequently, the computer response relates to the user focus on the wire between connectors 84 and 30. It is seen that dialog mode can lead to variable initiative dialog behavior through its effect on the computer's response selection process.

3.7 Putting the Pieces Together

3.7.1 What Is a Dialog?

Our notion of dialog is closely associated with the corresponding task to which the dialog pertains. Consequently, we define a dialog to be all the language interaction that occurs in conjunction with the associated task. Since a task

---

[5]A complete plan recognition process for inferring the user's exact goal is at the present time, a very costly computational process and not feasible in a system designed for real-time interaction. Consequently, our system uses the user focus as determined from the previous utterance as a basis for its beliefs about the user's current goals.

is composed of a set of task steps, we define a subdialog to be all the language interaction pertaining to one task step. To summarize, a dialog will be composed of a set of subdialogs where each subdialog is the language interaction that pertains to one task step.

The question may be asked, "why a *set* rather than *sequence* of subdialogs?" The answer is that the generality of natural language dialog allows somewhat arbitrary suspension and resumption of subdialogs (see Reichman [Rei85] for example). Consequently, the constraint that the subdialogs form a sequence is too restrictive. The ability to suspend and resume subdialogs must be allowed. Hence, the term *set*, which does not imply a rigid order, is used. Now that the fundamental notions of dialog and subdialog have been defined, we can look at the overall dialog processing architecture that reflects the theory we have developed.

3.7.2   Integrated Theory

This chapter presents an integrated theory of dialog processing. Interactive task processing is modeled via a reasoning approach whereby the domain processor iteratively recommends needed task steps based on the current situation without necessarily developing a complete plan. Language is used to supply missing axioms when attempts to prove these recommended task steps cannot proceed. Consequently, the attempt to prove a task step leads to a subdialog about the task step. The user model is maintained as axioms usable by this theorem proving process and is exploited to avoid needless repetition as well as to ensure that needed information is presented. Expectation is associated with specific subdialogs (task steps), is compiled from both domain and dialog knowledge, and is used for contextual interpretation. Finally, variable initiative dialog is made possible by variable types of processing in determining the current response topic (task step) according to the degree of allowed interruptibility. In the next chapter, we turn our attention to the specifics of the computational model. The model is based on the architecture and theory presented in this chapter.

Chapter 4

Computational Model

This chapter describes the computational model that has evolved from the theory of integrated dialog processing presented in the previous chapter. The organization of this chapter follows.

1. A high-level description of the basic dialog processing algorithm.

2. A detailed discussion of the major steps of the algorithm.

3. A concluding critique that evaluates the model's effectiveness at handling several fundamental problems in dialog processing.

The system software that implements this model is available via anonymous FTP. Details on obtaining the software are given in appendix C.

4.1 Dialog Processing Algorithm

4.1.1 Motivation and Basic Steps

Figure 4.1 describes the basic steps of the overall dialog processing algorithm that is executed by the dialog controller.[1] By necessity, this description is at a very high level, but specifics will be given in subsequent sections. The motivation for these steps is presented below.

Since the computer is providing task assistance, an important part of the algorithm must be the selection of a task step to accomplish (steps 1 and 2). Because the characterization of task steps is a function of the domain processor, the dialog controller must receive recommendations from the domain processor during the selection process (step 1). However, since a dialog may have arbitrary suspensions and resumptions of subdialogs, the dialog controller cannot blindly select the domain processor's recommendation. The relationship of the recommended task step to the dialog as well as the dialog status must be considered before the selection can be made (step 2).

Once a task step is selected, the dialog controller must use the *general reasoning facility* (i.e. the interruptible theorem prover, IPSIM) in step 3 to determine when the task step is accomplished. Whenever the theorem prover cannot continue due to a missing axiom, the dialog controller uses available knowledge about linguistic realizations of utterances in order to communicate a contextually appropriate utterance as well as to compute expectations for the response. After the response is received and its relationship to the missing axiom determined, the dialog controller must decide how to continue the task step completion process. Various possibilities are:

---

[1] Recall that "task steps" are represented as "goals" in the GADL representation. Consequently, the term "goal" will also be used during the discussion of the algorithm.

1. Obtain suggested goal from the domain processor.

2. Based on the suggested goal and the current state of the dialog, select the next goal to be pursued by the computer and determine the expectations associated with that goal.

3. Attempt to complete the goal.

4. Update system knowledge based on efforts at goal completion.

5. Determine next operation to be performed by the domain processor in providing a suggested goal.

6. Go to step 1.

Figure 4.1
Dialog Processing Algorithm

- Proceed with the proof as before. If the input indicates the need for clarification about the task step, the dialog controller may, before proceeding, insert completion of a substep into the proof.

- Initiate backtracking to complete the proof. This will occur when the input shows no particular relationship to the missing axiom.

- Prematurely terminate the proof attempt. This might occur as the result of an input requiring immediate attention that does not fit within the context of the task step being attempted. This is used to handle dialog phenomena such as interrupts where the orderly structure of a task-oriented dialog is disturbed.

A detailed discussion of step 3 is presented in section 4.4. Once the attempt at proving task step completion terminates, the dialog controller must send to the domain processor any newly acquired domain knowledge (step 4). After the update the dialog controller must decide upon the type of recommendation to obtain from the domain processor, and the cycle repeats (steps 5 and 6). However, the possibility of variable initiative dialog requires that the domain processor recommendation be a function of the computer's level of initiative. Consequently, the dialog processor must be able to specify the type of recommendation to be made, and the domain processor must be able to reason in a variety of ways according to the type of recommendation requested (see section 3.2.3).

With this overview of the dialog processing methodology in mind, we are now ready to look at an example.

1. C: Is there a wire between connector 84 and connector 99?
2. U: It is not there.
3. C: Add a wire between connector 84 and connector 99.
4. U: I need help.
5. C: Obtain a wire.
6. U: Okay.
7. C: Connect metal of one free end of the wire to connector 84.
8. U: How?
9. C: Bend back connector 84.
10. U: Done.
11. C: Insert free end of wire into connector 84.
12. U: The wire is connecting.
13. C: What is the LED displaying?

Figure 4.2
Main Example of Dialog Processing

4.1.2   Tracing the Basic Steps

The algorithm will be illustrated by using the sample dialog segment of figure 4.2. This segment is the one used in section 3.4.3 to illustrate the integration of task processing, dialog processing, and user model usage via interruptible theorem-proving. It will be used extensively to illustrate various details of the algorithm, and will be known as the "Main Example."

Prior to utterance 3, the suggested goal obtained from the domain processor was

$goal(user, ach(phys\_state(prop(wire(connector(84), connector(99)), exist, present), true)))$

or "have the user achieve the physical state that the wire between connectors 84 and 99 exists" (step 1). Step 2 of the algorithm selects this as the next goal to be pursued by the computer and the ensuing dialog (utterances 4 through 12) results from the completion attempt (step 3). At step 4 the dialog controller sends to the domain processor the knowledge that the "wire exists" (obtained from utterance 12). At step 5 the dialog controller selects the next operation to be performed by the domain processor in suggesting a new goal. The attempt at completion for this goal ensues with utterance 13.

This loop will repeat indefinitely until the next selected goal is to terminate the task, implying termination of the dialog. The ideas described previously on computational task processing, the role of language, context, expectation, and variable initiative dialog are used in the appropriate steps of this algorithm as will be seen in the following sections.

4.2   Receiving Suggestion from Domain Processor

As described in the previous chapter, the theory calls for interactive task
processing whereby

- A general architecture requires separate modules for domain expertise (the domain processor) and dialog supervision (the dialog
  controller).

- Robust goal selection requires frequent communication between the
  domain processor and dialog controller to monitor the changing
  task status.

- Variable initiative behavior requires the domain processor to have
  a variety of reasoning capabilities that are invoked by the dialog
  controller as needed.

Consequently, receiving a suggestion from the domain processor consists of:
(1) sending a message to the domain processor that specifies an operation code
(opcode) describing the required reasoning operation along with any needed
input, and (2) receiving a response from the domain processor that provides
a description of the suggested goal to be attempted next. GADL is used as
the domain-independent language for describing goals, actions, and states, as
needed. The following is the set of opcodes that instruct the domain processor
to suggest a goal to be accomplished. These operations are a subset of all
the possible reasoning operations that the domain processor may be asked to
perform (see section 3.2.3).

1. **next_step**: give the next task step to be performed according to the
   current goals of the domain processor.

2. **revise_goals**: revise the domain processor's goals based on state information obtained from a user input, then compute the next step to be
   performed.

3. **helpful_info**: give a domain fact to assist the user by giving priority to
   the state information obtained from user input.

To illustrate the difference between these three operations consider the
following dialog excerpt where the domain processor's primary goal is to "put
the switch up,"[2]

> C: Put the switch up.
> U: The LED is displaying only a flashing seven.

---

[2]For clarity, the domain processor suggestion is described using English rather than
GADL, the actual representation used within the system.

The suggestion provided by the domain processor at this point (step 1 of the algorithm) is a function of which of the three operations is requested. The **next_step** operation would yield "put the switch up," as the user's input provides no direct indication that putting the switch up has already been accomplished. The **revise_goals** operation would yield "what is the position of the switch when the LED is displaying a flashing seven?", as the domain processor revises its goals to take the user's statement into account, yielding the goal to learn the value for the dependent condition of the reported observation (i.e. the LED display is a function of the switch position). The **helpful_info** operation would yield "there is supposed to be a wire between connectors 84 and 99," a fact highly relevant to the user information about the LED display (i.e. when the wire between connectors 84 and 99 is missing, the LED will display a flashing seven instead of the correct display). Here the computer gives priority to the reported state information instead of to its own goals.

4.3 Selection of Next Goal

The second step of the dialog processing algorithm is to select the next goal to be pursued by the computer. It might be thought that once a suggested goal is received from the domain processor, it would automatically become the next goal that the computer would attempt to accomplish. However with variable initiative dialog, such an approach is inadequate because it:

- assumes the previous goal was successfully completed;

- does not consider the current dialog mode;

- does not consider the structure of the dialog.

Consequently, a function must be defined which selects the next goal to be pursued based on the suggestion of the domain processor as well as relevant factors in the dialog. The function *choose_action* will perform this selection. The inputs and outputs of this function are described below.

Inputs

Mode—the current dialog mode (passive, declarative, suggestive, or directive)

Input—specifies the result of the previous goal completion attempt (the possibilities are: a context shift, a theorem proving failure, or a theorem proving success)

Suggestion—suggested goal from the domain processor

DiscourseStructure—all discourse structure information about the current dialog

Outputs

Goal—selected goal

Expectation—list of expected responses to the performance of *Goal*

DiscourseOp—code that tells how a subdialog about *Goal* fits into the discourse structure

The rules of operation for *choose_action* are the following.

1. *Mode* = **passive**—in this case, the user has maximal initiative; consequently, the selection process does the following:

   - **If** the last subdialog involved satisfaction of a computer goal,[3] then set *Goal* = *Suggestion* to use the suggested domain goal as a response to acknowledge completion of the computer's previous goal; set *DiscourseOp* to indicate creation of a new subdialog.

   - **Else if** the last user input was a question, set *Goal* = *Suggestion*, as the suggested domain goal should be a response to the question; in addition, set *DiscourseOp* to indicate continuation of the subdialog that produced the question.

   - **Else** set *Goal* = "computer comprehends" and *DiscourseOp* to indicate continuation of subdialog; this corresponds to a simple acknowledgement of the user's last statement.

2. *Input* indicates that a context shift has occurred. Set *DiscourseOp* to indicate reopening the old context and set *Goal* to the suggested goal of this reopened context.

3. *Input* indicates that a theorem failure occurred. This indicates that the domain processor's previous suggestion should again be attempted, but by providing more details. *Goal* will be set to this previous suggestion, and *DiscourseOp* will be set to indicate amplification of the previous subdialog.

4. According to *DiscourseStructure*, there is an uncompleted subdialog previously suspended due to a context shift. If the primary goal of this subdialog was a learn goal (i.e. goal(user,learn(...)) in GADL), it will be assumed that this was achieved, and *choose_action* will be recursively invoked. Otherwise, set *DiscourseOp* to indicate reopening of this subdialog, and set *Goal* to be the primary goal of this reopened subdialog.

---

[3]That is, the form of the goal in GADL was *goal(computer,...)*.

5. The default situation. Set *Goal* = *Suggestion* and *DiscourseOp* to create a new subdialog for the next domain suggestion. Alternatively, the suggestion could be an auxiliary goal needed to complete the previous goal. In this case the last subdialog will be reopened. This possibility is discussed in more detail in the discussion of alternative domain goals (section 4.7.1).

4.4 Attempting Goal Completion

The third step of the dialog processing algorithm is to attempt completion of the selected goal. This attempt involves the use of the general reasoning system to prove goal completion. As previously indicated, it is when the theorem proving process is blocked due to a missing axiom that language is used. The computational specification of this step is given by the "Goal Completion Algorithm," which is presented below.

Goal Completion Algorithm

Inputs (first three were computed by *choose_action* as described in section 4.3)

> *Goal*—goal to be accomplished.
>
> *Expectation*—list of expected responses to the performance of *Goal*.
>
> *DiscourseOp*—code that tells how a subdialog about *Goal* fits into the discourse structure.
>
> *Mode*—gives the dialog mode in which dialog about *Goal* will be initiated.
>
> *Knowledge*—all knowledge resident in the *knowledge* module of the architecture is available for use.

As an example, before utterance 3 in the Main Example (figure 4.2), *Goal* would be instantiated as "add a wire between connectors 84 and 99." *Expectation* would then be the set of expected responses provided from the domain processor that pertain to this domain goal. *DiscourseOp* would denote "create a new subdialog."

Outputs

> *RelevantGoal*—goal that is completed; *RelevantGoal* ≠ *Goal* is possible; this can occur due to a context shift or when *Goal* is part of a hierarchy of active goals, any of which may be completed.
>
> *AxiomValue*—value for axiom that indicates goal completion or lack of goal completion depending on the circumstances.

Result—code that denotes if goal completion successfully occurred; possible values are:

- **success**, which indicates successful completion;
- **fail(X)** where **X** indicates the cause of failure, either a simple theorem failure, the completion of some other domain processor goal, or else a context shift to another theorem/subdialog.

Continuing the discussion of the Main Example, after utterance 12, theorem proving would produce *Result* = **success** and *RelevantGoal* = *Goal*.

Steps

1. Update discourse structure based on *DiscourseOp* and *Mode*.

2. Attempt goal completion by the following steps:

   a. Attempt to prove goal completion. The dialog controller will invoke the theorem prover IPSIM. IPSIM will return in *Message* the status information about the attempt.

      - *Message* = **halt** signifies success in proving goal completion; go to step 3.
      - *Message* = **known** signifies that a needed axiom was found in the knowledge base (part of the *knowledge* module); go back to step 2a.
      - *Message* = **unknown** signifies that a needed axiom was not found and that it is inappropriate for language to be used to acquire this axiom; continue with step 2a by trying an alternative way to prove goal completion.
      - *Message* = [**Action,UtteranceSpec**] signifies there is a missing axiom and that language can be used to try to supply the missing axiom; **Action** is a GADL description of the action which the user is to attempt as a consequence of the computer producing an utterance whose tentative specification is given in **UtteranceSpec**; continue with the following steps.

b. Compute the actual specification of the utterance based on **Action, UtteranceSpec,** and the dialog context. Send this specification to the generator module for utterance production.

c. Compute expectations for the user's response.

d. Activate the recognizer module to receive the user's response and return it to the dialog controller.

e. Use contextual knowledge to map the input into its world interpretation.

f. Adjust the context structure of the dialog to correctly reflect the theorem step to which the input pertained.

g. Update the discourse structure to include the new input.

h. Compute possible inferences based on the input.

i. Select from the input and its inferences the axiom that is the closest to satisfying a possibly missing axiom for its applicable theorem.

j. Return to step 2a and continue attempt at proving goal completion by either continuing same proof or trying alternative proof as indicated in the previous step.

3. Determine values for the outputs according to the result of the attempt at goal completion.

These steps can be illustrated by the Main Example. Suppose the current point in the dialog is just after utterance 2. *Goal* is "add a wire between connectors 84 and 99." *DiscourseOp* is "create a new subdialog." *Mode* is directive. Figure 4.3 shows the proof tree developed during the goal completion attempt spanning utterances 3 through 12.

Step 1—update discourse structure: The update shows the creation of a new subdialog pertaining to the task step of adding a wire between connectors 84 and 99.

Step 2a—attempt to prove goal completion: The initial attempt at proving completion results in determining there is a missing axiom—namely, an axiom asserting the designated wire has been added. Consequently, [**Action,UtteranceSpec**] will be returned in *Message* where **Action** = "add a wire between connectors 84 and 99," and **UtteranceSpec** = "request that the wire between connectors 84 and 99 be added."

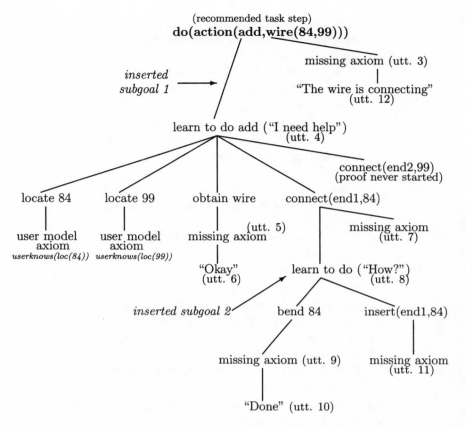

Figure 4.3
Proof Tree for Algorithm Trace

Step 2b—computing actual utterance specification: The actual specification will be the same as **UtteranceSpec**, and utterance 3 will be produced.

Step 2c—compute expectations: Expectations produced are: (1) the values given in *Expectation* that were provided by the domain processor; (2) general task expectations for the goal of achieving a property; and (3) general discourse expectations.

Step 2d—activate recognizer: The expectations produced in the previous step are sent to the recognizer module along with a request to return the user's response to the dialog controller. When the recognizer receives the user's input (utterance 4, "I need help."), it will use these expectations to determine that the action for which "help" is needed is the current action about adding the wire. Consequently, it will return to the dialog controller that the meaning of the user's response was, "I need to learn how to add the wire."

Step 2e—compute world interpretation: The meaning returned by the recognizer is mapped into the goal that the user wants to learn how to add the wire.

$$goal(user, learn(int\_know\_action(how\_to\_do(X))))$$

where $X = ach(phys\_state(prop(Z, exist, present), true))$.
and $Z = wire(connector(84), connector(99))$

Step 2f—adjust context: No adjustments are needed since the user input was an expected response to the current theorem step (adding the wire).

Step 2g—update discourse structure: Add information to indicate that the utterance is part of the subdialog about adding the wire.

Step 2h—compute inferences: These would include inferring that the user does not know how to add the wire.

Step 2i—select axiom: Since none of the inferences are more applicable to the missing axiom than the user input, it will be selected as the relevant axiom. However, this axiom does not satisfy the missing axiom for adding the wire. The axiom instead describes an "achievable subgoal" of adding the wire—learning how to perform the action. Consequently, this subgoal will be inserted into the theorem to immediately precede the point at which the theorem prover had previously suspended itself, the theorem step of looking for an axiom about adding the wire (see *inserted subgoal 1* in the proof tree).

Step 2j—continue proof attempt: The attempt will resume on the same proof which was just modified as noted.

Second iteration, step 2: After proving the user has located connectors 84 and 99 via the user model axioms, the proof will now be suspended due to a missing axiom about the user's ability to add the wire. This leads to an utterance specification that yields utterance 5 giving instructions on a substep for adding the wire. The user's response of "okay" maps into a world interpretation that the user has obtained a wire, satisfying the missing axiom for which the theorem prover had suspended itself during this iteration. Consequently, the system will continue the same proof on the next iteration of step 2.

Third iteration, step 2: The theorem prover will be suspended due to a missing axiom about connecting one end of the wire to connector 84, leading to utterance 7. Via expectations, the user's response of "How?" is mapped into a world interpretation that "the user wants to learn how to connect one end of the wire to connector 84," an achievable subgoal, which will be inserted into the theorem just before the theorem step of looking for an axiom about connecting an end of the wire to connector 84 (*inserted subgoal 2*).

Fourth iteration, step 2: The theorem prover is suspended due to a missing axiom about bending back connector 84, leading to utterance 9. The user's response of "done" maps into a world interpretation that the associated action that produced the expectation for "done" has been completed. The system will then continue to try to prove completion of all the substeps of connecting one end of the wire to connector 84.

Fifth iteration, step 2: The theorem prover is suspended due to a missing axiom about inserting an end of the wire into connector 84, leading to utterance 11. The user's response of "the wire is connecting," is not expected as a response to the current action or to its parent action of connecting the metal of one end of the wire to connector 84, but is an expected response to the original goal about adding the wire that was mentioned in utterance 3, where "the wire" refers to the wire between connectors 84 and 99. Thus, step 2f, adjusting context, will note this shift in the proper context of the utterance so that when step 2i for axiom selection occurs, it will use this context rather than the lower level goals where the user utterance was not expected. The axiom selection step will note that the utterance satisfies the missing axiom for the goal to add the wire, and the proof will be continued.

Sixth iteration, step 2: The proof will now be successfully completed since the computer has obtained verbal confirmation that the wire has been added. Ignored are the lower level substeps for which no explicit verbal confirmation of completion was ever received. Consequently, the value for *Message* will be **halt**. Go to step 3.

Step 3—determine output values for algorithm: Since the goal was completed successfully, *Result* = **success**, *RelevantGoal* = *Goal* (adding the wire), and *AxiomValue* = "the wire between connectors 84 and 99 now exists," the axiom that indicates completion of the goal. This example illustrates the processing done at the various stages in the Goal Completion Algorithm. We will now describe in more detail how this processing is done.

4.4.1   Step 2a: Attempt to Prove Completion

The IPSIM theorem prover is responsible for determining when goals have been completed. IPSIM is an interactive theorem prover operated by the dialog controller. Operation of the theorem prover is controlled by opcodes.[4] The three opcodes used by the dialog controller in proving goal completion are the following.

1. **next_goal**: Continue current attempt at proving goal completion.

2. **try_other**: Continue attempt at proving goal completion by selecting an alternative rule for proving the current theorem.

3. **input**: Check the supplied input to see if it satisfies the missing axiom.

next_goal initiates a normal proof attempt. If the proof is suspended due to a missing axiom and language is used to obtain user input for the proof, then the **input** command is used to determine the relationship of the input to the missing axiom. Upon each subsequent iteration of step 2 of the Goal Completion Algorithm (attempting goal completion), either **next_goal** or **try_other** may be invoked to continue the proof attempt. The operation selected will be a function of the result of the previous iteration as described at the end of section 4.4.8.

Whenever the theorem prover is invoked, *Message* gives the result of the theorem proving process. The possible values for *Message* were given in the steps of the algorithm. The value that needs elaboration is *Message* = [**Action,UtteranceSpec**]. This value is returned when IPSIM suspends itself due to a missing axiom that has been marked by a special marker that indicates outside interaction is permissible. This marker is the **axiom_need** marker. The form of this marker in a theorem specification is the following.

```
axiom_need(Action,AxiomList).
```

```
    Action---GADL description of the action for which the missing
                axiom is supposed to indicate completion.
    AxiomList---a list of GADL descriptions of axioms which
                satisfy the missing axiom.
```

For example, for the goal that the user add a wire between two connectors X and Y, the marker would have the following form.

```
axiom_need(ach(phys_state(prop(wire(connector(X),connector(Y)),
                               exist,present),TS)),
       [phys_state(prop(wire(connector(X),connector(Y)),
                        exist,Value),TS)]).
where Value and TS denote unknown values
```

---

[4]Recall that a detailed discussion of IPSIM is given in appendix B.

When one of these markers is encountered, the value for **Action** is returned as the `Action` value given in the marker. In addition, IPSIM invokes a procedure defined in the system's dialog knowledge that will compute **UtteranceSpec**, the specification of the utterance to be used in attempting to acquire the missing axiom. It indicates if the utterance will be a command, question, or assertion. While language can be used in different ways in trying to acquire missing axioms, the following simple approach is used.

- If **Action** is an "achieve" or "perform," then the utterance specification will be for a command (e.g. "put the switch up")

- If **Action** is an "observe," then the utterance specification will be for a question (e.g. "what is the position of the switch?")

- If **Action** is a "learn," then the utterance specification will be for an assertion (e.g. "the power is off when the switch is down.")

In addition, IPSIM must return a list of axioms that will satisfy the missing axiom. As previously noted, `AxiomList` of the **axiom_need** marker gives such a list of axiom descriptions. However, these descriptions are based on general dialog knowledge about the relationship between actions and language, independent of the specific domain. Consequently, when **Action** is a domain action, the domain processor can provide a more specific and detailed list of axioms that can satisfy the missing axiom. Thus, when **Action** is a domain action, a list of axioms supplied by the domain processor replaces the list given in `AxiomList`.

While language can be used to acquire the needed missing axiom, it may not be appropriate. Although the proof process should still be suspended, the decision not to use language may be due to linguistic and discourse factors that indicate difficulty in using language in certain situations. A general study of such factors has not been undertaken in this research. It is simply acknowledged that such a possibility exists and should be considered. When IPSIM returns *Message* = **unknown**, this situation has occurred, and the dialog controller will instead instruct IPSIM to try an alternative method for proving the theorem.

However, in the normal situation where the axiom is missing and a value for **UtteranceSpec** returned, the decision to speak has been made. The next step is to compute a final specification of the utterance based on context.

4.4.2   Step 2b: Computing Final Utterance Specification

Once the decision has been made to speak, one might assume that the value for **UtteranceSpec** will act as the input to the language generator. Normally, this will be the case, but not always. The original computation of **UtteranceSpec** is based strictly on the description of the action with which the utterance is associated. It does not consider any information about the state of the dialog. In particular, it does not consider the following.

1. The relationship of the action to the past. The action could be to observe a physical state that had previously been observed. In this case the utterance might need to question if the state is still true, or perhaps question whether the state ever actually existed. For example, a previous observation may have indicated that the power circuit was not working (i.e. that the LED is off), yet an exhaustive check finds no cause for the failure. The utterance produced as a result of **UtteranceSpec** would be "Is the LED off?" A more appropriate utterance would be "Is the LED still off?" or "Are you sure that the LED is off?"

2. The relationship of **UtteranceSpec** to the discourse structure. Consider the following possibility:

   ```
   C: Add a wire between connector 84 and connector 99.
   U: Should I turn the switch down?
   ```

   The resulting goal of the computer may be for the user to learn that it is not necessary to turn the switch down. The utterance produced as a result of **UtteranceSpec** would be something like, "the switch does not need to be put down." However, "no" is sufficient as a response.

3. The certainty about an assertion. For example, the action might be for the user to learn that a certain wire exists (i.e. that it is true that a particular wire exists). However, the computer cannot see the circuit board. It can only speak of such facts as that they "should" be the case. Similarly, when asserting that it is true that a user can use a particular object, the computer cannot really assert that the user actually uses the object, but it can assert that the user is "able" to use the object. Such considerations are based on discourse considerations independent of the specific action.

Consequently, a function must be defined which can map **UtteranceSpec** into the actual utterance specification to be used by the generator. This function considers the situations mentioned above before producing a final value for the utterance specification.

Once the final utterance specification is produced, it is sent to the language generator implemented by Robin Gambill (section 6.3), which produces an appropriate utterance. In addition, information about the utterance is recorded in the discourse structure.

4.4.3   Step 2c: Computing Expectations for the User's Response

The first phase is the production of *semantic* expectations, expectations based on the current dialog topic independent of the linguistic form used to initiate it. In task-oriented dialogs, the dialog topic is about completion of a task step or goal. Once the semantic expectations are computed, they are mapped into *linguistic* expectations according to rules for how various semantic meanings can be linguistically expressed. The discussion about producing semantic expectations will be given first, followed by a discussion of the mapping from semantic expectations to linguistic expectations.

Representation

Each semantic expectation is represented as a triple of the form:

$$[\text{Sef}, \text{Constraints}, \text{WorldMeaning}]$$

where **Sef** is a pseudo-linguistic representation of the semantic expectation; it will be mapped into an actual linguistic expectation; **Constraints** are a list of constraints on the values of the corresponding **Sef**; and **WorldMeaning** is a representation, in GADL, of the complete meaning of the utterance with respect to the context which is active as defined by the topic of conversation on which these expectations are based. As an example, consider the following semantic expectations for the goal,

ach(phys_state(prop(Obj,PropName,PropValue),_)),

a goal to achieve the value PropValue for the property PropName of object Obj:

1. `[affirmation(TS),[],`
   `phys_state(prop(Obj,PropName,PropValue),TS)]`
2. `[state_value(phys_state(prop(Obj,PropName,Value),true)),`
   `[(Value \== PropValue)],`
   `phys_state(prop(Obj,PropName,Value),true)],`
3. `[state_value(phys_state(prop(Obj,PropName,PropValue),TS)),[],`
   `phys_state(prop(Obj,PropName,PropValue),TS)]`

The first and third expectations have the same **WorldMeaning**, but different values for the **Sef**. The first expectation gives rise to responses such as "okay" or "done" while the last expectation gives rise to fully specified utterances such as, "there is a wire between connectors 84 and 99." The second expectation is for a response where the object has a value other than PropValue for property PropName. The constraint, `[(Value \== PropValue)]`, captures this notion.

In general, **WorldMeaning** provides the final interpretation of the utterance. In contrast, the **Sef** acts as an intermediate representation that connects the linguistic content of an utterance with its interpretation within the present context. The **Constraints** are a list of tests that filter unreasonable interpretations. For example, the value for a voltage measurement may be constrained to be a number. Thus, to the question, "what is the battery voltage?", a response of "off" is not expected because there is no numerical interpretation of "off", while a response of "five" would be expected according to the constraint. The number of constraints that could be specified is potentially huge. However, in the implementation the number has been kept small. Nevertheless, the notion of constraints is a useful one for filtering invalid interpretations.

Expectation Sources

Recall from section 3.5.2 that there were four types of semantic expectations: (1) Situation Specific Expectations (SSE), (2) Task Specific Expectations (TSE), (3) Situation Related Expectations (SRE), and (4) Task Related Expectations (TRE). The source for each of these expectations is given below.

> SSE—These expectations come directly from the domain processor and normally consist of possible state descriptions that can occur as a result of the performance of the current domain goal of observing, achieving, or learning about some physical state.

> TSE—These expectations come from the *knowledge* module of the system. They are based on the GADL representation of the goal that is the dialog topic and thus generalize over all task domains. These expectations are given for the following possible goals.

>> obs(phys_state(meas(Des,Val),TS))—observing a measure.

>> obs(phys_state(prop(Obj,PropName,PropValue),TS))—observing a property.

>> obs(phys_state(behav([Behavior],[Condition]),TS))—observing a behavior that consists of one conditional behavior, and one condition on which the behavior depends.

>> ach(phys_state(prop(Obj,PropName,PropValue),TS))—achieving a physical state which is a property of some object.

>> perf(Action)—perform a "primitive action."

>> learn(int_know_action(how_to_do(perf(Action))))—learning how to perform a primitive action.

>> learn(int_know(phys_state(prop(Obj,PrName,PrValue),true)))—learning about the intensional definition of some property (i.e. learning knowledge which will enable a person to be able to determine if an object has a specific value for a specific property).

>> learn(ext_know(phys_state(behav([Behavior],[Condition]),true)))—learning that a particular behavior is true, where Behavior and Condition either both describe properties or measures.

>> learn(ext_know(phys_state(meas(Des,Val),TS)))—learning that a particular measure is true or false.

>> learn(ext_know(phys_state(prop(Obj,PrName,PrValue),TS)))—learning that a particular property is true or false.

    learn(int_know_action(is_substep_of(ActionChild,Action)))—
    learning that one action, ActionChild, is a substep of
    performing another action, Action.

SRE—These are also computed by the domain processor.

TRE—These are computed by the dialog controller. This computation includes collecting all the expectations for actions that
are ancestors of the current action in the discourse structure. For
example, as part of determining the value of the switch position,
the user may need to learn how to locate the switch. The TRE
for the action of learning how to locate the switch would include
the expectations (SSE, TSE, and SRE) for the action of actually
locating the switch as well as the expectations for the action of
observing the switch position. The TRE also include a list of general expectations for whenever an action is occurring. These broad
expectations include the following.

- That the user understands the computer's statement.
- That the user does not understand the computer's state-
  ment.
- That the user is finished.
- That the user wants to know if he/she is finished.
- That the user wants to know the time.
- That the user wants something repeated.

A statement that is only expected as one of these general expectations is termed a *global interrupt*. Interrupt handling is discussed
in section 4.7.1.

Computing Linguistic Expectations

Once the semantic expectations are computed, they must be transformed into
linguistic expectations that describe the forms of utterances that are expected
as inputs. The representations of the linguistic expectations are called *snf*
forms for historical reasons relating to the research project. A description of
the various snf forms is given below.[5] In all cases, the possible values for TS
are "true" or "false" with the standard semantics associated with these values.
The descriptions given assume TS = true.

    assertion(TS,np(NP))—represents an abbreviated response (often
    a noun phrase) that can be interpreted within the surrounding
    context as part of a completed world interpretation

---

[5]This representation is also used for the utterance specifications sent to the generator.
Note that representations have been developed only for what is needed for the implemented
domain of circuit repair. More representations can certainly be specified as needed.

assertion(TS,affirmative)—indicates affirmation of some fact

assertion(TS,comprehension)—indicates understanding some fact

assertion(TS,do(user,Action))—indicates user did Action

assertion(TS,state(measure,X,Y))—indicates the measure of X is Y

assertion(TS,able(user,X))—indicates user is able to do X

assertion(TS,state(PropName,Obj,PropValue))—indicates that object Obj has value PropValue for property PropName

assertion(TS,want(user,X))—indicates user wants X

question(wh,location(Obj))—asking for the location of Obj

question(wh,definition(PropName,_))—asking for a definition or meaning description for PropName

question(wh,how_to_do(Action))—asking how to do Action

question(wh,time(_))—asking the time

question(wh,status(task,_))—asking the task status

question(yn,connected_to(X,Y,_))—asking if X should be connected to Y

question(yn,do_action(X))—asking if action X should be done

question(wh,StateDes)—asking for the missing value in StateDes

question(yn,StateDes)—asking if StateDes is true

command(X)—requesting X to be done

The list of forms for Action are the following:

perf(PrimAction) where PrimAction could be:

> ident(obj)—identify Obj
> add(Obj)—add Obj
> remove(Obj)—remove Obj
> replace(Obj)—replace Obj
> push(X,into,Y)—establish that X is in Y by pushing
> twist(X,to,Y)—twist X to value Y

ach(state(State))—achieve physical state State, where State is a GADL property, measure, or behavior state description

obs(state(State))—observe physical state State

Once the linguistic expectations are computed, they can be used by the recognition module to assist in interpreting the user's response as described below.

4.4.4   Step 2d: Receiving User Input

Once the expectations are computed the dialog controller sends a message to the recognizer module of the linguistic interface indicating the need for user input to be sent back to the controller. When the recognizer receives an input, it uses the expectations provided by the dialog controller to assist in computing the correct interpretation for the input. The basic idea for using the expectations is the following: given the errors inherent in speech recognition technology and given the "ungrammaticalness" that often occurs in spoken utterances, it is very likely that the input received cannot be directly parsed using *any* specified grammar. Consequently, the recognizer will use an error-correcting parser to produce a set of the n most likely correct parses by performing insertions, deletions, and substitutions of words to obtain a "grammatical" utterance. Each parse will be given a score estimating its likelihood of being the correct parse. In addition, each of these parses will be given an expectation cost based on the likelihood of its occurrence in the current context. Thus, the overall likelihood of a parse is a combination of its grammatical likelihood and expectation likelihood. Consequently, expectation helps to select the correct parse. Details of the parsing algorithm are provided in Chapter 5.

As an example, suppose that expectations for a response to the goal "put the switch down" were computed and sent to the recognizer. Furthermore, suppose the user responded with "the switch is in the down position," but the recognizer returned "the which is in turn position." The error-correcting parser may find no distinction between the following as the most likely correct parse.

The switch is in the up position.

The switch is in the top position.

The switch is in the on position.

The switch is in the down position.

The switch is in the off position.

The switch is in the bottom position.

However, there is greater expectation for a response of the form "the switch is down" than for the others since the goal was to put the switch down, and the correct interpretation would be returned. A selected parse is represented in the *snf* formalism.

4.4.5   Step 2e: Computing World Interpretation

After an input is received and returned by the recognizer, the complete meaning of the input with respect to the world model must be computed. When an input is returned from the recognizer, the representation of the input only reflects the actual words uttered. This usually does not provide a complete interpretation. Language allows a speaker to make connections to the surrounding world without having to explicitly mention all the features to which the speaker's utterance refers. Examples of such utterances include, "yes", "ok", "zero", "on", "up", "I fixed it", "done", "there is no wire", etc. Consequently, the semantic expectations must be used to connect the actual utterance to all the features of the world referenced. Recall that semantic expectations are represented as

$$[\textbf{Sef},\textbf{Constraints},\textbf{WorldMeaning}]$$

Computing the world interpretation is the process of making the connection between the utterance and the world as defined in the semantic expectations. Consequently, a match must be made between the utterance represented as an **Sef** and a semantic expectation. The matching process consists of the following operations:

1. Map the *snf* representation of the input into its equivalent **Sef** representation.

2. Search the current semantic expectations in the following order: SSE, TSE, SRE, and TRE for a match. A match occurs when the **Sef** representation of the input matches[6] the **Sef** representation of a semantic expectation, *and* the expectation's **Constraints** are satisfied. When a match occurs, return the corresponding **World Meaning** as the world interpretation for the input.

As an example, consider the following:

```
C: What is the switch position?
U: Down.
```

The **Sef** representation of the user utterance is simply the Prolog atom **down**. It will match the following TSE expectation for elliptical responses:

```
[PropValue,[is_prop_value_for(Obj,PropName,PropValue)],
  phys_state(prop(Obj,PropName,PropValue),true)]
```

where Obj=switch and PropName=position. down will unify with the variable PropValue, the constraint will be satisfied, and the world interpretation returned will be that it is now true that the switch position is down.

---

[6]The term "matching" can be considered equivalent to the notion of unification as defined by Nilsson [Nil80].

In addition to determining the world interpretation of the input, the context level to which the input is relevant is also computed. If the expectation for the input was found in the SSE, TSE, or SRE, then the context level is the current value for **Action** which was provided by the axiom_need marker when the theorem prover suspended itself. However, if the expectation is found in the TRE for **Action**, this indicates that the actual source of the expectation was in some ancestor goal of **Action** for which there is also a missing axiom. This situation is described next. It is also possible that the input could not be found in any of the current expectations. This corresponds to an "interrupt" or unexpected input. These are discussed in section 4.7.1.

4.4.6   Steps 2f and 2g: Updating Context and Discourse Structure

After the world interpretation is computed for the input, adjustments may be required in the context structures about the dialog as well as the discourse structure. These adjustments are required when the expectation for the input is not found in the SSE, TSE, or SRE of **Action**, the current action whose proof has a missing axiom. In this situation, the input is applicable to some other action for which there was a missing axiom. Suppose this action is an ancestor of **Action**. Call this action **AncestorAction**. The adjustment is to skip over the nodes in the proof tree between **Action** and **AncestorAction** to make **AncestorAction** the current action in the theorem. An example dialog that illustrates this is figure 4.4. After utterance 11 of this example, the proof tree structure is given in figure 4.5. There are now expectations for the five highlighted goals: (1) learning how to locate connector 41; (2) locating connector 41; (3) attaching the end of the wire with the large plug to connector 41; (4) making the complete wire connection; and (5) observing the voltage measurement. Whenever the goal to learn how to do an action is introduced, the goal to actually perform the action is added to the proof tree as well if it constitutes a substep of the original action.

After utterance 11, **Action** = "learn how to locate 41". Utterance 12 is an expectation for the original "observe the voltage" goal. Consequently, the four previously active subgoals are skipped in the proof tree, and "observe the voltage" again becomes the current action in the theorem. The subsequent continuation of the proof will be immediately successful since "zero" satisfies the missing axiom. If the proof had resumed with "learn the location of connector 41" as the current node in the proof tree, "zero" would not have satisfied the missing axiom for that goal, and an erroneous continuation of the dialog may have occurred. This example illustrates the importance of maintaining coherence between the goal completion proof and the dialog. Situations where the relevant action is not an ancestor of **Action** will be discussed in section 4.7.1.

1. C: What is the voltage between connector 41 and
        connector 110?
2. U: I do not know.
3. C: Locate the voltmeter.
4. U: OK.
5. C: Add a wire between the minus com hole on the voltmeter
        and connector 41.
6. U: How do I do that?
7. C: Connect the end of the black wire with the small plug to
        the minus com hole on the voltmeter.
8. U: OK.
9. C: Connect the end of the black wire with the large plug to
        connector 41.
10. U: Where is connector 41?
11. C: Near the left boundary and toward the middle is a green
        region. Now, in the middle of this green region is
        connector 41.
        (user makes all connections and measures voltage)
12. U: Zero.

Figure 4.4
Illustrative Subdialog for Context Search

4.4.7   Step 2h: Computing Inferences from the Input

This is the mechanism by which additional axioms are asserted and available
to the theorem prover. Once a disambiguated input is returned, an inferencing
procedure is invoked whereby some possible inferences defined in the *knowledge*
module of the system are attempted. A description of these inferences was
given in section 3.4.2 in discussing user model as these inferences mainly refer
to acquired knowledge about the user.

4.4.8   Step 2i: Selecting Applicable Axiom

Recall that the computational purpose of dialog is to supply missing axioms.
The determination of the world interpretation for the input and the subsequent
adjustment of the knowledge structures ensures that the input is associated
with the appropriate point in the theorem for which it may be a missing axiom.
The purpose of this step is to determine if the input or one of its inferences in
fact satisfies the requirements for the missing axiom. The possible relationships
an axiom can have with the missing axiom for an action are the following.

- Expected axiom—The axiom is one of the axioms specified as being
  acceptable as the missing axiom.

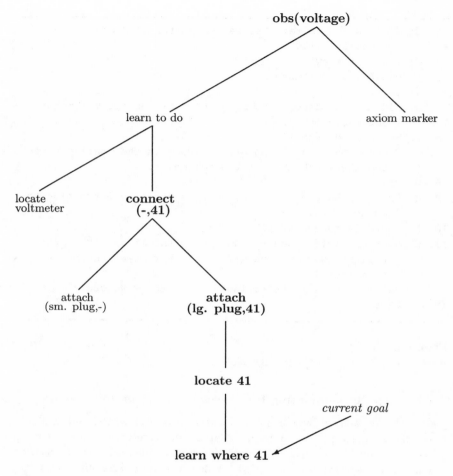

Figure 4.5
Sample Proof Tree for Context Search

- Not_expected—The axiom does not have any known relationship to the missing axiom. It is the default value for when none of the other cases occur.

- Other domain goal—The axiom indicates completion of a domain goal other than the one explicitly being attempted in the theorem. The expectations for axioms about possible alternative domain goals are given in the SRE (see section 3.5.2).

- Achievable subgoal—The axiom indicates a goal whose completion is a subgoal of the original goal *and* for which the computer can provide assistance. The relationships between an axiom and the original goal which satisfy the "subgoal" portion of this definition are the following.[7]

1. The axiom is a goal to learn about a property of an object where the main goal concerns the existence of the object. An example is: *the main goal is to achieve the existence of a wire; the axiom is a subgoal to learn what color the wire should be.*

2. The axiom is a goal to learn if something can be used to cause the existence of an object where the main goal concerns the existence of this object. An example is: *the main goal is to achieve the existence of a wire; the axiom is a subgoal to learn if another specific wire can be used to do this.*

3. The axiom indicates the user does not comprehend the definition of a state where the main goal is to observe this state. The subgoal will be to learn how to do the action associated with the main goal.

4. The axiom is a goal to learn how to do the action associated with the main goal.

5. The axiom indicates the user does not know anything about a physical state where the main goal is that the user learn about this physical state. The subgoal is to decompose learning about the physical state into more basic steps.

6. The axiom is a goal to learn how to do an action that is a subgoal of observing or achieving one of the states in a behavior where the main goal is to learn about this behavior. An example is: *the main goal is to learn that the power is on when the switch is up; the axiom is a subgoal to learn how to locate the switch.*

7. The axiom is a goal to do or learn how to do an action where the main goal is to learn about some attribute of this action (i.e. that the action is [not] necessary or desirable).

8. The axiom is a goal to learn how to achieve or observe a physical state where the main goal is to learn about this physical state.

9. The axiom is a subgoal of achieving or observing a physical state where the main goal is to learn about this physical state.

10. The axiom is a goal to learn the decomposition into substeps of the action associated with the main goal.

---

[7]Unless explicitly mentioned, the subgoal is specified by the axiom. In certain cases, the subgoal is related to the axiom, but is not equivalent to it.

11. The axiom is a goal to learn how to locate an object where the main goal is to observe or achieve some state involving the object or to learn intensional or extensional knowledge about the object.

12. The axiom is a goal to learn the definition of some state where the main goal is to achieve or observe this state.

13. The axiom is a goal to learn how to do an action where the main goal is to learn that this action is a substep of some other action.

14. The axiom is a goal to do some action or learn how to do some action which is a substep or a subgoal of a substep of the action associated with the main goal.

15. The axiom is a goal to do some action or learn how to do some action that is a substep or a subgoal of a substep of the action associated with the main goal where the main goal is to learn about some attribute of this action. An example is: *the main goal is to learn that putting the switch up is desirable; the axiom is a subgoal to learn how to locate the switch.*

The function *axiom_select(Input, Inferences, Goal, Action, SelAxiom, Relationship)* selects from among the input, *Input*, and its associated inferences, *Inferences*, the best axiom in terms of its closeness to satisfying the missing axiom for *Goal* that required action, *Action*. The selected axiom is returned in *SelAxiom* and *Relationship* indicates the relationship of *SelAxiom* to the missing axiom. *Relationship* will be one of the values described earlier. *axiom_select* operates as follows.

1. **If** the *Input* is an "expected axiom", set *SelAxiom* = *Input* and set *Relationship* = "expected axiom." An example is: *Action* = "put the switch up", *Input* = "the switch is up."

2. **Else if** one of the *Inferences*, say I_m, is an "expected axiom", set *SelAxiom* = I_m and set *Relationship* = "expected axiom." An example is: *Action* = "put the switch up", *Input* = "I fixed the switch", and one of the inferences would be "the switch is up."

3. **Else if** *Input* is an "other domain goal", set *SelAxiom* = *Input*, and set *Relationship* = "other domain goal" An example is: *Action* = "put the switch up", *Input* = "the LED is displaying nothing."

4. **Else if** *Input* is an "achievable subgoal", set *SelAxiom* = *Input*, and set *Relationship* = "achievable subgoal." An example is: *Action* = "put the switch up", *Input* = "where is the switch?"

5. **Else if** one of the *Inferences*, say I_m is either an "other domain goal" or "achievable subgoal", then set *SelAxiom* = I_m and set *Relationship* = to the appropriate value.

6. **Else** set *SelAxiom* = *Input* and set *Relationship* = "not_expected"

Examples of outputs from *axiom_select* from the Main Example include the following:

Utterance	Relationship
4. I need help.	achievable subgoal
6. Okay.	expected axiom
8. How?	achievable subgoal
10. Done.	expected axiom
12. The wire is connecting.	expected axiom

As noted in the previous discussion of the Goal Completion Algorithm, with respect to the Main Example, whenever *Relationship* = "achievable subgoal" the associated subgoal is inserted into the suspended theorem just prior to the theorem step where the suspension occurred (the theorem step of obtaining an axiom to indicate the completion of *Goal*). Consequently, when the proof attempt is resumed, the next theorem step will be for obtaining an axiom that indicates completion of the subgoal. Once the subgoal is completed, another attempt at completing *Goal* can be made.

In general, this is the last substep of step 2 of the Goal Completion Algorithm—attempting goal completion. On the next iteration of step 2, an opcode is given which controls how IPSIM attempts to prove goal completion (section 4.4.1). The choice for this opcode is a function of the result obtained from selecting an applicable axiom. If *Relationship* = "not expected," then the proof attempt will resume by selecting an alternative rule for proving the current theorem (the **try_other** opcode). Otherwise, the current proof attempt will be continued (the **next_goal** opcode).

4.5 Updating System Knowledge

Once goal completion is terminated, the fourth step of the dialog processing algorithm is to update system knowledge based on the attempt at goal completion. First, the discourse structure is updated. In the discourse structure, the status of the subdialog associated with the completed proof attempt must be updated. When the proof attempt completes successfully (*Result* = **success**), the subdialog's status is set to "closed." Otherwise, when the proof attempt does not complete successfully (*Result* = **fail(X)**), the subdialog's status is set to "suspend", as the subdialog was not completed, and may be re-entered later in order to complete the proof attempt. In either case, the parent subdialog of the just closed or suspended subdialog is reopened.

The other primary knowledge update is the transmission of information to the domain processor. If a value is transmitted, it will be *AxiomValue*, the axiom from which goal completion was inferred for a successful proof. Since the selected goal was a function of the goal recommended by the domain processor, this axiom should contain the information relevant to the domain processor. The relevant goal associated with *AxiomValue* is given by *RelevantGoal*. If *AxiomValue* is one of the domain expectations associated with *RelevantGoal*, then *AxiomValue* is sent to the domain processor, where the domain processor will update its task knowledge based on the input. Otherwise, no update is made.

4.6 Determine Next Domain Processor Operation

Because of the various possible outcomes of the goal completion process, the selection of the next reasoning operation of the domain processor cannot be based solely on the current dialog mode. The function *operation_selection* computes the value for *Operation*, the code which specifies the next reasoning operation to be performed by the domain processor in suggesting the next action to be performed in completing the task. The possible values for *Operation* are **next_step**, **revise_goals**, or **helpful_info**. These were described in section 4.2. The rules of the function are described below (let *Mode* denote the current dialog mode).

1. A context shift has occurred. Set *Operation* = "no new suggestion." The next goal selected by *choose_action* (section 4.3) will be based on the context shift that has occurred in the dialog.

2. The user input indicates the user is unsure how to proceed. Give the computer more initiative by setting the current mode to the next highest mode after *Mode*. Recursively invoke *operation_selection* with the new mode.

3. The user input indicates the user claims the task is finished. If the computer has the initiative, this claim is viewed skeptically. The computer will rely on the domain processor's judgment as to whether or not the task is completed. However, if the user has the initiative, the computer defers to the user's claim and ends the dialog since the task is supposedly complete.

4. The axiom returned for the Goal Completion Axiom was not expected. The domain processor will make no new suggestion. Instead, the dialog controller will try to complete the previous goal again by going into more detail.

5. If the axiom was expected for the relevant goal and *Mode* indicates the computer has the initiative, set *Operation* = **next_step**. This indicates a natural continuation of the domain processor's goals when the computer has the initiative.

6. The default case—choose the value for *Operation* according to the value for *Mode* as follows.

- *Mode* = *passive* or *Mode* = *declarative*—set *Operation* = **helpful_info.** The user has the initiative, so try to find a relevant fact.

- *Mode* = *suggestive*—set *Operation* = **revise_goals.** The computer has the initiative but is willing to modify its goals depending on the last user input.

- *Mode* = *directive*—set *Operation* = **next_step.** The computer has maximal initiative. Proceed with its intended goals without revision.

4.7 Solutions to Dialog Processing Problems

Now that a description of the computational model has been provided, an examination of how this model handles several important problems in dialog processing will be presented. The following problems were examined.

1. It is very commonly the case that a dialog utterance does not directly address the topic of the previous utterance. Such an utterance is termed an *interrupt*. There are several levels of interrupts ranging from clarification subdialogs to complete topic shifts. How does the model perform interrupt handling?

2. In a dialog system where speech recognition is used, recognition errors are going to occur. This means that the input received by the computer will often not be exactly what the user said. Furthermore, spoken language is frequently "ungrammatical," particularly with respect to written language, the basis for most grammars. How can dialog knowledge assist in the processing of misrecognized, ungrammatical inputs?

3. Finally, it has been mentioned that the capability for providing variable initiative dialog would greatly increase the utility of dialog systems. How does this model support variable initiative dialog?

4.7.1 Interrupts

A common phenomenon of dialog is the evolution in dialog topic as the dialog proceeds. When a new or related topic is introduced before another topic is completed, the introduction is termed an *interrupt* of the previous topic. There are various degrees of interrupts as indicated in the following example. Consider in the following sample dialog segment the set of five possible responses to the question, "What is the voltage between connectors 41 and 110?"

```
C: Put the knob to one zero.
U: Done.
C: What is the voltage between connectors 41 and 110?

U1: The voltage is zero.
U2: How do I measure voltage?
U3: Should I turn the switch down?
U4: Which knob?
U5: It is time for lunch.
```

Response U1 constitutes normal completion of the topic. Response U2 introduces a *clarification subdialog* that is closely related to the original topic, but the original topic cannot be closed until the clarification subdialog is complete. Response U3 introduces an *alternative domain goal* which may or may not be related to the original topic. Analysis is required by the domain processor to make this judgment. Response U4 is a *context shift*, referring to the context about setting the knob. Response U5 is a *global interrupt*. It introduces a topic that is possible at any time and which is usually unrelated to the current topic. Handling of each of these levels of interrupts is crucial. We will discuss how our model handles each of these levels of interrupt in turn.

Clarification Subdialogs

This is the most common and least severe type of interrupt. The initiation of a clarification subdialog is determined when selecting an applicable axiom as part of the Goal Completion Algorithm (section 4.4.8). When the selected axiom is determined to be an achievable subgoal, a clarification subdialog has been introduced.

When a clarification subdialog occurs, the proof structure is modified as follows. The goal associated with the clarification subdialog is inserted into the proof tree immediately before the proof tree marker that indicates language can be used to satisfy the missing axiom for the original goal. When the proof completion attempt resumes, proving completion of the clarification subdialog goal is attempted before completion of the original goal can resume. The expectations for the original goal become a part of the TRE (section 4.4.3) for the clarification subdialog goal. The TRE are computed by the dialog controller by examining the proof tree structure, traversing the ancestors of the current goal in the proof tree looking for nodes that reflect goals for which expectations are still active.

After the clarification subdialog is entered, dialog processing continues as before. However, as can commonly happen, subsequent user responses may refer back to the parent goal instead of the subgoal. When this occurs, the input was expected in an ancestor of the present goal. All active goals between the current goal and this ancestor goal are assumed to be satisfied, and the proof will resume with the ancestor goal as the current goal in the proof (section 4.4.6). The following detailed example, obtained from usage

1. C: What is the voltage between connector 41 and
      connector 110?
2. U: How do I do that?
3. C: Locate the voltmeter.
4. U: OK.
5. C: Add a wire between the minus com hole on the voltmeter
      and connector 41.
6. U: How do I do that?
7. C: Connect the end of the black wire with the small plug to
      the minus com hole on the voltmeter.
8. U: OK.
9. C: Connect the end of the black wire with the large plug to
      connector 41.
10. U: Where is connector 41?
11. C: Near the left boundary and toward the middle is a green
      region. Now, in the middle of this green region is
      connector 41.
12. U: Where is connector 110?
13. C: Near the lower left corner is a tan region. Now, in
      the upper right of this tan region is connector 110.
14. U: Zero.

Figure 4.6
Sample Subdialog with Clarifications

of the implemented system,[8] illustrates this method for handling clarification
subdialogs. The actual representation of the goals and actions is GADL. An
abbreviated representation will be used for display purposes. The sample subdialog is given in figure 4.6.

After utterance 1, the proof tree structure[9] is given in figure 4.7. Utterance 2 is interpreted as an "achievable subgoal" according to rule 4 of the
achievable subgoal definitions. This results in the proof tree structure of figure 4.8. The goal to learn how to measure a voltage has been inserted as
a subgoal of actually measuring the voltage. The theorem specification for
learning how to measure a voltage will consist of performing each step in the
action decomposition for measuring a voltage. These action decompositions
are also represented in GADL and reside in either the domain processor or
the knowledge modules of the system architecture (figure 3.3) depending on

---

[8]In the actual system, numbers are spoken using the digit representation. Thus, 110
would actually appear as one one zero. The reason for this is the vocabulary restriction
necessary with speech recognition.

[9]Throughout the sample proof trees, unproven active goals for which missing axioms
exist will be highlighted in boldface.

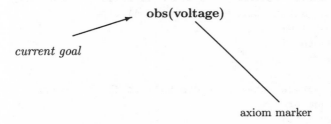

Figure 4.7
Proof tree after utterance 1

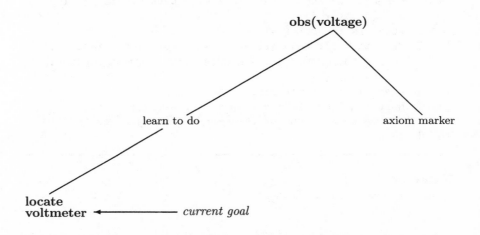

Figure 4.8
Proof tree after utterance 2

the domain specificness of the action. For example, the action decompositions for measuring a voltage reside in the domain processor module. Each action in an action decomposition may be further decomposed until the decomposition contains only primitive actions (actions represented by "perf" actions in GADL). The major steps in the action decomposition for measuring the voltage between H1 and H2 follow.

1. Locate the voltmeter.

2. Connect the negative terminal on the voltmeter and H1.

3. Connect the positive terminal on the voltmeter and H2.

4. Read the measurement on the voltmeter according to the dc 25 scale.

5. Disconnect the voltmeter wires.

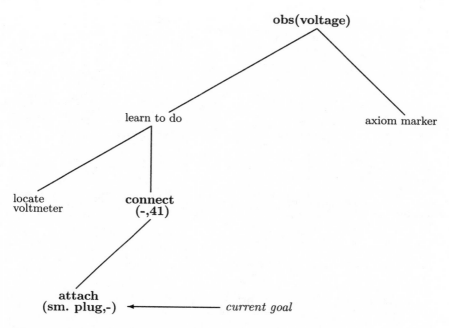

Figure 4.9
Proof tree after utterance 7

Figure 4.9 shows the state of the proof tree after utterance 7, the request to attach one end of the wire to the negative voltmeter terminal. To reduce the size of the tree, the node for "learning how to connect the negative terminal on the voltmeter and connector 41" will be omitted. It would have been inserted between **connect(-,41)** and **attach(sm. plug,-)**. At this point, there are active expectations for: (1) attaching the given end of the wire; (2) making the complete wire connection; and (3) observing the voltage measurement.

The state of the proof tree after utterance 10 is given in the proof tree of figure 4.10. By rule 11 in the achievable subgoal definition, the request to know how to locate connector 41 is an achievable subgoal of attaching the end of the wire with the large plug to connector 41. There are now expectations for five goals: (1) learning how to locate connector 41, (2) locating connector 41, (3) attaching the end of the wire with the large plug to connector 41, (4) making the complete wire connection, and (5) observing the voltage measurement. Whenever the goal to learn how to do an action is introduced, the goal to actually perform the action is added to the proof tree as well if it constitutes a substep of the original action.

Figure 4.11 shows the proof tree after utterance 12, "Where is connector 110?". This utterance was not expected at any of the four active subgoals. Consequently, it is analyzed as a subgoal of the top level goal (measuring

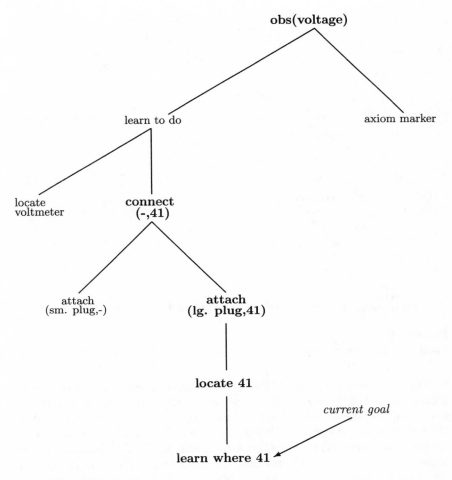

Figure 4.10
Proof tree after utterance 10

the voltage), and it is assumed that the other goals were completed. The theorem prover is commanded to skip over these other goals and to make the original goal the current goal. Again via rule 11 of the achievable subgoal definition, the dialog controller determines that utterance 12 is an achievable subgoal of the original goal. This determination causes the addition of the subgoals to locate and learn how to locate connector 110.[10] Finally, when the last utterance, "zero," is received, it is expected as a response to the original

---

[10]Note that if it turned out one of the other subgoals were not completed, there would be some type of user statement which would cause a context shift when interpreting the input about the subgoal because it would not be found in the currently active expectations.

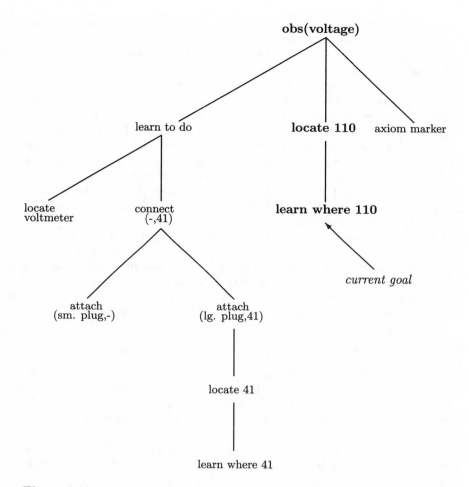

Figure 4.11
Proof tree after utterance 12

goal, and the two subgoals about locating connector 110 are skipped. The response is the expected axiom, and consequently the clarification subdialog and original subdialog are complete.

Alternative Domain Goals

The underlying principle for handling axioms that indicate completion of alternative domain goals is: *provide potentially useful information to the domain processor whenever it is obtained.* Satisfying this principle within the overall dialog processing algorithm (figure 4.1) requires terminating the current attempt at goal completion and updating the system knowledge based on the new axiom. The details describing the handling of this situation within the dialog processing algorithm are provided in the following paragraphs.

Recall that the main step of the Goal Completion Algorithm is a sequence of iterations for attempting goal completion. At the end of each iteration is the selection of an axiom via *axiom_select* (section 4.4.8). When *axiom_select* returns *Result* = "other domain goal," then it is known that the user input satisfies an alternative domain goal. Normally, the next iteration begins by trying to prove goal completion. The theorem prover is invoked according to an opcode whose selection is based on the result of the previous iteration. However as noted above, when an iteration indicates that the acquired axiom denotes completion of an alternative domain goal, the attempt at goal completion must be halted. Consequently, a special opcode is needed to signal that the iterative process for proving goal completion must halt. The opcode used is **fail(X)**, where **X = other_domain_goal**.

Thus, when the dialog controller obtains this special opcode after an iteration of attempting goal completion, it terminates the Goal Completion Algorithm with the values for the outputs being *Result* = **fail(other_domain_goal)**, *RelevantGoal = Goal*, and *AxiomValue* = the axiom denoting completion of the alternative domain goal. In the following dialog segment *RelevantGoal* = "putting the switch up," and *AxiomValue* = the LED description.

```
C: Put the switch up.
U: The LED is displaying one and seven at the same time.
```

Once the attempt at goal completion is terminated, the next step in the dialog processing algorithm is to update system knowledge. Part of this update is to send *AxiomValue* back to the domain processor. This update provides the domain processor with the required knowledge about the completed alternative domain goal.

Another interesting situation is when the user's input is classified as an "alternative domain goal," but the domain processor subsequently determines the two goals are related. Two examples of this are:

```
Example 1
    C: Add a wire between 84 and 99.  (Goal)
    U: Should I turn the switch down? (Alternative)
    C: No.
   U1: Okay.
   U2: I add the wire.

Example 2
    C: There is supposed to be a wire between 84 and 99. (Goal)
    U: There is a wire between 84 and 30.
    C: There is supposed to be a wire between 84 and 30. (Alt.)
   U1: Okay.
   U2: I add the wire.
```

In both examples U1 is a response to the alternative domain goal while U2 is a response to the original domain goal. Thus, the alternative domain goal may be addressed, but the original domain goal should remain in context as well. To maintain both goals in context requires the domain processor to be able to signal the dialog controller when a new goal is suggested (step 1 of the dialog processing algorithm) that the new goal is relevant to the previous goal. In some sense, the new goal is a "lemma" which is needed to complete the proof about accomplishing the original goal. In selecting the next goal to be pursued (step 2 of the dialog processing algorithm), the dialog controller must create structures which link the two goals together. The linkage consists of the following:

1. Create a separate proof tree about the new goal (i.e. the "lemma").

2. Reopen the subdialog about the original goal, making the subdialog about the new goal a part of the subdialog about the original goal.

3. Create a linkage between the proof trees about the new goal and the original goal to extend the current context beyond the current proof tree to the original goal. Normally, the current context consists of a hierarchy of active goals within one proof tree (e.g. figure 4.5).

This linkage will occur when updating the discourse structure prior to attempting goal completion (step 1 of the Goal Completion Algorithm). Once the linkage is established, an attempt to prove completion of the new goal ensues. However, if the response indicating completion of the original goal is given (response U2), then the output value for the Goal Completion Algorithm, *RelevantGoal*, is set equal to the original goal.

Context Shifts

This occurs when the input is unexpected in the current context but is expected in a previous context. Locating the proper context requires an orderly search of the previous contexts. This search is done as follows:

1. Search the most recent utterance in the current subdialog where the context differed from the already searched context. Initially, the "already searched context" will consist of the SSE, TSE, SRE, and TRE of the current action.

2. If expectation for the input is still not found, continue searching back to the most recent utterance without an already searched context. Within the subdialog where this utterance occurs, search all contexts before searching back in the utterances for the next subdialog.

This method for searching previous contexts will be illustrated by the sample dialog of figure 4.12 which was taken from actual system usage. Figure 4.13

---

1. C: This is the circuit fix it shop. How may I help you?
2. U: I want to fix an rs111 circuit.
3. C: I am familiar with that circuit. The LED is supposed to be displaying alternately flashing one and seven.
4. U: The LED is displaying only a not flashing one.
5. C: What is the switch at when the LED is displaying only a not flashing one on the left hand side?
6. U: Where is it?
7. C: Near the lower left corner is a tan region. Now, in the middle of this tan region is the switch.
8. U: The switch is up.
9. C: What is the knob at when the LED is displaying only a not flashing one on the left hand side?
10. U: One zero.
11. C: What is the voltage between connector one two one and connector three four?
12. U: I do not know.
13. C: Locate the voltmeter.
14. U: Done.
15. C: Add a wire between the minus com hole on the voltmeter and connector one two one.
16. U: How do I do that?
17. C: Connect the end of the black wire with the small plug to the minus com hole on the voltmeter.
18. U: Done.
19. C: Connect the end of the black wire with the large plug to connector one two one.
20. U: Which knob?

Figure 4.12
Sample Subdialog for Context Search

shows the collection of proof trees generated during this dialog through utterance 19. There is a separate tree for each task step recommended by the domain processor during execution of the dialog processing algorithm. When utterance 20 is received, the active contexts correspond to the highlighted goals which led to utterances 19, 15, and 11. Since utterance 20 is not expected as a response to any of these utterances, previously active contexts must be searched. Applying the search method, the contexts associated with utterances 17, 13, and 9 are searched before an expectation for utterance 20 is found within the context of utterance 9. Utterances 17 and 13 constitute contexts in the current subdialog which were not searched originally, while

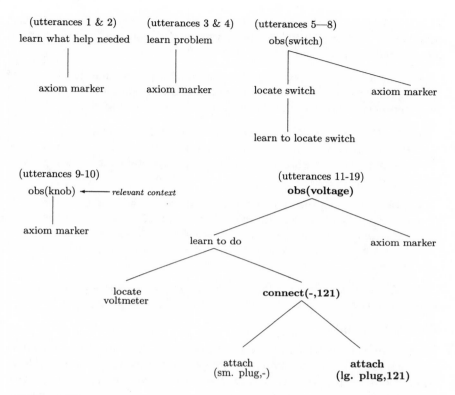

Figure 4.13
Sample Subdialog Proof Trees for Search

utterance 9 constitutes the next most recent utterance without an already searched context.

Once the proper context is found, coherent dialog requires that the computer proceed with the dialog in the reopened context as in the following:

20. U: Which knob?
21. C: Near the top boundary and in the center is a green region.
      Now, in the middle right of this green region is the
      control knob.

Within the framework of the dialog processing algorithm, handling the above context shift requires immediate termination of the goal completion attempt for the interrupted goal (measuring the voltage) and resumption of the reopened context (putting the knob to one zero) in the natural course of the algorithm. Note that it is possible that the result upon completing the reopened context might eliminate the need to resume the suspended context.

This is considered by the *choose_action* function (section 4.3). The remaining issue is how to properly update the context and discourse structure when a context shift occurs. The following rules are used.

- **If** the reopened context is in the same subdialog and same theorem as the current goal, **then** just redirect the theorem prover to the appropriate point where the input may be a missing axiom.

- **Else if** the reopened context is in the same subdialog but a different theorem from the current goal, **then** suspend the current theorem and redirect the theorem prover to the appropriate point in the old theorem.

- **Else if** the reopened context is in a different subdialog from the current goal, **then** suspend the current subdialog and redirect the theorem prover as in the previous case. Note that when the context is in a different subdialog it is of necessity in a different theorem as well.

In all cases the domain processor must be reset to the status that was active when the expectation for the input was originally produced.

Global Interrupts

These are interrupts which can occur at any time. They are either unrelated to the current topic or are completely independent of the topic content. These expectations are part of the TRE for the current goal, and the ones defined currently were given in section 4.4.3.

Due to their nature, once a global interrupt is handled, the original subdialog is ready for resumption. Consequently, every interrupt is processed in the following manner.

1. Suspend the current subdialog.

2. Invoke the interrupt handler. The interrupt handler could provide some type of response or enter a completely independent subdialog. It could also modify the proof structure and discourse structure of the original subdialog if it is a topic-specific expectation. For example, "I do not understand" would cause the addition of a subgoal for learning the required knowledge about the goal associated with the original subdialog. This addition would occur in the suspended subdialog.

3. Resume the "suspended" subdialog where the interrupt handler could have altered the direction of the suspended subdialog.

Completely Unexpected Inputs

These are inputs for which there is absolutely no expectation in the current or any previous context. In such a case the computer has absolutely no way of understanding how the utterance fits into the dialog. Consequently, the computer assumes that the input was a misguided attempt to talk about the current goal. The processing for this situation is to: (1) skip the axiom selection step of the goal completion algorithm; and (2) update the proof tree by inserting the goal that the user wants to learn how to do the current action. The dialog will continue by attempting to teach the user how to perform the action.

4.7.2 Robustness and the Handling of Speech Recognition Errors

The traditional approach of computational natural language understanding has been to take the input utterances and apply a parsing procedure that transforms the utterance into some type of usable machine representation. Parsing requires specification of a grammar that is intended to specify the set of legal utterances. It is assumed that a legal utterance will be received. Such an assumption cannot be used in a natural language dialog system with speech recognition for the user input. Even if the user only spoke "grammatical" utterances, it is quite likely that the speech recognizer will not correctly recognize the utterance. This often leads to ungrammatical inputs. An even more significant problem is when the speaker uses words that are not in the vocabulary of the speech recognizer. If the speech recognizer "recognizes" such utterances, it will do so by substituting other words for the unrecognizable word, and may lead to ungrammatical utterances whose interpretation may be different from the actual meaning of the utterance.

How can such utterances be parsed correctly? The solution lies in the usage of an error-correcting parser in conjunction with the expectations provided by the dialog controller. The parser, developed by the second author (Hipp), uses a dynamic programming approach similar to Ney [Ney91] to compute the best n parses for the input. What constitutes "best" is determined by a cost matrix for the possible words in the vocabulary and the given grammar. The cost matrix defines the cost for inserting or deleting words as well as the cost for a word substitution when such substitutions are allowed. The intent of permitting substitutions is for words which sound very similar, such as "do" and "two/to/too," words that are likely to be confused by the speech recognizer. The parser performs insertions, deletions, and substitutions in order to transform the input into a grammatical utterance. With each "grammatical" utterance is associated a *parse cost* (PC), which is the sum of the costs of each insertion, deletion, and substitution required. For each of the best n parses, an *expectation cost* is also produced according to how likely the input is to occur according to the expectations. The *total cost* of a parse is a weighted sum of PC and EC. There has been no attempt to determine the optimal values for these weights and costs, but the current system has produced an 81% success rate[11] in actual use. Chapter 5 provides a detailed discussion about the parsing algorithm. Figure 4.14 shows some of the utterances successfully

---

[11]This is the percentage of utterances *completely* understood correctly.

Computer: This is the circuit fix it shop. How may I help you?
User: Can you help me?   (you and me not in vocabulary)
Recognized: Same do help be.

Computer: Put the knob to one zero.
User: The knob is at one zero.
Recognized: Do of is at one zero.

Computer: What is the voltage between connector 121 and
              connector 83?
User: The voltage is five.   (voltage not in vocabulary)
Recognized: The will which is five.

Computer: The LED is supposed to be displaying alternately
              flashing one and seven.
User: LED is displaying one and seven.
Recognized: Be down it be is displaying one hand seven then.

Figure 4.14
Sample Misrecognitions Correctly Parsed

handled by the implemented system.

It is important to realize that robust behavior is crucial to the overall effectiveness of a dialog system and is not specific to the handling of misrecognized inputs. A common complaint of previous AI systems is their "brittle" ([LGK+90]) behavior in response to unexpected or illogical inputs. The integrated dialog processing theory presented in this book provides for robust behavior in handling unexpected inputs regardless of the cause. In addition to handling misrecognized inputs, robust behavior is also obtained via the interrupt handling mechanisms described in the previous section. In fact as reported in section 7.6.1, our implemented system based on this theory had only one software failure in processing 2840 user utterances during formal experimental trials. This contrasts with the previous results of Damerau [Dam81], Miller et al. [MHK78], and Biermann et al. [BBS83] that reported software failure rates of approximately 5, 2, and 2 percent respectively. The paradigm of equating subdialogs with theorems for completing goals, in conjunction with a dynamic theorem prover that can rapidly switch contexts as directed by the overall dialog controller, enables more robust and reliable system behavior even in the presence of misrecognized and unexpected inputs.

4.7.3   Variable Initiative Dialog

As discussed in section 3.6, the major factor concerning the usage of different modes of dialog is response formulation. Two major unresolved problems with variable initiative dialog include: (1) determining when it is appropriate to change dialog mode; and (2) maintaining dialog coherence when a mode change occurs. The following paragraphs discuss how the model supports solution and study for these aspects of variable initiative dialog.

Variable Initiative and Response Formulation

Response formulation as a function of dialog mode is handled in several stages. The first stage is the determination of the next domain processor operation (section 4.6). This operation defines how the domain processor will make its next suggestion for a user goal. This operation must specify the relative priority of user goals to the computer goals (i.e. the degree of interruptibility of computer goals). Consequently, the choice for operation is a function of, among other things, the dialog mode. Thus dialog mode, the indicator of the level of computer initiative, influences the domain processor recommendation by supporting the linkage between dialog initiative and task initiative.

Once the domain processor's suggestion is provided, the dialog controller must still select the next goal to be attempted (section 4.3) based on the domain processor's suggestion, the discourse history, and the current dialog mode. For example, selection of a "computer comprehends" goal when the current mode is passive, allows the user to retain maximal control.

Once the utterance topic is selected, the level of assertiveness in the actual utterance specification could also be made a function of dialog mode by defining a set of transformation functions from the initial utterance specification based on the associated action (section 4.4.1) into the utterance specification actually sent to the generator. Such transformations have not been needed in the implemented application domain. The generic utterance specifications as a function of the type of action have been sufficient. Nevertheless, the architecture readily permits the inclusion of the transformation function if needed (section 4.4.2). Thus, the use of dialog mode for response formulation reflects the idea that dialog initiative should reflect the task initiative.

Switching Dialog Mode

It should first be noted that the idea of dialog mode is a computational device and that no claim of psychological reality is being made for this mechanism. Consequently, there is no assumption that the human user is consciously aware of the means by which the computer is able to participate in a variable initiative dialog. Thus, the decision to switch mode is made strictly by the computer.

Determining an optimal automatic mode switching algorithm requires the acquisition of greater amounts of data on human-computer interaction by the implemented system. In the interim, a means for manual interaction to change mode is available in order to study the effects of mode changing on the dialog interaction. In addition, the following knowledge is available for use in the mode switching algorithm.

1. The current dialog mode.

2. Content of user input.

3. Relationship of the most recent input to the current and overall task goals. Possible relationships include: (a) introduces a clarification or subgoal, (b) pertains directly to the current task goal, (c) does not pertain directly to the current task goal, but does pertain to the overall task goal, and (d) is irrelevant to all possible goals. *axiom_select* (section 4.4.8) provides information on the relationship of an input to the current goal.

4. Historical record of the relevance of user inputs.

Currently, the only automatic mode switching rule occurs as part of the function for selecting the next domain processor operation. When the domain processor indicates it believes the outside agent is unsure how to proceed, the system transitions into the next mode which gives the computer more initiative (step 2 of *operation_selection*).

This project has not yet properly addressed the problem of how to automatically select the correct mode and little will be said about it. We have implemented the concept of modes throughout the system and can demonstrate the many aspects discussed here. As will be seen in chapter 7, we even conducted an experiment involving usage of our system where users interacted with the system under different preset dialog modes in order to demonstrate differences in dialog behavior as a function of mode.

Maintaining Dialog Coherence

Given that mode switching will occur, another key issue is how to ensure the coherence of the dialog when mode changes. For mode changes where the same conversational participant retains the initiative (i.e. between suggestive and directive or between declarative and passive), maintenance of coherence should be easy because the same participant's goals have priority. But for more extreme mode changes where the participant with control changes, there is the risk that coherency may be lost. For example, the following dialog segment occurred in an early version of the system. Initially, the mode was declarative, with the user in control.

```
C: The LED is supposed to be displaying alternately flashing
      1 and 7.
U: The LED is displaying nothing.
C: The power is on when the switch is up.
U: The switch is in the up position.
C: The switch is connecting to the battery when there is a
```

```
wire between connector 111 and connector 120.

<User observes there's no wire, but says nothing about this>

U: Now what should I do?

<mode switch to suggestive>

C: Turn the knob to 10.
```

In selecting a response topic, the computer ignored the context previously established and simply used the topic recommended by the domain processor based on its own goals. The problem is in the failure of the computer to adequately consider the established context in choosing the next topic of the dialog when it regained the initiative.

Thus, maintaining dialog coherence during mode switching is related to maintaining task coherence since the structure of the dialog should reflect the structure of the task. Consequently, the domain processor must maintain knowledge of its goals and the externally supplied information in such a way as to facilitate task coherence in its recommendations. It is possible that the dialog controller could play a larger role in the coherence issue by evaluating the domain processor's recommendation with respect to the current dialog situation, but this has not been extensively explored. One difficulty with doing this is that the dialog controller does not have domain expertise. Consequently, what the dialog controller may perceive as a radical shift in conversation based on a radical shift in domain goal may be very logical from the perspective of the domain processor. Perhaps the role of the dialog controller in such situations is the need to produce a "metastatement," or dialog about the dialog, to indicate a transition in the dialog from one goal to the next via an explicit statement. Such uses of the dialog controller still need to be investigated.

4.8   Integrated Dialog Processing: A Summary

The key to integrating problem solving, subdialog usage and movement, user model usage, expectation usage, and variable initiative lies in the Missing Axiom Theory for the role of language. The goal oriented behavior essential to problem solving is supplied by the theorem proving paradigm for determining action completion, while the Missing Axiom Theory provides the mechanism for determining the use of language. The interruptible theorem prover permits subdialog movement by maintaining a set of partially completed proofs, each of which corresponds to a subdialog, where the prover can be instructed to work on the most appropriate one at any given time by the dialog controller. A user model is provided by a continuously changing set of axioms inferred from the user utterances that can be referenced during theorem proving to enable or inhibit the use of language. Expectation is associated with individual subdialogs, is compiled from domain or dialog knowledge related to each specific computer utterance, and is used to improve speech recognition and enable movement between subdialogs. Finally, variable initiative behavior is made possible by making utterance production a function of the level of initiative through control of the degree of freedom the user has in interrupting to a different subdialog.

Chapter 5

Parsing

5.1 Introduction

Both the user of the system and the dialog controller communicate using language. The user's language consists of strings of English words ordered according to the rules of English syntax. The dialog controller's language is made from strings of ground logic terms, variables, and punctuation symbols all connected according to the syntax of Prolog expressions. This chapter describes the design of a parser whose task is to translate strings from the user's language into strings with approximately the same meaning in the dialog controller's language.

Some difficulties encountered by the parser follow.

1. Because of the less than flawless performance of speech recognizers, the parser will not know exactly what the user has said. Instead, the parser will receive as input one or more estimates of what was spoken, none of which may be absolutely correct.

2. Even what was spoken might not be what the user was thinking. The user may have mispronounced part of the utterance, or may make simple grammatical errors in the utterance.

3. The user may deliberately omit small structure words, such as "the" and "of", from what is said. This is a natural and subconscious response of native speakers when speaking to a machine which has less than perfect language skills.

4. The parser's grammar of the English language is probably not identical to the user's. Thus, even without recognition errors, mispronunciations, or omitted words, the input to the parser may not be syntactically well-formed.

5. The mapping from the user's language to the dialog controller's language is not one-to-one. Many inputs will have multiple meanings, and will thus need to be translated into two or more outputs. Conversely, a particular output may result from several syntactically unsimilar inputs.

Together with [EM81], [HHCT86], [HM81], and [YHW+90], we argue that due to the above problems, the traditional natural language parsing techniques that accept written or typed input are not adequate for systems which accept speech input. New parsing architectures are required to deal with the high level of uncertainty that is inherent to speech input.

Some prior efforts at robust parsing have used the assumption that most inputs are well-formed, and that a traditional parser will fail only occasionally.

The cases where the parser does fail are resolved by using a hodgepodge of error-correction heuristics or "meta-rules" [WS81]. This approach works for parsing clean text-based input, but the assumption that the input is usually well-formed is not valid for speech inputs, and the technique breaks down.

Least deviant parsing [Leh92] is another possible technique that was previously mentioned in section 2.3.3. Inputs that deviate from the grammar are parsed by determining the way in which the input deviates from the grammar, and a new individualized grammar rule may be added to account for the user's preference for an unusual language construct. However, this method assumes typewritten input and does not consider deviations due to signal error in processing speech input. It only considers reasonable deviations based on a user's particular input style.

Another common approach is to use case-frames [HHCT86] in which phrases of the input are parsed separately, rather than as part of a complete sentence, and then the meanings derived from the phrases are used to fill in slots of a template sentence meaning. This approach works better than meta-rules because it avoids the assumption that most sentences are syntactically well-formed, but is still inadequate for much speech input because it assumes that individual phrases are well-formed. Nevertheless, some recent success has been reported using the case-frame approach [DGA+93] [War91].

Probably the most common approach to robust parsing in recent years has been the use of Probablistic Context-Free Grammars (PCFGs) [JLM90]. In this technique, a grammar is used which gives very broad language coverage—sufficiently broad to cover even most ungrammatical utterances. Each production rule of the grammar is augmented with a probability such that the sum of probabilities on all production rules with the same left-hand side is 1.0. Each candidate parse of an input (and there are typically many parses since a grammar with broad coverage is usually also highly ambiguous) is assigned a likelihood which is the product of the production rules used to complete the parse. The parse with the greatest likelihood is chosen as the meaning of the utterance.

The recent surge in the popularity of PCFGs is perhaps due to the success of similar methods used in speech recognition systems. Indeed, it is increasingly common to combine the speech recognizer and the parser of a speech understanding system into a single monolithic entity. However, there are some valid objections to the use of PCFGs for natural language parsing.

- The computation of the most likely parse using a PCFG uses the assumption that each selection of a production rule to expand a non-terminal symbol is an independent random event. One can easily question the validity of this assumption.

- Estimating the probabilities that are attached to each production rule normally requires a very large training set.

- Parsing techniques for PCFGs are computationally expensive.

All of these problems are being actively addressed by other researchers in the field, but good solutions are only now beginning to emerge.

The parser used in our system and that is the topic of this chapter is fundamentally different from any previously reported natural language parsing technique. The new parsing system addresses the concerns about the difficulty of understanding spoken input while remaining relatively easy to program and operating in real time. While no parser can be expected to perform perfectly in an environment of such uncertainty, the parser described in this chapter has demonstrated success and shown promise for continued improvement.

5.2 Overview of the Parser

The basic idea behind our parser is *minimum-distance translation*—a combination of minimum-distance parsing [AP72][Lyo74] and syntax-directed translation [AU69]. Ambiguities in the output of the minimum-distance translator are resolved by dialog expectation.[1] A block diagram of the parser is shown in figure 5.1.

The principal input to the parser is the speech recognizer's guess of what was spoken by the user. This guess is represented as a single-source, single-sink, acyclic directed graph (hereafter called a *lattice*) in which each arc is labeled with a word and a measure of the recognizer's confidence that the word was spoken. The specific lattice that is the input to the algorithm is called the *parser input lattice*. Additional description and an analysis of lattices is given in section 5.3.

Within the parser there is a *translation grammar* that specifies a mapping between the *input language* spoken by the user and the *output language* understood by the dialog controller. The translation grammar formalism used by the parser requires that the input and the output languages both be context-free.

The heart of the parser is the minimum distance translation algorithm (hereafter referred to as MDT). Input to this algorithm is the translation grammar and the parser input lattice. The output is a set of no more than K strings from the output language, which is called the *hypothesis set*. Each string in this set is an hypothesis. K is a positive integer parameter to the algorithm and is normally set to about 10. Each hypothesis has an utterance cost, U, which is the MDT algorithm's estimate of how close the hypothesis is to the correct meaning for what was spoken by the user. The utterance cost is based on the *minimum edit distance* [WF74] between strings of the input language and the parser input lattice. The MDT algorithm works by looking for strings in the input language that are close to (have a small edit distance from) the sequence of words on any path from the source to the sink of the parser input lattice. When a close match is found, the matching string from the input language is mapped into a corresponding string from the output language and the output language string is added to the hypothesis set. A

---

[1]Recall that dialog expectation was discussed in sections 3.5 and 4.4.3. Throughout the remainder of this chapter we will refer to dialog expectation simply as expectation.

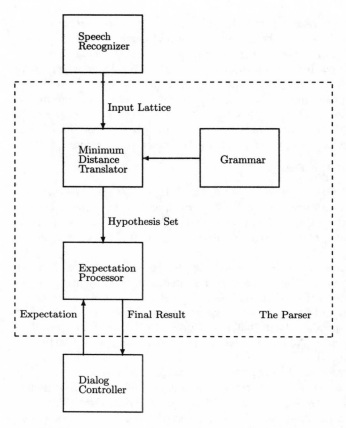

Figure 5.1
Block Diagram of the Parser

formal description of what MDT does is given in section 5.5. A description of
an efficient algorithm for MDT is given in section 5.6. Finally, some extensions
and embellishments to MDT, which improve the parser's performance, are
described in section 5.7.

A secondary input to the parser is the expectation. The expectation is a set
of strings from the output language each labeled with an expectation cost, W.
The expectation is input to the parser from the dialog controller. Each string in
the expectation corresponds to a set of inputs that the dialog controller expects
the user might say next. The expectation cost is the dialog controller's estimate
of how likely any of the corresponding inputs might be spoken. Expectation
strings will often contain instances of a special vocabulary symbol known as
the *wildcard*, which is a place holder for one or more unknown symbols. The
use of wildcards in expectation strings enables the dialog controller to say that

it expects to see any of a large class of related inputs.

The expectation and the hypothesis set are both input to the *expectation processor*. This module first finds an expectation cost for every hypothesis by matching with strings in the expectation. After computing W for each hypothesis, the expectation processor selects as final output of the parser that hypothesis which minimizes $g(U, W)$ where g is the *expectation function*. Full details regarding expectation, wildcards in both expectation and hypotheses, matching of expectation and hypotheses, and final parser output selection may be found in section 5.8.

Let N be the number of nodes in the input lattice, and let M be the size of the translation grammar. The parser executes in time $O(N^3 M)$. This complexity result, as well as computational complexity measures for individual components of the parser, is derived in section 5.9.

5.3 The Parser Input Lattice

Data is transmitted from the speech recognizer to the parser in a structure called a lattice. The specific lattice that is input to the parser will be referred to as the *parser input graph*. This section will describe what a lattice is, how it works, and why it was chosen as the vehicle for communication between the speech recognizer and the parser.

5.3.1 What is in a Word?

The parser input lattice conveys the speech recognizer's estimate of what words were spoken by the user. Before going further, it is appropriate to define exactly what is meant by the term "word." In this text, the term "word" will be used to mean any of the following.

- A traditional word of English (or any other language) such as one would look up in a dictionary.

- A morpheme. That is a part of a word which embodies an indivisible particle of "meaning."

- A syllable.

- A phoneme. A fundamental sound of the language.

- An acoustic parameter vector.

- Some other unit of speech.

For conciseness, let us say that a word is the smallest unit of speech which the speech recognizer will recognize.

The selection of what units of sound to designate as a word in the system is influenced by a number of factors.

- The set of all words should be finite and should preferably be small. This criterion eliminates the possibility of calling phrases or sentences the words of the system, because there are infinitely many sentences in any natural language.

- There should be no syntactically complex structure embedded within a single word.

- Each word should cover as much sound as possible. This will reduce the number of words in each utterance. Reducing the number of words in each utterance is important because the time used by the MDT algorithm (see section 5.9) is proportional to the cube of the number of words.

5.3.2   Uncertain Inputs

If the speech recognizer were able to perfectly transcribe speech into words, then it could simply pass the string of spoken words to the parser. However, no speech recognizer is perfect.[2] Cases will often arise where the speech recognizer has difficulty choosing between several alternative word sequences. Some method is needed whereby the speech recognizer can communicate its uncertainty to the parser. In our system, that method is the use of a directed graph.

The directed graph used to transmit speech information to the parser has the following properties.

- It contains no cycles. There is no path from a node back to itself.

- There is a distinguished node called the "source" from which there is a path to every other node in the graph.

- There is another distinguished node called the "sink" to which there is a path from every other node in the graph.

We will call any graph that satisfies the above conditions a *lattice*.

In the parser and speech recognizer, each arc in the parser input lattice represents a word heard by the speech recognizer. A path from the source to the sink represents one possible interpretation of what was spoken by the user. The set of all paths through the lattice represent all possible interpretations of the user's speech.

As an example, suppose the user spoke thus: "What do I do", and the speech recognizer was unable to tell if the second word spoken was suppose to be "to" or "do." An appropriate lattice for this situation is shown in figure 5.2.

Observe in this figure that the arcs for the words "to" and "do" span exactly the same nodes, indicating that these are alternative interpretations of the spoken utterance at that point.

---

[2]Even human experts make speech recognition errors. In an experiment conducted by the authors, words selected at random from a 122 word vocabulary and read over the telephone were misrecognized about 3% of the time.

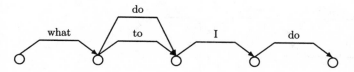

Figure 5.2
A possible lattice for "What do I do"

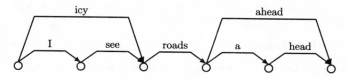

Figure 5.3
A possible lattice for "Icy roads ahead"

A more complex example occurs in the utterance "Icy roads ahead." A possible lattice for this utterance is shown in figure 5.3. In this example, the single word "icy" may be misunderstood as two separate words "I" and "see." Similarly, "ahead" might be interpreted as "a" followed by "head."

In the previous two examples, there was at least one path through the input lattice that visited every node. This need not be the case. Consider, for example, the lattice in figure 5.4. Here the two words "ice cream" were confused with "I scream." It would not be acceptable to simply have parallel arcs for "I" and "ice", or for "cream" and "scream", because that situation would have allowed for inputs such as "ice scream" or "I cream."

5.3.3 Arc Weights

In the above examples, every arc in the input lattice represents a possible interpretation that is just as likely to have occurred as any other parallel arc. In practice it is seldom the case that all possible interpretations of a speech input are equally likely, and so there needs to be some method for expressing different likelihoods in the parser input lattice. Therefore, each arc is allowed to be labeled with a weight, which is a measure of confidence that the word that labels the arc is what was actually spoken. The confidence measure will be a cost. This means that lower numbers are better. Complete confidence is expressed by a cost of zero. Extreme uncertainty is expressed by a large value for the cost. Most arcs will have a cost in between these two extremes.

Immediately the question arises of how to compute lattice arc costs. This is a difficult problem worthy of further research. In the work reported here, the problem is dealt with mostly by ignoring it. The heuristic employed to assign costs to word arcs in our experimental system is to give a cost of zero

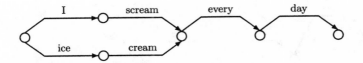

Figure 5.4
A lattice for "I scream every day"

to the speech recognizer's best guess and to any close alternative guess, and
to assign a small cost (less than the cost associated with inserting or deleting
a single word—see section 5.5.1) to other alternatives.

5.3.4 Indexing Lattice Nodes

Before a lattice is used by the MDT algorithm, each node of the lattice should
be assigned a unique index from 1 to N such that the following conditions
hold.

- The source node has an index of 1.

- The sink node has an index of N.

- If x and y are the indexes of two nodes N_x and N_y and there is an arc
  from N_x to N_y, then $x < y$.

Assigning indexes to lattice nodes in this way simplifies the code for the MDT
algorithm, and allows for a constant factor speed improvement. This subsection will describe an efficient algorithm for assigning indexes to nodes in the
parser input lattice.

Algorithm 5.1 *Sequential node indexing in a lattice.*

Input: A lattice with N nodes and E edges.

Output: The input lattice with an integer index assigned to each node as
   follows.

- The source node is assigned the value 1.
- The sink is given the value N.
- No two nodes have the same index.
- If A and B are both nodes in the lattice, and there is a path from
  node A to node B, then the index assigned to A is less than the
  index assigned to B.

Method: The algorithm will use two variables. The "active set" is a set of
   zero or more nodes from the input lattice. The counter is an integer
   variable. The algorithm is as follows.

1. Initialize the active set to contain only the source node.

2. Initialize the counter to 1.

3. While the active set is not empty, do the following.

   (a) Set the value of the node index of every node in the active set to the value of the counter. This applies even if the node index has already been set to some smaller value in a previous iteration of this step.

   (b) Increase the value of the counter by 1.

   (c) Create a new active set, which is the set of all nodes that can be reached by a single arc from any node in the old active set.

4. Sort the nodes according to their indexes. Nodes that have the same index may be placed in any order relative to each other.

5. Beginning with the source node, visit each node of the lattice in the order chosen by the previous step and set the index of each node to successive integers.

The purpose of step 3 in the algorithm 5.1 is to create a numbering for the lattice such that any path through the lattice always visits nodes with successively higher numbers. When this step results in two nodes with the same index, then there is no path which visits both nodes and they can be arranged in any order. Step 3 is guaranteed to terminate because the lattice is acyclic. Step 4 orders the nodes so that arcs always go from an earlier node to a later node. Step 5 renumbers the nodes so that each node has a unique index.

5.3.5   Inputs Used in the Experiments

Most of the data for experiments reported later in this book were gathered using a parser that accepted as input only lattices in which arcs span adjacent nodes (e.g. figure 5.2). There are several reasons for this limitation. First, and perhaps most important, is that the commercial speech recognizer used in our experiments was only capable of providing a single "best guess" and would not give alternative outputs. Alternative arcs had to be inferred from the best guess, and this is most easily done by restricting the alternative arcs to exactly parallel existing arcs. The second reason for this limitation is our desire to make the system work in real time. The MDT algorithm requires time proportional to the cube of the number of nodes in the input lattice, and so we very much desired to keep the number of input lattice nodes to a minimum. Alternative arcs of the type shown in figures 5.3 and especially figure 5.4 require more than the minimum number of nodes to express, and were therefore disallowed.

5.4 Translation Grammars

The grammar is what makes the parser programmable. It allows the parser to be adapted to use different languages for input, output, or both. This section will describe the notation used to represent the grammar in our system, and explain how this grammar defines an appropriate mapping between input and output languages.

Both the input and the output languages of the parser must be context free. It is assumed that the reader is already familiar with basic ideas behind context-free languages, such as described in [HJ79]. Therefore, this section will not discuss general properties of context-free languages, but will concentrate on the notation and special properties of the grammar used for the parser.

The grammar formalism for our system is essentially the *translation grammar* formalism developed in [LS68] and [AU69], though we use a different notation. In our system, each production rule begins with a single non-terminal symbol called the left-hand side (hereafter LHS). Following the LHS is the special symbol "->" and a string of terminal and non-terminal symbols which are the right-hand side (hereafter RHS). After the RHS there may be semantics, though the semantics might also be omitted. The semantics consists of the special symbol ":" followed by another list of terminal and non-terminal symbols. The entire production rule is closed by a period.

Non-terminal symbols are written in all uppercase letters. Terminal symbols are in lowercase letters. Individual punctuation characters (except those that are part of the grammar specification itself) are also interpreted as terminal symbols.

Each non-terminal in the semantics of a production rule must be linked to an instance of the same non-terminal on the RHS of the same rule through the use of a special notation.[3] The link between a semantic and a RHS non-terminal is accomplished when both non-terminals have exactly the same name, and both non-terminals are followed by the same number of apostrophes. The meaning of the linkage will be explained later.

Some examples will help clarify the notation used to express the grammar, and will serve as a vehicle for explaining what the rules of the grammar mean. Consider first the following simple grammar without semantics.

```
S -> NP VP.
NP -> DET N.
NP -> N.
DET -> the.
DET -> a.
VP -> is V.
N -> girl.
N -> boy.
```

---

[3]The converse is not true: a non-terminal in the RHS of a production rule need not have a corresponding non-terminal in the semantics.

```
V -> walking.
V -> sleeping.
```

The above grammar specifies an input language that contains exactly twelve sentences, (some of which are not considered correct English), namely:

> boy is walking
> a boy is walking
> the boy is walking
> girl is walking
> a girl is walking
> the girl is walking
> boy is sleeping
> a boy is sleeping
> the boy is sleeping
> girl is sleeping
> a girl is sleeping
> the girl is sleeping

The way in which these sentences are derived from the grammar is simple and should come as no surprise to those who are familiar with context-free grammars.

We will now augment our simple grammar to include some semantics.

```
S -> NP' VP'        : VP'(NP').
NP -> DET' N'       : N',DET'.
NP -> N'            : N'.
DET -> the          : specific.
DET -> a            : unspecific.
VP -> is V'         : V'
N -> girl           : female-child.
N -> boy            : male-child.
V -> walking        : ambulates.
V -> sleeping       : slumbers.
```

In this latter grammar, a colon and a string of terminal and non-terminal symbols has been added to each production rule in order to form the semantics of the rule. The four symbols in the semantics of the first rule, for example, are as follows: VP', (, NP', and).

Notice that the semantics of the first production rule contain the non-terminal symbols NP and VP, which are linked to the equivalent symbol in the RHS of the rule. This linkage is indicated by the presence of an apostrophe following the non-terminal's name in both the RHS and the semantics. More than one apostrophe could have been used, but one was sufficient in this case. If the non-terminal NP had occurred twice in both the RHS and in the semantics, and had been linked both times, then each linkage would have required a different number of apostrophes in order to distinguish one from the other.

The semantics of a rule are used to specify an appropriate translation from a string of the input language that matches the RHS of the rule to a string in the output language with the same meaning. When part of an input string matches the RHS of a production rule, then the translation of that part of the input string is the semantics of the production rule. Non-terminals are translated recursively, until all parts of both the RHS and semantics of the production rule have been fully translated.

The output language translations of each of the sentences in the input language of our example grammar are listed below. Notice that each of the non-terminals in the semantics of the first production rule have been replaced by the semantics associated with the corresponding non-terminal on the RHS of the production rule.

boy is walking	ambulates(male-child)
a boy is walking	ambulates(male-child,unspecific)
the boy is walking	ambulates(male-child,specific)
girl is walking	ambulates(female-child)
a girl is walking	ambulates(female-child,unspecific)
the girl is walking	ambulates(female-child,specific)
boy is sleeping	slumbers(male-child)
a boy is sleeping	slumbers(male-child,unspecific)
the boy is sleeping	slumbers(male-child,specific)
girl is sleeping	slumbers(female-child)
a girl is sleeping	slumbers(female-child,unspecific)
the girl is sleeping	slumbers(female-child,specific)

5.5   Minimum Distance Translation

The minimum distance translation (MDT) algorithm is the most important component of the parser. The MDT translates the input language spoken by the user into the output language understood by the dialog controller. The MDT generally uses much more computing resources than all other parts of the parser combined. It is certainly the most complicated component in the parser, and may be the most difficult to understand as well. This section will describe exactly what the MDT does and how it works.

5.5.1   Distance Between Strings

The concept of distance between two strings is central to the MDT algorithm. The following few paragraphs will explain the meaning of distance within the context of language translation.

Suppose we have two strings, A and B, each consisting of tokens chosen from a finite alphabet. The distance from A to B, written $D(A, B)$, is defined to be the minimum number of token insertions and deletions required to transform A into B. As an example, consider the following two strings.

$$A = \text{the quick dog runs}$$
$$B = \text{the brown dog runs home}$$

In this example, A and B are both strings of English words. A minimum of 3 changes are required to convert A into B: delete the word "quick", insert "brown", and insert "home". Hence $D(A, B) = 3$.

It is instructive to consider the range of the distance function. For all strings A and B,

$$0 \leq D(A,B) \leq |A| + |B|. \tag{5.1}$$

The inequality 5.1 says that the distance between two strings is non-negative (it is zero only if the strings are identical) and is less than the sum of the number of elements in each string. The upper bound on distance arises from the fact that any string can be converted to any other by deleting every element of the starting string, and then inserting every element of the target string.

The above definition of distance applies only to two strings. The definition will now be extended to define the distance between an individual string and the language defined by a lattice. Let X be the set of strings derived from a lattice. Each element of this set is a sequence of words found by tracing a path from the source of the lattice to the sink. For a lattice defining k different possible inputs we would have:

$$X = \{A_1, A_2, A_3, \ldots, A_k\}.$$

Associated with each $A_i \in X$ is a cost $D(A_i)$, which is the sum of the weights on each arc that was used to construct A_i. The distance from X to any individual string B (or from B to X) is defined to be the minimum of the distances from B to any A_i plus $D(A_i)$.

$$D(X,B) = \min_i \left(D(A_i, B) + D(A_i) \right).$$

One final extension to the definition of distance is required. Suppose now that instead of taking the distance from an individual string to a lattice, we instead want to find the distance between an entire set of strings and a lattice. The definition of such a distance is similar to what is defined above and is easily guessed. Let X be a lattice, and let $Y = \{B_1, B_2, B_3, \ldots\}$ be any non-empty, possibly infinite, set of strings. The distance between X and Y is defined to be the minimum of the distances between X and any element of Y.

$$D(X,Y) = \min_j D(X, B_j).$$

5.5.2   A Precise Definition of What the MDT Algorithm Does

The input to the MDT algorithm is the parser input lattice and a translation grammar. Define $X = \{A_1, A_2, \ldots, A_k\}$ to be the set of k strings derived from the parser input lattice. Intuitively, X is the set of all the speech recognizer's estimates of what was spoken by the user. As before, we define the primitive distance $D(A_i)$ of each $A_i \in X$ to be the sum of the distances on arcs of the parser input lattice that generate A_i. Define Z to be the set of all strings in the output language (the language understood by the dialog controller). Let m_i be the i-th element of Z in dictionary order. Let Y_i be the set of strings in the input language (the language spoken by the user) that map to m_i according to the translation grammar. Define the set H as follows:

$$H = \{(m_i, d_i) \mid d_i = D(X, Y_i)\}.$$

The output of the MDT algorithm is a subset of H consisting of the K elements from H with the smallest values of d_i.

The above explanation of exactly what MDT computes may be a little difficult to follow. In an effort to elucidate the meaning of MDT, we will now give a simple "algorithm" that computes the same result as MDT. The word "algorithm" is in quotes in the previous sentence because the procedure we provide is not an algorithm in the strict sense as it requires an infinite amount of memory and computer time. The method described is therefore not useful for actually implementing MDT. However, it is helpful as a mnemonic and descriptive aid.

Pseudo-algorithm 5.2 *Minimum Distance Translation*

Input: A lattice representing all of the speech recognizer's guesses of what was spoken and a translation grammar.

Output: A set of up to K strings from the output language of the translation grammar, each labeled with a cost.

Method:

1. Compute the set S of all strings in the input language of the translation grammar. $S = \{s_1, s_2, s_3, \ldots\}$.

2. For each string in S, compute the distance between that string and the parser input lattice. Store this distance together with the string in the set P. $P = \{(s_1, d_1), (s_2, d_2), (s_3, d_3), \ldots\}$

3. From the set P, compute a new set Q as follows: For every pair (s_x, d_x) in P, use the grammar to find all strings of the output language that correspond to the input language string s_x. For each of these output language strings, add a pair to the new set Q consisting of the output language string and the distance d_x from the original pair. $Q = \{(r_i, d_x) | (s_x, d_x) \in P$ and r_i is an output language string corresponding to the input language string s_x according to the grammar$\}$.

4. Sort the elements of Q in order of increasing distance.

5. In the sorted set from the previous step, if (B, d) is any pair in that set, then delete from the set all pairs containing the string B that

occur after the pair (B, d). In other words, of all pairs of the form $(B, *)$, where $*$ represents any distance value, retain only the single pair with the smallest distance.

6. Output the first K elements of the set which remain after the previous step.

5.6 An Efficient Algorithm for MDT

This section will describe an efficient dynamic-programming based algorithm for MDT.

5.6.1 Data Structures Used by MDT

It is expedient to begin the description of the MDT algorithm by defining a data structure called a *semset* and an operation on that data structure.

A semset is a collection of between zero and K string and distance pairs. Within each pair, the string is a "meaning." That is to say, the string is an element of the output language defined by the semantic rules of the grammar. The string need not be fully expanded into terminal symbols of the output language. It can, and frequently will, contain non-terminals. The distance part of the pair is a measure of how far away from the input lattice is the corresponding string.

A semset will not contain two string and distance pairs that have the same string. Every string within a semset must be unique. A semset may contain more than one pair with the same distance, however.

The operation to be defined for semsets is *insert*. This operation will add a new string and distance pair to the semset while simultaneously insuring that the total number of string and distance pairs in the semset does not exceed the preset maximum K. The insert operation happens exactly as you would expect.

Algorithm 5.3 *Add a string and distance pair to a semset.*

Input: A semset X and a string and distance pair (m, d).

Output: A modified version of the semset X, called Y.

Method:

1. If X is the empty set, then Y is the single pair (m, d).

2. Else if X contains an element of the form $(m, \hat{d})$, then do the following.

   (a) If $d < \hat{d}$ then Y is a copy of X, except that (m, d) replaces $(m, \hat{d})$.

   (b) Else if $d \geq \hat{d}$, then Y is an exact copy of X.

3. Else if X contains fewer than K elements, then Y is the union of X with (m, d).

4. Else

   (a) If (m_{max}, d_{max}) is the element of X which has the largest distance value, and $d_{max} > d$, then Y is a copy of X except that (m, d) replaces (m_{max}, d_{max}).

   (b) Else Y is exactly X.

5.6.2 The Outer Procedure

The outer procedure of the MDT algorithm adds additional arcs to the parser input lattice. But, unlike the arcs that originally composed the input lattice and were labeled by a single terminal symbol from the input grammar and a fixed cost, the new arcs added by the MDT algorithm's outer procedure are each labeled by a non-terminal symbol from the input grammar and a semset. Each added arc represents a parse of the section of the input lattice which the arc spans. The final output of the algorithm is the semset for the arc that begins at the lattice source and goes to the lattice sink. It is labeled with the distinguished non-terminal, or start symbol, of the grammar.

The outer procedure is recursive. This procedure, and in fact the entire MDT algorithm, is initially invoked to compute an arc from the source to the sink of the input lattice with the start symbol as the arc's label. When this procedure returns, the semset attached to the newly constructed arc is the output of the MDT algorithm. However, the first invocation is not the only time that the outer procedure is called. The outer procedure will call itself, using the inner procedure as an intermediary, as many times as necessary to compute other arcs in the lattice.

Algorithm 5.4 *The outer procedure of MDT: computation of a non-terminal arc with semantics.*

Input:

1. The parser input lattice.

2. The translation grammar.

3. The index of the node in the parser input lattice from which the new arc is to originate. Call this index f (for "from").

4. The index of the node at which the new arc should terminate. Call this index t (for "to").

5. The non-terminal, Λ, with which the new arc should be labeled.

Output: The parser input lattice augmented with a new arc. The new arc has an attached semset.

Method: The procedure uses two temporary semsets A and B.

1. Initialize semset A to the empty set.

2. For each production, P, in the translation grammar, which has Λ as its LHS, do the following.

    (a) Execute the inner procedure to compute the semset associated with production P and spanning the subtree from f to t. Store the results in B.

    (b) Execute algorithm 5.3 repeatedly to add each element of B to A.

3. Construct a new arc in the parser input lattice from nodes f to t. Label this arc with the non-terminal Λ and the semset A.

5.6.3 The Inner Procedure

The inner procedure of the MDT algorithm matches a subgraph of the parser input lattice against the RHS of a single production rule from the grammar. The result of the inner procedure is a semset that embodies potential meanings of the subgraph as understood by the given production rule.

Let the number of nodes in the subgraph be L and let the number of symbols on the RHS of the production rule be $M - 1$. The inner procedure operates by computing an L by M element matrix of semsets as shown in figure 5.5. This matrix of semsets is called the *dynamic programming matrix*. Call the i by j-th element of the dynamic programming matrix $a_{i,j}$. Intuitively, $a_{i,j}$ records the possible output language interpretations and their respective distances when the first i nodes of the input subgraph are matched against the first j symbols of the production rule RHS. The matrix is initialized by putting the single string and distance pair $(m, 0)$ into element $a_{0,0}$ where m is the semantics of the production rule. All other elements of the dynamic programming matrix are then recursively computed using rules described below. The output of the inner procedure is the semset in the lower right-hand matrix element, $a_{L-1,M-1}$.

Algorithm 5.5 *The inner procedure of MDT: Matching of a grammar production to a subgraph.*

Input:

1. The parser input lattice.

2. A single production, P, from the translation grammar.

3. The index, f, of the first node in the input lattice over which pattern matching should occur.

4. The index, t, of the last node in the input lattice to use.

Output: A semset that describes the semantics of matching the subgraph from node f to node t against the input production rule.

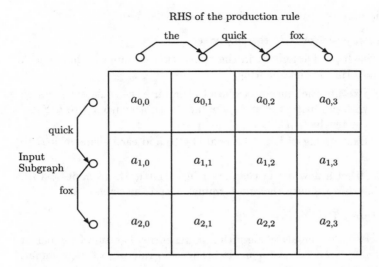

Figure 5.5
Diagram of the dynamic programming matrix for the inner procedure

Method: Processing is broken into a main procedure which is executed once, and a subprocedure which is recursively executed once for each semset computed.

The main procedure. The following code executes only once for each time that algorithm 5.5 is called.

1. Allocate an L by M dynamic programming matrix as shown in figure 5.5. Initialize element $a_{0,0}$ of this matrix to the single string and distance pair $(m, 0)$ where m is the semantics from production rule P. Initialize all other elements of the dynamic programming matrix to the empty set.

2. Execute the subprocedure below to compute the value of $a_{L-1,M-1}$.

3. Return the semset $a_{L-1,M-1}$.

The subprocedure. The following subprocedure is executed recursively to compute element $a_{i,j}$ of the dynamic programming matrix allocated in the main procedure above. *Note: Because of the length and complexity of this subprocedure, commentary intended to aid comprehension is printed in italics before each step. Also, a discussion of the role of each step of the subprocedure is given in the text following the presentation of this algorithm.*

1. *(This step causes the word on the input lattice arc spanning nodes k to i to be ignored.)* If $i > 0$, then for every k such that $f \le k < i$

and an arc from node k to node i is labeled with a terminal, do the following.

(a) Execute this subprocedure recursively to compute $a_{k,j}$, if it hasn't already been computed.

(b) For each pair (m, d) in $a_{k,j}$, add the pair $(m, d+1)$ to $a_{i,j}$ using algorithm 5.3.

2. *(This step causes the j-th symbol on the RHS of the production rule to be matched against nothing.)* If $j > 0$, then do the following.

(a) Refer to the j-th symbol on the RHS of the production rule as α. Find the deletion cost for α and name it δ. If α is a terminal, then δ is 1. If α is a non-terminal, then the deletion cost is computed by summing the deletion costs on the RHS of every production rule which has α as its LHS and taking the minimum of these sums.

(b) Execute this subprocedure recursively to compute $a_{i,j-1}$, if it hasn't already been computed.

(c) For each pair (m, d) in $a_{i,j-1}$, add the pair $(m, d + \delta)$ to $a_{i,j}$ using algorithm 5.3.

3. *(This step matches the j-th symbol on the RHS of the production rule against a single word in the input lattice.)* If $i > 0$ and $j > 0$ and the j-th symbol of the production rule is a terminal symbol α, then for every arc in the parser input lattice from node k to node i with $f \leq k$ which is labeled with α do the following.

(a) If it hasn't already been computed, calculate $a_{k,j-1}$ by a recursive execution of this subprocedure.

(b) Let the cost of the α arc from k to i be δ.

(c) For each pair (m, d) in $a_{k,j-1}$, add the pair $(m, d + \delta)$ to $a_{i,j}$ using algorithm 5.3.

4. *(This step matches the j-th symbol on the RHS of the production rule against a sequence of arcs on the input lattice.)* If $i > 0$ and $j > 0$ and the j-th symbol of the production rule is a non-terminal symbol Λ, and this symbol has no corresponding symbol in the semantics of the production rule, then do the following.

(a) Consider the set of arcs that are labeled with Λ, that begin at node k where $f \leq k < i$, and that terminate at node i. If any of these arcs have not been computed, then recursively execute the outer procedure to compute them.

(b) For each arc labeled with non-terminal Λ that spans nodes k to i where $f \leq k < i$, do the following steps.

  i. If it hasn't already been computed, calculate $a_{k,j-1}$.

  ii. Find the minimum distance of all the string and distance pairs in $a_{k,j-1}$. Call this minimum distance δ.

       iii. For each pair (m, d) in $a_{k,j-1}$, add the pair $(m, d + \delta)$ to $a_{i,j}$ using algorithm 5.3.

5. *(This step, like the previous one, matches the j-th symbol on the RHS of the production rule against a sequence of arcs on the input lattice. This step, however, has the added complication of updating the semantic information in the semset $a_{i,j}$ because of a linkage between the j-th RHS symbol and some symbol in the semantics of the production rule.)* If $i > 0$ and $j > 0$ and the j-th symbol of the production rule is a non-terminal symbol Λ, and this symbol has a corresponding symbol in the semantics of the production rule, then do the following.

    (a) Consider the set of arcs that are labeled with Λ, that begin at node k where $f \leq k < i$, and that terminate at node i. If any of these arcs have not been computed, then recursively execute the outer procedure to compute them.

    (b) For each arc labeled with non-terminal Λ that spans nodes k to i where $f \leq k < i$, do the following steps.

       i. If it hasn't already been computed, calculate $a_{k,j-1}$.

       ii. Let a_Λ be the semset that is attached to the arc with label Λ that spans k to i. For all pairs (x, y) where $x = (m, d)$ is an element of $a_{k,j-1}$ and $y = (\chi, \delta)$ is an element of a_Λ, do the following.

         A. Find the non-terminal symbol in m that corresponds to the RHS non-terminal symbol Λ. Replace this single symbol with the entire string χ, and call the result $\hat{m}$.

         B. Add the pair $(\hat{m}, d + \delta)$ to $a_{i,j}$ using algorithm 5.3.

The following paragraphs will attempt to better elucidate the recursive subprocedure of algorithm 5.5.

The first part of the procedure deals with omitted and inserted words. Step 1 handles the problem of words in the input that are not allowed by the grammar. The offending word is skipped and a penalty distance of 1 is added to the resulting parse semantics. In Step 2 the opposite problem is addressed. This step makes allowance for words that the grammar requires but that are not in the input lattice. As in step 1, the offending symbol is skipped and a penalty is added to the distance of all associated semantic strings. The penalty is 1 for each terminal symbol that is skipped.

The latter part of the procedure, steps 3, 4, and 5, is concerned with matching symbols of the grammar against words of the input lattice. When a terminal symbol in the grammar exactly matches a word in the parser input lattice, the semantic information is carried forward with an increase in distance equal to the arc cost (see section 5.3.3) of the arc in the input lattice. This operation is performed by step 3. Step 4 handles the case where a non-terminal symbol in the grammar, which has no associated semantics, is matched against zero or more words of the input lattice. The processing is the same as in step 3 except there is an extra loop to handle the flexibility of being able to match any number of input words.

The most complicated and difficult to understand part of the semset computation, and indeed of the entire MDT algorithm, is step 5. This step handles the complex case of matching a non-terminal with associated semantics against zero or more words in the input lattice. The outer loop of this step handles the actual matching of words and is identical to the outer loop of step 4. The complication arises in the inner loops where strings within the semset must be changed according to the semantic rules associated with the non-terminal being matched. An example will illustrate what is happening within step 5(b)ii. Assuming the non-terminal being matched is X, let the semset on the arc labeled by this non-terminal contain the following string and distance pairs:

$$\begin{array}{ll} \text{running} & 0 \\ \text{sleeping} & 1. \end{array}$$

Let the semset $a_{k,j-1}$ contain the string and distance pairs:

$$\begin{array}{ll} \text{sent(horse,X)} & 0 \\ \text{sent(boy,X)} & 1. \end{array}$$

With the above conditions, step 5(b)ii will insert the following string and distance pairs into the new semset $a_{i,j}$.

$$\begin{array}{ll} \text{sent(horse,running)} & 0 \\ \text{sent(horse,sleeping)} & 1 \\ \text{sent(boy,running)} & 1 \\ \text{sent(boy,sleeping)} & 2 \end{array}$$

5.6.4   An Important Optimization

In the above description of the inner procedure, the value returned is the lower right-hand corner semset in the dynamic programming matrix. All other elements of the dynamic programming matrix are discarded. It turns out, however, that this is computationally wasteful. If the number of nodes in the parser input lattice is N, then the MDT algorithm can be made to run faster by a factor of N by caching the entire dynamic programming matrix.

Suppose the input to the parser is a lattice with the single path, "I see a quick fox." Figure 5.5 shows the dynamic programming matrix for the subgraph consisting of the two words "quick fox" on a particular production rule of the grammar. Compare this to figure 5.6, which shows the dynamic programming matrix for a different subgraph, namely the single word "quick." Notice that the dynamic programming matrix of figure 5.6 will be exactly the upper two rows of the dynamic programming matrix of figure 5.5. This is because the computation of any individual semset in a dynamic programming matrix depends only on the values of other semsets above it and to its left,

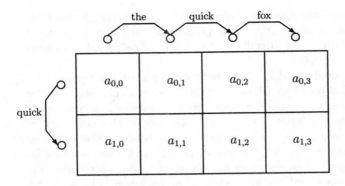

Figure 5.6
Diagram of another dynamic programming matrix for the inner procedure. Compare with the previous figure.

never on the value of semsets below.

In general, if two dynamic programming matrixes share the same production rule, and the source node of their subgraphs is the same, then they will have one or more rows of semsets in common. When the entire parser input lattice has N nodes, then given any subgraph there will be $O(N)$ other subgraphs with the same source. If all of these subgraphs compute their dynamic programming matrixes separately, then each semset will be computed $O(N)$ times. If, however, elements of the dynamic programming matrix are shared among the subgraphs, each semset need be computed only once, and the MDT algorithm requires $O(N)$ less computation.

5.7 Enhancements to the MDT Algorithm

In an effort to make the material more understandable, the MDT algorithm presented previously, and in particular the long recursive subprocedure in algorithm 5.5, was simplified. There are several changes and embellishments that can be made to the MDT algorithm. If used carefully, these can enhance the overall performance of the parser. This section will describe some of these changes.

5.7.1 Lexicon Dependent Deletion and Insertion Costs

As pointed out before, step 1 of the recursive subprocedure in algorithm 5.5 is responsible for skipping words in the parser input graph that do not fit on the RHS of the production rule. A penalty distance of 1 is added (see step 1b) each time an input graph word is skipped. In step 2 the opposite happens—symbols in the production rule are skipped, which is essentially the same as inserting words into the parser input graph. Again, a penalty distance of 1 is added for each word inserted. (The number of words inserted is computed in step 2a and this number is added to the distance in step 2c.) The first embellishment to the

MDT algorithm will be to make the insertion and deletion penalty distances depend on the input word that was added or removed.

Why should there be varying insertion and deletion costs? Some input words may be inserted or deleted with little or no change to the meaning of the utterance. Such words as "the" and "a" may usually be inserted or deleted from the input graph without altering the user's intended meaning. It also happens that these short, unaccented words tend to be spuriously inserted and deleted by speech recognizers. Hence, it makes sense to assign a low cost for inserting and deleting these words. Longer words, which carry stress and have significant meaning, such as "displaying" or "alternately", are much less likely to be accidentally inserted or deleted either by the user or the speech recognizer, and therefore carry a larger penalty distance. Some words, like "not", can result in vast changes to the meaning of the utterance if ignored or added, and are therefore given large insertion and deletion costs.

The insertion and deletion costs on a word need not be the same. The interjection "uh" is often added by speakers as a space filler, and so the parser should assign it a low deletion cost, but such a word should never be inserted by the parser, and should thus receive a large insertion cost.

5.7.2 Grammar Dependent Insertion Costs

Sometimes the importance of a word, and hence its insertion and deletion cost, depend not so much on what the word is but how it is used. As an example, consider the homophones "two" and "to."[4] We spell these words differently, but they are pronounced the same, and so as far as the speech recognizer and parser are concerned they are exactly the same word. Yet they have very different meanings. The preposition "to" is a small unstressed word that does not usually contribute significantly to the overall meaning of the utterance, and would thus normally be given a small insertion cost. The digit "two", on the other hand, is often critical to understanding an utterance and should hence be given a larger insertion cost. But one can't give "to" a small insertion cost and "two" a larger cost, because to the parser they are both the same word. (The speech recognizer returns the word "to" regardless of whether "to" or "two" is spoken.)

The solution to this dilemma is to give the word "to" a different insertion cost depending on how it is used in the grammar. If it is used in the sense of the preposition, give it a small cost; but if it used as a digit, give it a larger insertion cost. Recall that a word is effectively inserted into the input by deleting it from the production rule in step 2 of the subprocedure in algorithm 5.5. Instead of giving every instance of a particular terminal symbol the same insertion cost, we can record a case specific insertion cost in the RHS of every production rule in which that symbol is used.

---

[4]The vocabulary used in the experiments reported later in this book contains two other homophone pairs: for/four and know/no. The system also treats the pair an/am as homophones, since our speech recognizer has great difficulty in distinguishing between them.

The translation grammar notation will have to be expanded to allow insertion costs to be specified for individual symbols within production rules. We specify an insertion cost by a number enclosed in curly braces that immediately follows the symbol in question. Consider the following example.

```
A -> the to{10} are going to{2} town.
```

The first instance of "to" in the above rule is a noun that is important to the meaning of the utterance, so it is given a larger insertion cost or 10. The second occurrence is less important so it receives a smaller insertion cost of 2. (Presumably, the default insertion cost for "to" is somewhere between 10 and 2, perhaps 6.)

In practice, the ability to specify a precise individual insertion cost for each symbol on the RHS of a rule is more control than is needed. Usually, one only uses two values of the insertion cost—zero to indicate that the word is optional, and a very large number to indicate that the word is required in the current context. Special notation is used for these two cases because they are so frequent. The question mark character, ?, will mean the same as {0}, and the exclamation point, or bang character, !, will mean the same as {999999}. Consider the following example.

```
A -> the? switch is? up! : switch(up).
A -> the? switch is? down! : switch(down).
```

In both production rules, the words "the" and "is" are given a zero insertion cost. This means that they may be omitted from the input without causing a distance penalty to be added when the utterance is parsed. They are effectively optional words. The words "up" and "down", on the other hand, will bear a very large penalty if they are missing from the input, a penalty that is so large that these words are effectively required for a successful parse.

5.8   Expectation Processing

Besides the parser input graph, the only input to the parser is the expectation. The expectation is a set of output language strings and costs that is sent to the parser from the dialog controller. As its name implies, the expectation is a description of what the dialog controller expects that the user will say next. The expectation is used by the parser to select which one of the K hypotheses generated by the MDT is to become the final result of the parser.

Each expectation string has an associated expectation cost that is a measure of how much the string is expected. A zero expectation cost indicates that the string is very probable. A large expectation cost indicates an unlikely string.

5.8.1   Wildcards

The parser allows for the vocabulary of the output language to contain a symbol that serves as a place-holder for one or more unknown symbols in the midst of a string. This special symbol will be called the *wildcard*, and will be represented here by an asterisk.

The parser allows wildcards to appear anywhere that output language symbols are allowed—in the semantics of translation grammar productions, or as part of the final output of the parser—but wildcards find their more prolific use in the expectation. This is because a wildcard allows many statements to be anticipated with a single expectation string. For example, suppose the dialog controller has just asked the user to "report the voltage displayed by the DVM." The expectation for the response to this request could be something like the following.

voltageis(0.00)
voltageis(0.01)
voltageis(0.02)

⋮

voltageis(9.99)

But, to express the expectation this way, 1000 separate expectation strings are required. Clearly, it is simpler to replace the explicit voltage value in the expectation with the wildcard, and thus collapse the list of 1000 expectation strings into the single string:

voltageis(*).

Not every use of wildcards in expectation gives the 1000-fold reduction in the number of expectation strings, as in this example, but the savings are substantial.

Wildcards may also be used in the semantics of the translation grammar to hold a place for aspects of meaning that were actually omitted from the spoken utterance, due to anaphora, ellipsis, or some other form of abbreviation. For example, if the translation of "the dog is sleeping" is "sent(dog,sleep)", and the translation of "the cat is sleeping" is "sent(cat,sleep)", then it is quite natural to allow the translation of "it is sleeping" to be "sent(*,sleep)."

5.8.2 Wildcard String Matching

Were it not for wildcards, it would be a simple matter to determine if a hypothesis generated by MDT were the same as a particular expectation string. The use of wildcards introduces a level of complication into this determination, however, that will be the topic of this subsection.

What does it mean for a wildcard string to match? If A is a string containing wildcards and C is a string without wildcards, then A and C will be said to match if every wildcard in A can be replaced by some sequence of one or more symbols so that A is converted into an exact copy of C. If B is another string with wildcards, then A and B will be said to match if there exists some string C without wildcards that matches them both. In this second case, C will be called the *matching string* of A and B.

When comparing two strings that both contain wildcards, it may happen that the matching string is not unique. Therefore, we define the minimum matching string as follows.

- If one matching string is shorter (has fewer vocabulary symbols) than all the others, then select it as the minimum matching string.

- If there is more than one matching string that has the fewest number of symbols, then compare all of these shortest strings, and in every symbol position at which the strings disagree, put the wildcard in the corresponding symbol position of the minimum matching string.

Some examples will serve to clarify the concept of the minimum matching string. Each of the strings in the following examples uses the vocabulary of lower case letters, with asterisk serving as the wildcard.

Input A	Input B	Minimum Matching String
ab*	abc	abc
ab*	*bc	abc
ab*	a*c	abc
ab*	ab*c	ab*c
a*c	a*b*	a*bc
a*c	a*b	*nil*

The final output of the parser is not really one of the hypotheses, as has been stated earlier, but is the minimum matching string that results from the comparison of one of the hypotheses to one of the expectation strings. Algorithm 5.6 below describes an efficient dynamic programming algorithm for computing the minimum matching string.

Algorithm 5.6 *Computation of the minimum matching string*

Input: Two strings $A = \{a_1, a_2, a_3, \ldots, a_p\}$ and $B = \{b_1, b_2, b_3, \ldots, b_q\}$. Each may contain zero or more wildcards.

Output: A string $C = \{c_1, c_2, c_3, \ldots, c_n\}$ which is the minimum matching string for A and B, or nil if A and B do not match.

Method:

1. Allocate a p by q array, x, of variables each of which can store one of the following values:

   - MATCH-A
   - MATCH-B
   - MATCH-AB
   - MATCH-BA

- NO-MATCH

Initialize every element of x to NO-MATCH.

2. If a_1 is the wildcard, then $x(1,1) \leftarrow$ MATCH-BA.

3. If $b_1 = a_1$ or b_1 is the wildcard, then $x(1,1) \leftarrow$ MATCH-AB.

4. For i from 1 to p and for j from 1 to q do the following steps: (It makes no difference whether the i is nested inside or outside of the j loop, but both loops must be increasing. Assume that the values of $x(0, \ldots)$ and of $x(\ldots, 0)$ are both NO-MATCH.)

   (a) $x(i-1, j) \neq$ NO-MATCH and b_j is the wildcard, then $x(i,j) \leftarrow$ MATCH-A.

   (b) $x(i, j-1) \neq$ NO-MATCH and a_i is the wildcard, then $x(i,j) \leftarrow$ MATCH-B.

   (c) $x(i-1, j-1) \neq$ NO-MATCH and b_j is the wildcard, then $x(i,j) \leftarrow$ MATCH-AB.

   (d) $x(i-1, j-1) \neq$ NO-MATCH and a_i is the wildcard, then $x(i,j) \leftarrow$ MATCH-BA.

   (e) $x(i-1, j-1) \neq$ NO-MATCH and $a_i = b_j$, then $x(i,j) \leftarrow$ MATCH-AB.

5. If $x(p,q) =$ NO-MATCH, then return nil and halt because the two input strings do not match. Otherwise, continue with the next step.

6. Initialize a counter variable k to 1.

7. Set $i \leftarrow p$ and $j \leftarrow q$.

8. While $i \geq 1$ and $j \geq 1$ do the following.

   (a) If $x(i,j) =$ MATCH-A or $x(i,j) =$ MATCH-AB, then $C_k \leftarrow a_i$. Otherwise, $C_k \leftarrow b_j$.

   (b) $k \leftarrow k + 1$

   (c) $\hat{i} \leftarrow i$.

   (d) If $x(i,j) \neq$ MATCH-B, then $i \leftarrow i - 1$.

   (e) If $x(\hat{i}, j) \neq$ MATCH-A, then $j \leftarrow j - 1$.

9. C now contains the k symbols of the minimum matching string in reverse order. Unreverse the order of the symbols in this string and return the string as the final result of the algorithm.

A brief intuitive description of algorithm 5.6 will help the reader to understand how the algorithm works. The matrix element $x(i,j)$ stores the results of matching the first i symbols of the A string against the first j symbols of the B string. Hence in step 5, if $x(p,q)$ is not a match, then the two strings do not match. The four MATCH-* values of matrix elements are used to reconstruct the minimum matching string after it is determined that the input strings do in fact match. The interpretation of each is as follows.

MATCH-A means that b_j is the wildcard and that a_i is not the first symbol in the sequence that matches the wildcard at b_j. Hence, a_i should be added to the minimum matching string, and i should be decremented, but j should be unchanged.

MATCH-B is the analogue of MATCH-A where a_i is the wildcard.

MATCH-AB means either that b_j and a_i are the same symbol, or that b_j is the wildcard and a_i is the first symbol to match that wildcard. a_i is copied onto the minimum matching string and both i and j are decremented to the previous symbol.

MATCH-BA is used when a_i is the wildcard and b_j is the first symbol matching that wildcard.

5.8.3   Enhancements to the Minimum Matching String Algorithm

As will be seen in section 5.9.4, if the size of a string that is input to algorithm 5.6 is N then the running time for the algorithm is proportional to N^2. This is slower than one would hope. It is therefore worth mentioning the existence of several simple tricks for making this algorithm much faster in many cases.

Before a pair of strings are given to algorithm 5.6, any prefix and suffix that is common to both strings should be removed. This common prefix and suffix should later be added back to the minimum matching string (assuming the algorithm finds a match). The common prefix and suffix can be removed and restored in linear time, and removing them has the advantage of reducing the size of N in the $O(N^2)$ algorithm.

In actual use within the parser, most attempts to find a minimum matching string using algorithm 5.6 will discover that no matching string exists. Since this is the most common result, changes to the algorithm that find this result quickly will decrease the average running time of the algorithm. The following are a few fast and efficient ways to detect that the inputs will not match.

- After the common prefixes are removed, if the first symbol of neither string is the wildcard, then the strings cannot match.

- After removal of the common suffixes, one of the two input strings must end with the wildcard, or else the strings cannot match.

- If nothing is left of one of the two strings after the common prefix and suffix are removed (that is, if the string consists of nothing but the common prefix and suffix), but there are symbols left in the second string, then the two strings cannot match.

Another case that arises frequently is when one of the two input strings to algorithm 5.6 contains only a single wildcard, and after the common prefix and suffix have been removed that wildcard is all that remains of the string.

In such cases, the other of the two strings is always the minimum matching string, regardless of how many wildcards it may contain.

5.8.4   Wildcard String Matching Versus Unification

As used in this system, wildcard string matching is actually a special case of unification (see Nilsson [Nil80]) in which all variables are singletons. In the original implementation, Prolog unification was used to accomplish wildcard string matching. This was found to be a speed bottleneck. Consequently, the wildcard string matching was recoded in C using algorithm 5.6.

5.8.5   Expectation Based Hypothesis Selection

The algorithm by which expectation is used to select the final output of the parser is simple. For every hypothesis string that matches a string in the expectation, a cost is computed based on the utterance cost of the hypothesis and the expectation cost of the expectation string. The minimum matching string for the expectation and hypothesis pair that yields the lowest cost becomes the final output of the parser. This procedure is formalized in algorithm 5.7. The most interesting part of the algorithm is the method by which the utterance cost and expectation costs are combined. This detail is handled by the expectation function, which is the subject of the next subsection.

Algorithm 5.7 *Expectation based hypothesis selection*

Input: A set of K hypotheses, $H = \{(m_1, u_1), (m_2, u_2), \ldots, (m_K, u_K)\}$, and a set of r expectations, $E = \{(x_1, w_1), (x_2, w_2), \ldots, (x_r, w_r)\}$.

Output: A single string, which will become the output of the parser.

Method:

1. $z_{min} \leftarrow$ nil, and $s_{min} \leftarrow +\infty$.

2. For each pair of i and j such that $1 \leq i \leq K$ and $1 \leq j \leq r$ do the following.

   (a) $u \leftarrow$ the minimum matching string of m_i and x_j.

   (b) $s \leftarrow g(u_i, w_j)$ where $g(\cdot)$ is the expectation function.

   (c) If $u \neq$ nil and $s < s_{min}$ then $z_{min} \leftarrow u$ and $s_{min} \leftarrow s$.

3. Return the string z_{min}.

5.8.6   The Expectation Function

Intuition tells us that the expectation function should be an important part of the parser, since it alone determines the relative importance of utterance cost and expectation cost. However, intuition is not an effective guide to predicting what the best expectation function might be. This section will describe three candidate expectation functions, each of which may be tuned to change the relative importance of utterance and expectation costs.

All of the expectation functions below are based on the *normalized* utterance cost, written $\hat{u}$. The normalized utterance cost is defined to be the ordinary utterance cost divided by the longest path from source to sink of the input lattice. One might think of the normalized utterance cost as the utterance cost per word of input.

The first expectation function is simply a linear combination of the normalized utterance cost and expectation cost.

$$g(u, w) = \beta\hat{u} + (1 - \beta)w. \tag{5.2}$$

The parameter β in this function is a constant between 0 and 1 that controls the relative importance of utterance and expectation cost in arriving at the final output. When β is close to 1, the utterance cost becomes the dominant factor in selecting an output for the parser. When β is close to zero, expectation becomes more important.

One may note that the value of β depends to some extent on the difference in ranges of possible values for the $\hat{u}$ and w. For example, if $\hat{u}$ can take on values between 0 and 10^6, but range of w is between 0 and 1, then we would expect β to be very close to 0 since this would reduce the range of $\hat{u}$ to be comparable to the range of w. Conversely, if w has a much larger possible range of values than $\hat{u}$, we expect β to be near 1 so that the term $(1 - \beta)$ will be close to 0 and therefore reduce the range of w. In order to eliminate this variability of β, we will henceforth assume that the possible range of values for both the normalized utterance cost, $\hat{u}$, and the expectation, w, are the same. Exactly what these ranges are is unimportant, since it is only the relative values of $\hat{u}$ and w that make a difference.

What is the best value for β? An experiment was conducted to answer this question. The results are reported in section 8.4. The short answer is that β greater than about 0.75 but less than 1 should give the best parser accuracy.

The second expectation function gives greater importance to utterance cost, and uses expectation only as a tie-breaker between hypotheses with basically the same utterance cost.

$$g(u, w) = \begin{cases} w & \hat{u} \leq \hat{u}_{min} + \gamma \cdot u_{max} \\ +\infty & \text{otherwise.} \end{cases} \tag{5.3}$$

The variable $\hat{u}_{min}$ is the smallest utterance cost of any hypothesis in the current hypothesis set. The factor u_{max} is the largest possible value of the utterance cost in any hypothesis. The parameter γ determines a range of utterance costs that are considered to be in a tie for first place. The multiplication of γ by u_{max} constrains γ to values between 0 and 1, and thus makes the value of γ independent of u_{max}.

Equation 5.3 shows an additive γ, but this same idea can also be used with a multiplicative γ (which henceforth shall be written as $\bar{\gamma}$ to distinguish it from its additive cousin) as shown in equation 5.4.

$$g(u, w) = \begin{cases} w & \hat{u} \leq \hat{u}_{min} \cdot \bar{\gamma} \\ +\infty & \text{otherwise.} \end{cases} \tag{5.4}$$

Experiments conducted to determine the best values for γ (or $\bar{\gamma}$) in each of these latter two expectation functions (see section 8.4) reveal that $\gamma = 0$ and $\bar{\gamma} = 1$ are best.

5.9 Computational Complexity

This section will derive expressions for the computational complexity of the entire parser. The derivation begins with a definition of notation used throughout this section (and chapter). The computational complexity of various components of the parser is developed first. Finally, these individual results are collected to derive the computational complexity of the overall parser algorithm.

5.9.1 Notation

Six parameters are defined for use in the subsequent complexity formulas.

1. The number of nodes in the parser input lattice is N.

2. The number of arcs in the parser input lattice is E.

3. The total size of the grammar measured in tokens is M.

4. The maximum number of string and distance pairs in any semset is K.

5. The number of expectation strings and costs is r.

5.9.2 The Complexity of Input Lattice Node Renumbering

The first operation of the parser is the input lattice node renumbering operation described in section 5.3.4. The following discussion will derive the computational complexity of algorithm 5.1.

Step 3 is a loop which will execute at most N times. This limit occurs because the input lattice is acyclic, and therefore can not contain a path which is longer than the number of nodes in the lattice. Each active set can contain $O(N)$ elements, so $O(N)$ operations are required for each iteration of step 3a. The number of operations required by step 3c is $O(E)$. Hence, the total computational complexity of step 3 is $O(NE + N^2)$. Steps 4 and 5 require respectively $O(N \log N)$ and $O(N)$ operations. These do not contribute to the asymptotic complexity. The total computation time for the algorithm is determined by step 3 as $O(N^2 + NE)$.

In most parser input lattices, E and N are related as $E = O(N)$. Under this assumption, the total number of operations required by algorithm 5.1 is $O(N^2)$.

5.9.3 The Complexity of MDT

The number of operations required by the MDT algorithm will be computed as the product of the number of dynamic programming matrix elements and the number of operations required to compute each such matrix element.

The number of dynamic programming matrix elements computed by MDT is $O(N^2M)$. To see this, consider first that the algorithm computes arcs between every pair of nodes in the parser input lattice, and that there are $O(N^2)$ node pairs. For each pair of arcs, a single row of dynamic programming matrix elements must be computed for each production in the grammar. The length of each row is the length of the production, so that the total number of matrix elements computed per node pair is $O(M)$. (This value would be $O(NM)$ if the optimization of section 5.6.4 were not used.)

If the ratio of non-terminals to terminals in the grammar is constant (a reasonable assumption), then the time needed to compute a single dynamic programming matrix element is determined by the total execution time of the slowest of the steps in algorithm 5.5. Each of these steps will be examined separately in the following paragraphs.

The main procedure of algorithm 5.5 requires constant time. It will not be considered further since other steps in the algorithm clearly dominate the computational complexity. Subsequent discussion will refer to the recursive subprocedure of algorithm 5.5.

The number of operations required by step 1 is the product of the number of applicable arcs and the number of operations required to process each arc. The number of arcs connected to each node and that are labeled with terminals is $O(EN^{-1})$. A balanced tree scheme can be used to implement step 1b in time $O(K \log K)$; however this implementation carries a large time constant. For the small values of K normally used by the MDT algorithm, a $O(K^2)$ implementation is much faster. Therefore, let us say that the total time complexity of step 1 is $O(K^2EN^{-1})$. (For the same reason, subsequent paragraphs will also make use of $O(K^2)$ when $O(K \log K)$ would suffice.)

Within step 2, the computation of deletion costs for a non-terminal (step 2a) seems rather involved. However, this computation depends only upon the grammar and not on the input lattice. Hence it can be done off-line, and step 2a can be reduced to a constant-time table lookup. The computational complexity of step 2 then becomes $O(K^2)$.

The complexity of step 3 is $O(K^2EN^{-1})$, the same as step 1.

Step 4 of the algorithm contains nested loops. The outer loop at step 4b executes $O(N)$ times. The inner loop at step 4(b)iii uses time $O(K^2)$ so the total complexity is $O(NK^2)$.

The portion of the inner procedure which dominates in all practical cases is step 5. As in step 4, there is an outer loop at step 5b that executes $O(N)$ times. However, there are nested inner loops at step 5(b)ii that run $O(K^2)$ times. The semantic string rewriting operation at step 5(b)iiA can be made to run in time $O(K)$, with a careful choice of representation. Time of $O(K)$ is also required for step 5(b)iiB. Thus the complexity of step 5 is $O(NK^3)$.

Pulling together the computational complexity of all steps in the inner procedure shows that the number of operations needed to compute a single element of the dynamic programming matrix is $O(NK^3+EN^{-1}K^2)$. This gives a total complexity for the MDT algorithm of $O(N^3MK^3 + ENMK^2)$. With the reasonable assumptions that K is constant, $E = O(N)$, and $M = O(N)$, this expression for the complexity reduces to $O(N^4)$.

The computational complexity reported for the minimum-distance parsing algorithms in [AP72], [Lev85], [Lyo74], and [Ney91] is $O(N^3)$. The reader should not be misled by this and assume that MDT is asymptotically slower than minimum-distance parsing. The asymptotic complexities of minimum-distance parsing and MDT are actually the same. In the previously cited minimum-distance parsing references, the size of the grammar, M, is assumed to be a constant. This is a valid assumption for any particular implementation, but as a system is expanded in order to handle longer and more complex inputs, the size of the grammar will tend to increase proportionally. Hence, for purposes of estimating the computational requirements of new systems, we feel that $O(N^4)$ is a better measure of the algorithm's complexity.

5.9.4 The Complexity of Expectation Processing

Because the expectation functions can all be computed in constant time, the computational complexity of algorithm 5.7 is $O(rK)$ times that for algorithm 5.6. In the worst case, algorithm 5.6 requires time proportional to the square of the length of its inputs. We can make the assumption that the length of a hypothesis string is proportional to the length of the user's input[5], so we say that algorithm 5.6 requires time $O(N^2)$. This gives a total computational complexity of all expectation processing of $O(N^2rK)$, or if we make the assumption that $r = O(M)$, $O(N^2MK)$.

5.9.5 Overall Parser Complexity

A review of the asymptotic complexity of the various component algorithms of the parser shows that the time to compute MDT dominates the calculation. Our experimental observations confirm this. Let us therefore say that the asymptotic computational complexity of the complete parsing algorithm relative to the size of its input is $O(N^4)$.

An implementation of the parser on a Sun-4/280 has demonstrated acceptable performance for utterances of 8 words or less. We conjecture that a robust commercial speech understanding system must be able to process utterances of up to 32 words in length. If current trends in hardware improvement continue, then the level of performance needed for such a system should be available on desktop in about the year 2010.

---

[5]It makes sense that the length of a string in the input language should be proportional to the length of a string in the output language, since both strings will convey the same amount of meaning. Aho and Ullman [AU69] prove that this is always the case when the translation grammar specifies a many-to-one mapping from input to output.

Chapter 6

System Implementation

Without development of an actual working system it is impossible to empirically validate the proposed computational model. Thus, the architecture introduced in section 3.1 has been implemented on a Sun 4 workstation and later ported to a Sparc II workstation. The majority of the code is written in Quintus Prolog[1] while the parser is written in C. The system software is available via anonymous FTP as described in appendix C.

The overall hardware configuration is illustrated in figure 6.1. Speech recognition is performed by a Verbex 6000 user-dependent connected-speech recognizer running on an IBM PC. The vocabulary is currently restricted to the 125 words given in table 7.1. Users are required to begin each utterance with the word "verbie" and end with the word "over" (e.g. "verbie, the switch is up, over"). The Verbex speech recognizer acknowledges each input with a small beep. These sentinel interactions act as a synchronization mechanism for the user and the machine. Speech output is performed by a DECtalk[2] DTCO1 text-to-speech converter.

This chapter discusses the following technical aspects of the implementation.

- The various knowledge representation formalisms.

- The implemented domain processor, an expert system for assisting in simple circuit repair.

- The implemented generation component.

- The basic physical resource utilization of the system.

---

[1]Quintus Prolog is a trademark of Quintus Computer Systems, Incorporated.
[2]DECtalk is a trademark of Digital Equipment Corporation.

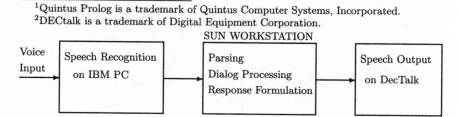

Figure 6.1
Hardware Configuration

6.1   Knowledge Representation

6.1.1   Prolog

The basis for the implementation has been the logic programming language, Prolog. Clocksin and Mellish [CM87] provide an introduction to this language. Pereira and Shieber [PS87] and McCord [McC87] can be consulted for a discussion of the usage of Prolog for natural language analysis. Prolog allows the expression of rules and facts in a subset of first-order logic called Horn clauses. Prolog is supplemented with non-logical features that aid in efficient computation as well, but as a representational formalism, its utility in representing rules and facts in a declarative format provides a basis for the representation of knowledge and rules within the model.

6.1.2   GADL

The Goal and Action Description Language was introduced in section 3.2.2. A detailed description is provided in appendix A. It is used as a standard formalism for representing goals that may be accomplished during a task. It provides a common representation that generalizes over various task domains. All knowledge within the system about domain processor recommendations, action decompositions, achievable subgoal definitions, world meanings in expectation definitions and discourse records, and axiom information is represented in GADL.

6.1.3   snf

In order to perform computational natural language dialog, the user inputs must be translated into a representation for which computational processes must be defined. *snf* is the representation used for describing the linguistic content of utterances. A description of the various snf forms is given in section 4.4.3.

6.1.4   Sef

Sef is a pseudo-linguistic representation of the semantic expectation (section 4.4.3). It is used as an intermediate representation between actual linguistic representations (represented in snf) and world interpretations (represented in GADL). A description of the various Sef forms is given below.

affirmation(_,TS)—indicates affirmation (TS = true) or negative affirmation (TS = false) of some fact. The connection to the actual fact is provided by the world interpretation given in the expectation description. For example, for the goal:

obs(phys_state(prop(switch,position,up),_))—"Is the switch up?", the associated expectation description would be:

[affirmation(_,TS),[],phys_state(prop(switch,position,up),TS)].

Thus, a response of "no" would map to the world interpretation that it is false that the switch is up (i.e. the switch is not up).

understand(_,TS)—indicates understanding (TS = true) or not understanding (TS = false) some fact.

state_value(StateDescription)—indicates assertion of a GADL state description.

want(Agent,Want)—Agent (computer or user) has the goal described in Want (a GADL action description).

command(X)—indicates the computer should do X.

atom—this represents an abbreviated response that can be interpreted within the surrounding context as part of a completed world interpretation. For example, a response of "up" to "What is the switch position?", is an abbreviated response where the world interpretation would be:

$$phys\_state(prop(switch,position,up),true).$$

need_value(Characteristic,Entity)—need a value to satisfy Characteristic of Entity. Entity may be an object, action, or state_value. The current possible values for Characteristic follow.

- definition—need a definition or explanation of Entity.
- location—need the location of Entity
  (e.g. need_value(location,switch)).
- help—need assistance with Entity (an action).
- time—need the time.
- status—need "status" information for Entity.
- wh—need to fill in the missing values for Entity, a state_value, to make it a true proposition in the current world state. An example is:
  need_value(wh,state_value(phys_state(prop(X,true)))), where X denotes (switch,position,_), which indicates a need to determine what the switch position should be.
- yn—need to know if Entity, when evaluated as a proposition in the current world state, is true or false.

6.1.5   IPSIM

IPSIM is the interruptible theorem prover described beginning in section 3.3.2. Usage of IPSIM requires specification of rules and axioms in a notation that is basically a subset of Prolog with some minor differences. Details on the usage of IPSIM are provided in appendix B.

6.1.6   Discourse Structure

Discourse structure information is represented in the following manner. For each utterance there is a clause of the form:

utterance_record(ID,SegID,Speaker,Snf,WorldMeaning).

- ID—Unique identification number.

- SegID—Identification number of the subdialog of which the utterance is a part (refers to a discourse_record clause).

- Speaker—Denotes who made utterance (computer or user).

- Snf—Linguistic representation of the utterance (in snf).

- WorldMeaning—Semantic representation of the utterance within full context; = **repeat** if same as snf; otherwise, represented in GADL for an input; snf for an output.

For each subdialog/discourse segment there is a clause of the form:

discourse_record(ID,ParentID,DSP,Mode,Initiator,UtteranceSequence,Status).

- ID—unique identification number of the subdialog.

- ParentID—identification number of parent subdialog (refers to another discourse record).

- DSP—subdialog purpose. Gives the primary goal of the subdialog. Normally a domain goal represented in GADL.

- CurrentMode—dialog mode in which subdialog is currently being conducted.

- Initiator—denotes who initiated subdialog (computer or user).

- UtteranceSequence—list of ID numbers of utterance records for the utterances that compose the subdialog.

- Status—gives the subdialog status. Possible values are open, closed, or suspend. A subdialog may be suspended due to an interrupt or due to failure of the theorem prover to complete the associated goal (the DSP) of the subdialog.

- NOTE: The global dialog record has ID = 0 and DSP = task. It is the parent subdialog of all top level subdialogs.

6.1.7 Axioms

As dialog is pursued in order to prove the completion of task steps, the user's inputs are translated into axioms about the world. In addition, other axioms may be inferred that can be useful in proving the completion of future task steps. The representation used for describing axioms is the following.

axiom(ID,ProofNum,StateDescription,HowKnown).

- ID—unique identification number.

- ProofNum—identification number for the theorem active when the axiom was acquired.

- StateDescription—GADL state description that represents the axiom content.

- HowKnown—tells how the axiom was acquired; possible values are:

  said(UID)—indicates that the axiom was said by the user and that the identification number of the corresponding utterance record is given by UID.

  infer(X)—indicates the axiom was inferred from the axiom with identification number X.

As an example, for the following subdialog:

```
C:  Is there a wire between connector 84 and connector 99?
U:  It is not there.
```

The axioms added to the knowledge base during execution are shown in figure 6.2. Axiom 15 is the world interpretation of the user's statement (which was utterance 13 of the dialog, hence the value "said(13)" in the HowKnown field), while axioms 16 through 19 are inferences. Note that axioms 17 and 18 are the two inferred axioms that allow the system to skip mentioning the substeps of locating connectors 84 and 99 when engaging in the subdialog about providing help in adding the wire between the two connectors that was discussed in section 3.4.3. The complete details of the GADL representation of state descriptions is specified in appendix A.

As a dialog ensues, certain axioms may no longer be valid. Such axioms include physical state descriptions as well as descriptions of goals. Such axioms are called *proof-specific* and are valid only for the duration of the theorem in which they are acquired. In contrast, *proof-independent* axioms are ones that remain valid unless evidence to the contrary occurs. For example, axioms about user abilities are proof-independent. These user model axioms can be used during the proof of any theorem. Thus, from figure 6.2, axiom 15 is an example of a proof-specific axiom while the others are proof-independent axioms since they are user model axioms.

```
axiom(15,6,phys_state(prop(wire(connector(84),connector(99)),exist,absent),
    true),said(13)).
axiom(16,6,mental_state(user, int_know_action(how_to_do(
    perf(ident(wire(connector(84),connector(99)))))),true),infer(15)).
axiom(17,6,mental_state(user,int_know_action(how_to_do(perf(ident(
    connector(84))))),true),infer(15)).
axiom(18,6,mental_state(user,int_know_action(how_to_do(perf(ident(
    connector(99))))),true),infer(15)).
axiom(19,6,mental_state(user,int_know_action(how_to_do(obs(phys_state(
    prop(wire(connector(84),connector(99)),exist,absent),true)))),true),
    infer(15)).
```

Figure 6.2
Sample axioms

6.1.8 Interfaces

As shown in section 3.1, the system architecture consists of a collection of modules. There must be a consistency between the various knowledge representations used. The primary representation of the dialog system is GADL. Consequently, as part of the interface between the dialog processor and domain processor there must be a mapping function, defined in the domain processor, for mapping between its internal knowledge representation and GADL. Mappings defined within the dialog processor are the following.

- Between sef and snf when computing expectations and input interpretations.

- Between sef and GADL in performing contextual understanding; these are defined in the semantic expectations (section 4.4.3).

- Between GADL and snf in computing utterance specifications for computer utterances. Normally, missing axioms pertain to unproven goals. There must be a mapping from the goal to an snf representation of the utterance that will hopefully lead to accomplishment of the goal.

6.2 Domain Processor

Testing the dialog controller requires the development of a domain processor with which to use the dialog system. The developed domain processor is a system for assisting with circuit repair on a Radio Shack 160 in One Electronic Project Kit. The specific circuit being used causes the LED to alternately display a one and seven, and the type of errors that can be detected are missing wires or a dead battery. The following pages give a description of various aspects of this system, beginning with a general description of the circuit debugging methodology, and progressing to a discussion of the actual decision strategies and the method for interfacing this system to dialog. Technical details on the knowledge representation, which uses a Prolog-style syntax, are given in Smith [Smi91]. The code is available as part of obtaining the entire system software as described in appendix C. Here we provide the intuitive overview necessary to understand the system and the method for interfacing the domain processor to the dialog controller.

6.2.1 Debugging Methodology

The goal was to design and implement a computer program that could assist in the debugging of an electric circuit. Here we describe the debugging process for an entity with complete knowledge in a way that is amenable to implementation by computer program. The main topics of discussion are the following.

- Background information and terminology.

- Description of the structural hierarchy of a circuit.

- Presentation of a debugging paradigm usable by an entity with complete knowledge.

- Discussion of complications that arise when an entity with complete knowledge must communicate via natural language with a "slave" who performs the required sensory and mechanical operations necessary for debugging.

Background and Terminology

Debugging an electric circuit implies that the circuit has a particular set of behaviors that is deemed to be the correct set of behaviors for the circuit. This set of behaviors will be called the *defining behavior* for the circuit. The defining behavior is a subset of the behaviors and structural descriptions about the circuit. Behaviors are properties of the circuit such as: "the voltage between terminals 82 and 120 should be 7.5 volts," or "when the switch is on and the control knob is at 10 the LED should be alternately blinking a 1 and a 7 at a frequency greater than once per second." Structural descriptions describe the constituents of portions of the circuit. An example of a structural description is the list of objects/physical components that make up a subcircuit such as a transistor circuit. For example, a transistor circuit may be composed of a transistor, two resistors, a capacitor, and a set of wires providing the connections from the power circuit and through the transistor on to the LED. It may be possible to use structural descriptions exclusively to get the various portions of the circuit constructed properly, but behavioral descriptions are required to specify the defining behavior. Circuits are useful for what they do, not what they look like. When the defining behavior is observed, the circuit is considered to be working correctly. The non-defining behaviors and structural descriptions can be used to determine when various parts of the circuit are functioning correctly. However, they are more often used when the circuit is not functioning correctly in order to isolate and correct the problems in the circuit.

The Structural Hierarchy of a Circuit

A circuit consists of *components*. A component may be either a physical object (such as a battery), or a conceptual object (such as the power circuit). Conceptual components are decomposed into other conceptual and physical components. Physical components are not normally decomposed into constituent objects, but they may be. The highest level conceptual component is the *system*. Each component has a set of behavioral and/or structural descriptions that help define when the component is considered to be functioning correctly. These descriptions are called *specifications* or *specs*. Specs consist of: (1) a description of an observation to be made; (2) a list of prerequisite conditions that must exist in order to make the observation; and (3) a set of actions to be performed; the actions can be described by the "IF-THEN-ELSE" paradigm—IF obs1 THEN action1 ELSE IF obs2 THEN action2 ELSE .... An example of a part of a spec would be the following (some of the actions have been omitted).

```
Observation:  Observe the behavior of the LED.
Conditions:   The switch must be on, and the control must be
              set to 10.
Actions:   IF the LED is alternately displaying a 1 and a 7
           with a frequency of > once per second, THEN
           assert the spec is satisfied
        ELSE IF the LED is not on, THEN assert the battery
           is suspicious, but if it's been checked,
           then assert the power-circuit as suspicious
        ELSE IF the LED is on but not blinking, THEN assert
           that the transistor circuits are suspicious
        ELSE IF the LED is blinking but not alternately
           displaying a 1 and a 7, THEN assert that
           the LED circuit is suspicious
        ELSE IF ...
```

In general, possible actions as the result of an observation are the following.

1. Raise the suspicion level for some components. The suspicion level measures the likelihood that a component is a source of error in the circuit.

2. Assert that the spec is checked (and as a consequence the associated component may be checked).

3. Assert that the spec is not checkable (because the prerequisite conditions are unobtainable or the observation is not achievable).

4. Replace or add a component. The only types of repair allowed are the replacemeɪt or addition of a component. Thus, this debugging method only handles problems of missing components, faulty components, or disconnected components. It does not handle the problems of extra components or misconnected components (such as short circuits).

In order to believe that a component is functioning properly it may be necessary to examine all or only some of its specs. The specs for the system component specify the defining behavior of the circuit.

A Debugging Paradigm

The basic approach to debugging seems simple at first glance. It is based on the following steps.

1. Has it been determined that the system is functioning correctly (i.e. have observed the defining behavior)? If so, then stop with success; otherwise, go to step 2.

2. Are there no longer any productive steps to take? If so, then stop with failure; otherwise go to step 3.

3. Choose a component to be examined.

4. Choose a spec of the component selected in 3 to be tested.

5. For the spec chosen in 4 do the following.

   (a) Set the conditions required by the spec.
   (b) Make the observation required by the spec.
   (c) Perform the appropriate actions based on the observation made.

6. Go to step 1.

For a person with complete knowledge and the ability to carry out all necessary physical and sensory actions, the basic approach to debugging is simple. However, that is not the environment in which a computer program assisting in the debugging of an electric circuit will operate. The operating environment for the computer program is described next.

Complications

We assume that the user and computer are dependent upon each other for successful completion of the task. Natural language is assumed to be the medium of communication between the computer and user. The debugging process should be a cooperative venture between the computer and human user that leads to one of two conclusions.

- The circuit is considered to be functioning correctly by the computer and user.

- The computer concludes that it cannot assist the user any further—
  that it cannot enable the circuit to be repaired.

The debugging paradigm given previously can be used. Intuitively, debugging proceeds by first checking to see if the defining behavior has been observed. If it has, debugging is complete. If it has not, the observation performed provides clues about the source of the problem. Components that became suspicious as a result of the aberrant behavior are examined. Eventually, the problem or problems are found and the repair or repairs are made, and the circuit is eventually repaired. In reality, it is not this simple.

The first difficulty is caused by the complex interactions between various electrical and mechanical components. Until the defining behavior is observed, there is never absolute certainty that the error has been found. Thus, provision must be made for examining all possible sources of error when necessary. Since any component can be a source of error, the automatic selection process must be capable of eventually selecting any component in any situation. As an example of a complex interaction, suppose there is a circuit where the LED should light when the switch is turned on. If the switch is turned on and the LED does not light, then the greatest suspicion is on the battery. Suppose that the LED does not light up when the switch is turned on, the battery is ok, but the voltmeter is broken and the actual problem is a missing or broken wire between the switch and the battery. Because greatest suspicion is on the battery, its voltage is checked. The voltage reads zero because the voltmeter is broken; thus, it is erroneously concluded that there is a dead battery. The battery is replaced, but still the circuit does not work. If the component of greatest suspicion, the battery, is continually examined, the circuit will never get repaired. At some point it must be conceded that no progress is being made by replacing the battery and less suspicious components must be examined in order to try and find the problem. The process of choosing a component to be examined is not clear cut.

The second difficulty is in maintaining information about the behavior of the circuit. Observations are dependent on the circuit configuration. The LED may behave differently when the switch is on from when the switch is off or when a control knob is at different settings. When the configuration is changed, the observation under the old configuration cannot be assumed to be the correct observation under the new configuration. Similarly, when a component is replaced or added, none of the previous behavioral observations are necessarily valid. Furthermore, even when the configuration does not change it may be necessary to go back and request old observations to be repeated. Language is an inexact medium of communication because of the differing knowledge of the participants for which neither is completely aware of the knowledge of the other. Thus, detecting and recovering from miscommunication is crucial. It is possible that the user may make a mistake or describe an observation incorrectly. A component that was reported as being present may really be missing. Eventually, old observations may require rechecking.

Thus, absolute belief in reported information cannot be assumed if debugging is to be successful in some situations.

6.2.2   Decision Making Strategies

The previous section presented the basic debugging paradigm which is the basis for the implemented system. Two critical problems with this paradigm are:

- Developing a method for selecting the next component to be examined such that all components will be selected or reselected after a finite amount of time if no progress is being made.

- Developing a method for deciding when a repair has fixed the circuit such that the defining behavior will be checked after a finite amount of time after any repair.

This section presents the details of the solution strategy for these two problems.

Analysis

The most crucial decision involves selection of the next component to be examined. Initially, the system is examined. If it is determined that the system is not functioning properly, one of its constituent components is selected to be examined for the source of error. In most cases the observation of system error points to one or two components as being the most likely source of error. However, this does not mean that they will be the actual source of error. At some point when examining the components of greatest suspicion is not helping to correct the circuit behavior, other components must be examined.

Another decision concerns the component to examine next after a repair is made. If it is believed the circuit may have been fixed, the overall system should be examined next. If it is believed the circuit has many errors and only one has been repaired, another component should be examined.

These decisions about when to skip over a more suspicious component and when a repair may have fixed the circuit are somewhat arbitrary in nature in that just about any criteria can be used for making the decision. It is necessary to decide to skip a component of higher suspicion after some finite amount of time in order to correctly repair the circuit when the actual source of error is a component or components of lesser suspicion. The decision about when a repair may have fixed the circuit can be made using any desired criterion. It may be decided that any repair may have fixed the circuit, or that no repair has fixed the circuit, or anything in between. All that must be done is that at some finite time following the repair that fixes the circuit, the system must be examined for correct functioning. Since it is not known in advance which repair fixes the circuit, this is equivalent to saying that at some finite time following any repair, the system must be examined if nothing else is found to be wrong with other components.

Selecting the Next Component

The selection process requires the following information about components and their corresponding specs.

1. A status value for a component (and its associated numerical rating). Possible component status values are: checked (3.0), unchecked (2.0), partially checked (1.0), or suspicious (0.0).

2. A status value for each spec. Possible spec status values are: checked, unchecked, uncheckable, or suspicious(N), where N is a positive integer. The greater the value of N, the higher the suspicion about the spec. Specs can be uncheckable if the user is unable to perform one of the prerequisite actions required to set the conditions or cannot carry out the required observation. For instance, if a spec requires measuring a voltage and there is no voltmeter available (or if it is broken, or if the user can't or won't use it), then the corresponding spec is uncheckable.

3. A function that computes the status of a component as a function of the status of its specs.

4. An iteration counter for each spec that represents the number of iterations that this particular spec has been selected to be examined. At the end of each iteration of the debugging loop, the iteration counter for the spec selected will normally be incremented. There are a few cases where the counter will not be incremented, but these cases can only occur a finite number of times.

5. A node value for each component, which is the sum of the numerical rating associated with its status and the average of the iteration counters for its specs. A smaller node value implies that either (a) the component is more suspicious than other components, or (b) the component has been selected fewer times for examination.

The rule for selecting components follows.

> *Choose the component with lowest node value; in case of a tie, choose the component that has a spec of greatest suspicion; if there is still a tie, choose the component arbitrarily among the components of lowest node value and most suspicious spec.*

The rule for selecting a spec after selecting the component follows.

> *Choose the spec of greatest suspicion; in case of a tie, choose the spec that has the lowest iteration counter; if there is still a tie, choose the spec arbitrarily among the specs of greatest suspicion and minimum iteration counter; if there are no suspicious specs, then look for unchecked specs, uncheckable specs, and checked specs, respectively, using the same tie breaking rule on iteration counter if more than one unchecked, uncheckable, or checked spec is found.*

Analysis of the Selection Mechanism

This selection mechanism ensures that all components will be examined in a finite amount of time if the defining behavior is never observed. The key factor is the use of the iteration counters in computing node value. Eventually, the iteration counters will dominate the numerical rating for component status. This domination occurs because the numerical rating cannot grow arbitrarily big; it can range only between the rating associated with suspicious (0.0) to the rating associated with checked (3.0). There is no upper bound on the iteration counters. Thus, if after several iterations of choosing a suspicious component no success is obtained in repairing the circuit, the iteration counters will grow sufficiently large, thus causing the node value of the suspicious component to exceed the node value of an unchecked component, and then the unchecked component will be examined. This domination by the iteration counters can even cause the debugger to choose checked components at a later step if examining other components is unsuccessful in getting the system repaired. This corresponds to the potential situation where the user erroneously reported some information that caused the debugger to conclude that a faulty component was actually working.

Another effect of this selection mechanism is what will be called the *dovetailing effect*. This can occur when there is a set of components with minimal node value that have the same status. After one iteration, one of these components is selected and processed, and its iteration average increases by a small amount. This puts its node value slightly greater than these other components; thus, another component is selected the next iteration. The second component will then have its iteration average increased by a small amount, and then another component is selected the next iteration. This process will keep repeating, resulting in a different component being selected each iteration. The set of components will be selected cyclically if they each have the same number of specs because each iteration will increase a component's iteration average by the same amount. If they do not have the same number of specs, the order of selection will vary. As an example, consider three unchecked components (associated rating of 2.0) which have 3, 4, and 5 specs, respectively. Thus, after each iteration selecting the given component will increase the iteration average for the component by $1/3$, $1/4$, and $1/5$, respectively. Figure 6.3 demonstrates how the selection process would proceed. It shows how the debugging process can alternate between components under certain conditions.

One should not conclude that dovetailing is necessarily bad. If in the current situation there appear to be many errors in the system, or it is not clear where the errors occur, then alternately examining different components for possible errors is not a bad strategy for more quickly finding which component or components are faulty (i.e. breadth-first search). However, in cases where progress is being made, that is, cases where the spec examined is checked as satisfactory, it is unfortunate if the debugger chooses to go look at another component when progress is being made on the most recently selected component. In a certain sense there is momentum for continuing to work on the component on which progress is being made. The component will not be selected on the next iteration due to the increase in iteration average. Consequently, if incrementation of the iteration counters is temporarily suspended, the same component will be selected at subsequent iterations as well. However, it is due to the increasing of the iteration average that guarantees the debugging process will eventually examine all components—under all situations if necessary. Consequently, the suspension of incrementation must be for a finite amount of time, and it should only be done in situations where it is clear that progress is being made. These considerations are captured in the following rule that describes the situation under which the iteration counter for a spec is not incremented at the end of an iteration in which it was examined.

```
             IF
Condition 1:       the spec (S) is checked,
Condition 2:   AND the component (Node) corresponding to S is
                   NOT checked
Condition 3:   AND there exists another spec of Node that is
                   unchecked or suspicious,
Condition 4:   AND this has not occurred a consecutive number
                   of times > than the number of specs of Node,
             THEN do not increment the counter for S.
```

Condition 1 is the basic requirement that the spec that was examined has been checked as satisfactory. Condition 2 ensures that the momentum rule is not unnecessarily used—if the component is checked as satisfactory, then there is no overriding need to continue examining it. Condition 3 ensures that the momentum rule is not used in a situation where it is not warranted—namely, the only other specs have an uncheckable status, which means it is probably unnecessary to continue looking at this component. Condition 4 ensures that the momentum rule will only be used at most an average of once on each spec of the component. This ensures that suspension of incrementing the iteration counters will only occur for a finite amount of time.

Handling Repairs

Recall that the main issue concerning the repair of components is deciding whether or not the change has caused the system to be repaired. If it has, then the system component should be examined next. If it has not, the debugger should just continue, choosing the component of lowest node value to be examined next. The following strategy for this decision has been adopted.

```
    If this were the first change, reinitialize the status of
everything to its initial conditions (all specs except the
system specs are marked unchecked, the system specs are
marked suspicious(1)).
```

Initially,

	# of Specs	Rating	Iteration Average	Node Value
Component 1	3	2	1	3.0
Component 2	4	2	1	3.0
Component 3	5	2	1	3.0

Suppose on iteration 1 component 1 is arbitrarily chosen.
Status after update:

	# of Specs	Rating	Iteration Average	Node Value
Component 1	3	2	1.333	3.333
Component 2	4	2	1	3.0
Component 3	5	2	1	3.0

Then on iteration 2 component 2 is arbitrarily chosen over
component 3. Status after update:

	# of Specs	Rating	Iteration Average	Node Value
Component 1	3	2	1.333	3.333
Component 2	4	2	1.25	3.25
Component 3	5	2	1	3.0

Now component 3 would be chosen (minimum node value).
Status after update:

	# of Specs	Rating	Iteration Average	Node Value
Component 1	3	2	1.333	3.333
Component 2	4	2	1.25	3.25
Component 3	5	2	1.20	3.20

Subsequent iterations will select the component of minimal node
value, which is equivalent to selecting the component of minimal
iteration average.

Choose Component 3. Status after update:

	# of Specs	Rating	Iteration Average	Node Value
Component 1	3	2	1.333	3.333
Component 2	4	2	1.25	3.25
Component 3	5	2	1.40	3.40

Choose Component 2. Status after update:

	# of Specs	Rating	Iteration Average	Node Value
Component 1	3	2	1.333	3.333
Component 2	4	2	1.50	3.50
Component 3	5	2	1.40	3.40

Choose Component 1. Status after update:

	# of Specs	Rating	Iteration Average	Node Value
Component 1	3	2	1.667	3.667
Component 2	4	2	1.50	3.50
Component 3	5	2	1.40	3.40

Choose Component 3. Status after update:

	# of Specs	Rating	Iteration Average	Node Value
Component 1	3	2	1.667	3.667
Component 2	4	2	1.50	3.50
Component 3	5	2	1.60	3.60

Figure 6.3

Demonstration of Component Selection Dovetailing

If this were the second change, reinitialize the status of
the component changed as well as all components that are
descendants or ancestors of it in the component hierarchy;
leave the rest unchanged.

If this were the third or any subsequent change, only
reinitialize the status of the component changed; leave
the rest unchanged.

It should be noted that reinitialization implies resetting the iteration counters to zero during the first or second change. The only spec whose iteration
counter is not zeroed is the spec that was being processed when the reinitialization occurred. Its counter will be zeroed, but then will be incremented after
completion of the debugging loop. This will bias the debugger against immediately selecting the same spec again after reinitialization. Zeroing the iteration
counters also causes the node values to be reset to their original values. In
subsequent changes, when the debugger believes there are many errors, the
counters of the reinitialized specs are not zeroed.

In addition, reinitialization causes the removal of knowledge from the debugger about observations previously made. All external observations are
recorded by the debugger, but some of them become invalid when a component is added or replaced. All voltage measurements except for the battery
and all observations about the status of an object (i.e. its physical appearance)
are removed unless an object's status is considered to be independent of the
board configuration. For the circuit being used, only the switch position and
the knob position are considered independent. Thus, when a component is
added or replaced, all knowledge about observations of the LED display are
removed. This knowledge about observations is used to skip over specs whose
observation has already been made, although at some point it may be desirable to be able to go back and recheck an old observation when no progress is
being made.

Intuitively, the strategy reflects the idea that there is probably either only
one error, or there are a lot of errors. After the first correction, reinitialization
of everything means first examining the defining behavior of the system. After
the second correction, the defining behavior may or may not be examined first.
After the third correction, there is a continuation of looking for more problems
until the system component is examined in the natural course of events. Of
course, when dialog is interfaced with the debugger the potential of having
user input cause a change of strategy becomes possible.

6.2.3   Debugging Control Strategy Modifications for Dialog

The debugger control loop presented in section 6.2.1 is very effective when
allowed to run unimpeded. In an ideal situation, where the slave that is
required to carry out necessary actions does so faithfully, debugging is a simple
task. However, the realities of human nature and dialog preclude the possibility

of the ideal situation. Consequently, the debugger cannot run unimpeded in this rigid loop, requiring modifications and additions to this simple loop. These changes are the topic of this section.

Consequences of Human Nature and Dialog

One of the major consequences is that the human user may not respond with what the computer debugging system wants to hear. Cooperativeness by the user is assumed, but in trying to be helpful the user may respond with what the user believes to be helpful instead of what the debugger considers most helpful. For example, if the debugger decides it wants the switch set to a particular position, the most helpful response to the debugger would be a statement that the switch has been set to the desired position. Instead, the user might respond with a statement about a changed circuit behavior without any verbal indication that the switch has been set (e.g. "The LED is now flashing."). In order to be able to use this volunteered information, the debugger must be able to suspend or terminate processing of a chosen spec. This requires the ability for the debugger to be more flexible than allowed by the control loop.

Another consequence is the flexibility that interactive dialog permits. This flexibility can help with decisions such as deciding when a repair may have caused the circuit to begin functioning properly. Once an observation of errant behavior is made, such as, "The LED is off", the computer could say, "Let me know when the LED comes on", and then proceed under the assumption that a given repair does not cause the LED to come on unless the user voluntarily provides the information. Eventually, the debugger may conclude that the LED should be on, although the user has not mentioned this. Consequently, the computer may again prompt with, "Is the LED still not on?". The freedom of dialog also gives the user the opportunity to provide additional information that can cause the debugger to reevaluate the suspicion levels of various components, allowing quicker determination of the error source than by mechanically forcing the user at each step through the paradigm of examining a spec chosen solely on the basis of the requested observation. However, to be able to accept additional information from the user requires the debugger to be capable of more flexible control than permitted by the control loop.

Other major consequences due to the general nature of dialog, language, and task performance include the following.

- User responses can be concerned with the conversation about the task instead of the task itself.

- There are details of the task that are not relevant to the debugger. For example, the debugger is only concerned with the value from a voltage measurement, not how it is performed.

- There are many ways of expressing a given statement/request. Choosing the most appropriate one is not a concern of the debugger. For example, the debugger may want the switch to be in the up position. Depending on the state of the dialog, any of the following could be appropriate.

```
Turn the switch up.
Is the switch up?
The switch needs to be up.
        .
        .
        .
```

The conclusion is that the debugger should not communicate directly with the user. It must communicate with some computational process that will handle the details of interaction with the user in order to provide the debugger with the required information.[3] Furthermore, the debugger should be capable of more general assistance than stepping through the proposed rigid control loop. Different users have different knowledge and abilities. Some users may require the computer to dictate every action to be taken while other users may know virtually every step required for debugging and only require the computer to fill in a few missing details. It is required that the debugging system be capable of providing helpful assistance to this wide spectrum of users.

To provide this varying assistance while communicating indirectly with users requires the development of a new control loop for communicating with the intermediate computational process. In addition, while the debugger must still be able to independently develop a strategy for debugging, it must also be able to provide direct assistance based on external ideas for completing the debugging task. These topics are covered in the following.

New Control Loop

Based on the considerations just described, the steps of the new control loop follow.

1. Receive message from an external process (normally the dialog controller).

2. Perform processing based on this message.

3. Send response back to the external process.

Each message is either a request for information from the debugger, or provides input for the debugger to process. Each message from the external process will be of the form [**Code,Input**], where **Code** is the operation code describing what the debugger should do, and **Input** is the semantic representation of any input to be processed or used; most often it will be a semantic

---

[3]In our system architecture this process is of course, the dialog controller.

representation of user input but could be the semantic representation of the current debugger goal. Now, the debugging process is controlled by an external process with which the debugger exchanges messages. A general description of how the debugger functions in this new environment is provided below.

Modified Debugger Processing

First, some terminology must be established. The original debugger control loop will now be known as the *computer-directed debugging strategy*. This change is necessitated by the development of the new control loop for interacting with the outside world. Nevertheless, this strategy can still be used by the debugger when the user must be directed step by step through the debugging process. However, other procedures are required in order to deal with the wider range of interactions possible with dialog. Consequently, the debugger has to be modified to add these new procedures and to integrate them smoothly with the already established strategy in order to change between methods of assistance as the requests from the external world dictate. Under the new control loop there are three basic types of actions performed by the debugger.

1. Select relevant fact or recommended next action.

2. Compute expectations for external response to selected fact or action.

3. Update knowledge based on input provided by external process.

Action type 1 is the action by which the debugger provides assistance for the user. The fact or action may be selected according to a variety of criteria depending on the state of the dialog. However, it is up to the external process to decide which criterion is most relevant in determining the processing to be performed by the debugger. These possible criteria follow.

- Select according to the computer-directed debugging strategy. This is for when the computer is guiding the user step by step through the debugging process.

- Select according to an item of volunteered information. In this situation the computer-directed debugging strategy is still being used, but the user may occasionally provide inputs that may be helpful to the debugging process although they may not come in the desired order for the computer-directed strategy. The computer may have to suspend its strategy in order to first obtain all the items necessary about the volunteered information that were not initially supplied. Once this is done, the information may be integrated into the computer-directed strategy, altering the course of the debugging process.

- Select according to an inferred external strategy. This leads to a user-directed debugging strategy, which was added to complement the computer-directed strategy. This strategy is simply to infer from the input the external strategy for debugging and then provide facts that are relevant to that strategy. For example, if the user observes the LED is off when it should be displaying something, then the inference would be that there is interest in repairing the power circuit. Consequently, the debugger would consult its information about the power circuit and select some fact not already considered and provide that to be communicated. An example of such a fact would be, "the power is on when the switch is up." If the user had already reported that the switch was up, then supply another fact such as, "the switch is connected to the battery by a wire between connectors 111 and 120." Other types of possible facts include stating that a particular action, such as measuring a voltage, observing the LED, or adding or removing a wire, might be desirable or necessary. This strategy depends on making a plausible inference about the external strategy and being able to access knowledge about the circuit appropriately. Currently, the method for strategy inference is based on the result of the key observation that determines if the circuit is functioning properly.[4]

- Select according to direct question from the user. Whether the debugging process is computer-directed or user-directed, questions may arise which need to be answered.

Action type 2, computing expectations, arises because of the need to determine when an input is directly relevant to a computer-directed strategy or is simply a helpful response that was volunteered. It may also provide assistance in helping the computer to understand user utterances in a dialog system. The expectations are based on the fact or action provided in **Input**. Normally, it will be the most recently selected fact or action of the debugger, but the external process could specify a different fact or action. This permits the external process to choose a different fact or action if the one provided by the debugger is not deemed sufficiently relevant to the dialog. The two main categories of expectation are: (1) *direct*—responses that are directly relevant to the fact or action; and (2) *helpful*—responses that fit the category of helpful responses; an example of such a response would be, "there is a wire from connector 84 to 30," in response to, "Is there a wire from connector 84 to 99?"

Action type 3, updating knowledge based on input, is necessary for the computer to continue providing assistance throughout the task. The update operations are a function of the level at which the input was expected, *direct* or *helpful*, as well as the active debugging strategy, computer-directed or user-directed.

---

[4]For our implemented system, this would be the LED display.

Maintaining Debugger Status

As a result of the new control scheme, the debugger must have a means for maintaining information about the status of the debugging task while waiting for the next message from the external process. Status information includes: (1) an indication of whether the debugging process is computer or user-directed; (2) information about its status within the computer-directed debugging strategy if the debugging process is computer-directed; or information about the external strategy if the debugging process is user-directed.

Multiple Domain Goals

In most situations, the debugger suggests a goal, receives input, and chooses a new goal. However, in some cases the external input indicates that the original goal should remain active while another supplementary goal should be recommended. Currently, this can occur in the following situations.

1. The user asks a specific question. For example:

>   C: Add a wire between connector 34 and 69.
>   U: Should I turn the switch down?

   The goal of adding a wire should remain active, but a supplementary goal that the user learn it is not necessary to turn down the switch, should also be added.

2. The user makes a statement about a second wire when learning the existence of another wire is the active goal while within user-directed debugging. For example:

>   U: The LED is flashing seven.
>   C: There is supposed to be a wire between 84 and 99.
>   U: There is a wire from 84 to 30.

   The goal of learning there should be a wire between 84 and 99 should remain active, but a supplementary goal, that the user learn there should also be a wire between 84 and 30, should also be added.

In these cases, the debugger status structure is modified by adding a description of the extra goal. This causes both goals to remain active and expected. When the user response occurs, the action to which the response is relevant will be returned to the domain processor, and the debugger status updated appropriately.

Questioning Old Observations

When the computer-directed strategy is active, the default rule when checking
a spec is, "if a value for the observation has already been made, do not question
the observation, but proceed directly to performing the actions." This prevents
redundant dialog such as the following.

```
U: The LED is flashing seven.
C: What is the knob at when the LED is displaying
   a flashing seven?
U: 10.
C: What is the LED displaying?
```

However, observations may eventually need to be requestioned if progress
is not being made. The actions defined by a spec are a function of the observation made. These actions normally include the marking of other components
and specs as suspicious because the given observation indicates that these
components are the likely source of the circuit error. However, if the user mis-
informed the debugger about the observation or the debugger misunderstood,
then the debugger could undertake an unsuccessful search because the source
of error is elsewhere. Consequently, the following rule was defined for labeling
a previous observation as suspicious.

```
IF   the spec associated with an observation (Obs) is still
     suspicious
AND  all specs that were marked suspicious as result of Obs
     are now checked,
THEN mark Obs as suspicious
```

Consequently, the next time the spec associated with Obs is chosen, the
observation will be questioned.

Goal Status Information

In addition to providing the external process with a suggestion of the goal,
the debugger also provides the external process with the status of the goal.
Possible values follow.

> extra_goal—indicates the previous suggestion should remain active
> as well as the current suggestion.

> verifying—indicates a previous observation is to be verified. This
> is returned when an old observation is being requestioned.

> new_goal—the normal case. It indicates a completely new goal is
> being suggested.

This information may be used in computing the final utterance specification
for a computer utterance (see section 4.4.2).

Changing Strategies

The debugger is capable of operating in either a computer-directed or user-directed debugging strategy. In variable initiative dialog, it is possible there could be a need to switch between strategies during a debugging task, perhaps several times. How can the debugger maintain coherence between the strategies? Switching from computer-directed to user-directed is easy since all the information collected is available for use in the strategy inference process. Changing from user-directed to computer-directed is not as easy due to the reliance of the computer-directed strategy on the setting of specs and components to various levels of suspicion. The setting of suspicion values are defined in the actions associated with observations where these observations are defined as a part of specs, the basic unit of knowledge utilized in the computer-directed strategy (section 6.2.1). Although the user-directed strategy relies on the circuit knowledge defined in specs, there is no use of the actions for setting suspicion levels. Consequently, a series of rules have been defined in the circuit description that approximate the suspicion setting operations of the regular specs based on the relevant fact selected during the user-directed strategy. Thus, when a switch to the computer-directed strategy is made, the suspicion levels of the various components and specs will reflect the information acquired while the user-directed strategy was active. The technical details about these rules are provided in Smith [Smi91].

Summary of Modifications

The modifications made to the debugger control strategy in order to adapt to the nuances of dialog can be summarized as follows.

1. The control loop has been replaced by a simple loop that consists of message exchanges with an external process that controls the operation of the debugger. The old control loop has become a subsidiary, computer-directed debugging strategy that may be invoked by the external process if the user is to be guided step-by-step through the debugging task. In addition, a user-directed strategy has been implemented whereby the debugger performs a strategy inferring process to respond with helpful information according to the perceived external debugging strategy.

2. The subsidiary role of the debugger has been implemented by defining a set of actions the debugger can perform along with a set of operation codes for use by the external process in invoking the debugger. In addition, an internal structure has been implemented in order for the debugger to maintain status information about the debugging task while it awaits further instruction from the external process. This state information is a function of whether the computer-directed or user-directed strategy is currently being used.

6.3 Generation

6.3.1 Overview

The linguistic generator was developed by Robin Gambill. It uses rule-driven techniques similar to those described in Allen [All87]. Generator input is an utterance specification represented in snf (section 4.4.3) while the output is an English string that is sent to a DECtalk DTC01 text-to-speech converter for enunciation. Before actual transmission to the DecTalk the string is passed through a procedure that modifies words to assist in proper pronunciation. For example, "LED" is mapped into "eleedee" and "omega" is mapped into "ohmayga." This procedure was augmented to cause the rate of speech to be decreased when a request for "repeat" has been given. This was done based on the assumption that a subject needed an utterance repeated because the information was provided too rapidly.

Due to resource constraints in developing snf representations, some utterance specifications provided to the generator are precoded English strings that are simply output verbatim (i.e. "canned text", McKeown [McK85]). The two main sources of such strings are GALOP (see below) and some domain specific information about certain physical and existence properties.

6.3.2 Natural Language Directions for Locating Objects

Given the application domain of circuit repair, it was necessary to develop a method for providing directions to assist users in locating objects on the circuit board. The underlying theory for a computational method for producing such directions is presented in Smith [Smi87] and in summary form in [Smi88]. The Generalized Assistant in Locating Objects Program (GALOP), a programming implementation of a portion of this theory, has been installed as a subroutine in the dialog architecture. Whenever the current goal is of the form

$$goal(user, learn(int\_know\_action(how\_to\_do(perf(ident(Obj))))))$$

(i.e. the user has the goal to learn how to locate Obj), where Obj is some object on the circuit board, GALOP is invoked to produce the utterance specification[5] for the response which will then be spoken by the computer. In its original development, GALOP maintained its own discourse structure for representing information about the objects on the circuit board with the intention that when it was integrated with an actual dialog system, its discourse structure would be integrated with that of the overall dialog system. However, that has not currently been implemented. What such an integration would allow is the use by GALOP of objects otherwise mentioned in the dialog as possible landmarks for locating the target object. The purpose of this is that these mentioned objects obtain a higher salience due to their usage in dialog. Cur-

---

[5]In addition to the utterance specification, GALOP also produces the actual English response. Because GALOP's utterance specifications are not represented in snf, the general purpose generator of Gambill cannot translate them to English at this time.

rently, GALOP only knows about objects used in previous utterances where directions were provided.

6.4 Resource Utilization

Including comment lines, the dialog processing system consists of over 17000 lines of Prolog and 43 lines of C code. The parser consists of over 7600 lines of C code, while the grammar consists of 560 rules, and the parser dictionary contains 450 entries. The system can occupy over 25M bytes of memory, with the parser consuming about 22M bytes of this. The initially loaded dialog processor uses 1.8M bytes of memory, which expands to nearly 4M bytes of memory at the conclusion of a dialog due to all the extra user model and discourse information acquired during a dialog.

In terms of speed, the system had an average response time of 8.1 seconds during the formal experiment, the results from which are discussed in the next chapter. Parsing took an average of 3.9 seconds while the dialog processing took an average of 4.2 seconds. Later, a faster parsing algorithm was implemented and the system was ported to a SPARC II workstation from the Sun 4 used during the experiment. For an experimental subject using the enhanced system, average response time was 2.2 seconds.

Chapter 7

Experimental Results

One of the main goals of this research was to develop a computational model that could be implemented and tested. Testing could serve at least two purposes: (1) Demonstrate the viability of the Missing Axiom Theory for dialog processing; and (2) Determine the ways that varying levels of dialog control influence the interaction between user and computer. Consequently, an experiment involving use of the system was constructed to test the effects of different levels of dialog control. The format and results of this experiment are reported in this chapter.

7.1 Hypotheses

The following hypotheses are proposed as performance differences by users as they gain experience and have the initiative.

- Task completion time will decrease.

- The number of utterances per dialog will decrease.

- The percentage of "non-trivial" utterances will increase (a non-trivial utterance is any utterance longer than one word).

- The average length of a non-trivial utterance will increase.

- The rate of speech (number of utterances per minute) will decrease.

These hypotheses are consistent with the intuition that as the user has more initiative, the user will put more thought into the process, reducing the rate of interaction. In addition, it is expected that when the user has more initiative, there would be an attempt to convey more detailed information in each non-trivial utterance. Finally, it is also believed that increased user initiative will be more helpful when the user gains experience and has more knowledge about performing the task independent of computer guidance.

7.2 Preliminary Results

Two graduate students in computer science volunteered to use the system. Each subject received about 75 minutes of training on the speech recognizer with the 125 word vocabulary (see table 7.1). The subjects then participated in three sessions on differing days. Each session consisted of four different problems where each problem consisted of a single missing wire. The results from these subjects tended to support our hypotheses.

However, the experimental control for this testing was not well-defined. The two subjects are involved in AI and NL research and consequently have strong preconceptions about NL systems and what constitutes "proper" behavior toward such systems. In particular, it was very difficult to provide them

Vocabulary List

a	done	know	over	the
add	down	LED	part	then
alternately	each	left	point	there
an	eight	light	position	this
and	every	longer	power	three
another	faster	lower	problem	through
any	five	make	put	time
are	fix	move	red	to
at	flashing	need	repeat	top
back	for	nine	right	turn
be	forth	not	rs111	understand
between	frequency	nothing	same	up
both	from	now	say	use
bottom	going	number	second	verbie
brighter	half	of	see	want
can	hand	off	seven	what
cancel	have	OK	should	when
circuit	help	on	side	where
color	here	once	six	which
connecting	how	one	slower	will
connector	I	ones	stays	wire
control	in	only	still	with
corner	is	or	switch	working
displaying	it	other	than	yes
do	knob	out	that	zero

Table 7.1
Subject Vocabulary

with appropriate instruction to indicate that they had control of the dialog without explicit direction about what could be said. As a result, there was not a consistent set of instructions given to the two subjects.

Another complicating factor was the issue of misrecognitions by the Verbex speech recognizer, which caused incorrect interpretations of the user's input. In certain situations, this would only cause a small increase in the number of utterances while in other situations the time required to finish the task would increase greatly. This is especially true when the computer has the initiative and is less willing to adjust its goals in response to user input that deviates from the computer's already chosen goals. There was not an established policy for what to do in the case of misrecognitions. In general, a major unresolved issue was the interaction between experimenter and subject. It was clear that some interaction was needed due to the system complexity and the potential for confusions such as the following.

1. Misrecognitions.

2. Providing responses before the system had a chance to respond to the user's previous utterance. Normal response time was five to ten seconds. However, sentences of longer than eight to ten words could take more than thirty seconds to process.

3. All utterances were supposed to start with the word "verbie" and end with the word "over" to facilitate the recognition process (e.g. "verbie, the switch is up, over"). Subjects would sometimes forget to start the utterance with "verbie" or end the utterance with "over."

4. The subject would say something that was not recognized and not realize it. Successful recognition was always indicated by a beeping sound from the Verbex, but a subject might not realize the beep was never issued. Consequently, the subject would be waiting for a response to an input never transmitted.

5. The subject might use a word not in the vocabulary.

6. The subject might say multiple sentences.

7. The subject might start speaking with a different tone, volume, or rhythm than used during training of the speech recognizer, causing poor recognition of words. Stress was a particularly important factor. A subject who let stress affect speaking had worse recognition, leading to more confusion and more stress.

8. The subject might try to ask the experimenter questions instead of working with the system.

9. The subject might go into a loop in trying to fix the system by refusing to follow the computer's guidance.

However, the intent of any proposed experiment was to study the interaction between subject and computer. Interaction between subject and experimenter needed to be minimized, and certainly lessened from that which occurred with the preliminary subjects. Based upon these concerns as well as the preliminary results, a specific experimental design was devised. Before the actual experiment was conducted two pilot subjects were run using the proposed experimental design. From the knowledge gained from running the pilot subjects certain modifications to the experimental design were made which led to the actual design reported in the following section. The insights gained from the pilot subjects include the following.

- The proposed experimental design included the display of charts that could be used by subjects to assist in the structuring of utterances. The usefulness of these charts was demonstrated. Consequently, further effort was spent on more effective charts.

- The proposed experimental design included a set of guidelines for allowed verbal interaction between experimenter and subject during testing. This guide needed reorganization. It was difficult to access the appropriate interaction in a timely fashion.

- There was a need for more explicit instruction at the beginning of a session about the mode of interaction between subject and computer to be used during the session. This resulted in the development of the session specific instructions that were used.

- There was a need to ensure better speech recognition performance. The pilot subjects' level of success in interacting with the system was greatly dependent on achieving a sufficiently high speech recognition rate. When the input words coming from the Verbex closely paralleled what was actually said, the system functioned well. Consequently, it was suggested by the second author (Hipp) that in training the subjects on the speech recognizer that we should emphasize that they use *connected* rather than *continuous* speech. Continuous speech is normal conversational speech where words tend to run together. In connected speech it is not necessary to emphasize a pause between words, but it is necessary to emphasize the enunciation of each word distinctly, as if it were being said in isolation. With this form of speech, there is less confusion for the speech recognizer in determining the boundaries between words, and each word tends to sound the same in all usages. By using connected speech, it was hoped that all the subjects would achieve a sufficiently good recognition rate to be able to interact effectively with the system. As the results will show, this was achieved a high proportion of the time.

7.3 Experimental Design

7.3.1 Overview

Subjects participated in the experiment in three sessions. The first and third sessions occurred a week apart, and the second session normally occurred three or four days after the first session.[1] The first session consisted of: (1) the primary speech training lasting approximately 60 to 75 minutes; (2) approximately 20 minutes of instruction on using the system; and (3) practice using

---

[1]The only exception was the last subject, where the second session occurred two days after the first session, and the third session occurred one week after the second session.

the system by attempting to solve four "warmup" problems with the system operating in directive mode, the mode where the computer has maximal control. A maximum of two and one half hours was spent on the first session. The second and third sessions each consisted of: (1) review work with the speech recognizer; (2) a review of the instructions; and (3) usage of the system on up to ten problems depending on how rapidly the problems were solved. One group of subjects would work with the system in directive mode during the second session and in declarative mode during the third session while the other group would work with the same modes, but in opposite sessions. The time allowed for the second and third sessions was two hours each. After a discussion of the problem selection and ordering, a detailed description of the procedure used in each session will be provided.

7.3.2 Problem Selection

The subjects worked with a Radio Shack 160 in One Electronic Project Kit (catalog number 28-258). The particular circuit being used causes the LED to alternately display a one and seven, and the implemented domain processor could detect errors caused by missing wires as well as a dead battery. The basic debugging process consists of the following steps.

1. Determine if the LED display is correct.

2. If it is not correct, perform zero or more diagnostic steps to further isolate the problem. Possible diagnostic steps are voltage measurements or an LED observation under a different physical configuration of the circuit board.

3. Check for the absence of one or more wires until a missing wire is located.

The wires are attached to metal spring-like connectors which are identified by numbers on the circuit board. Thus, a wire is identified by the numbers of the two connectors to which it is connected. There are a total of twenty wires on the circuit board, but due to complications involving the natural language descriptions of certain LED displays, only fourteen of the wires were viable candidates for usage in the experiment. In order to balance the difficulty of the problems between the second and third sessions, the wires were classified according to the difficulty with which the error could be detected. Based on this classification, the assignment of missing wires to each session was made. The basic details of this assignment were the following.

- Four of the fourteen wires were used in the four warmup problems of the first session.

- For the ten remaining wires, five were used for the first five problems of session 2 and the other five were used for the first five problems of session 3.

- Problems six through eight of sessions 2 and 3 consisted of two missing wires for each problem. The two missing wires were selected from the five missing wires used during the first five problems of the session. Each of problems six through eight differed by one missing wire.

- Problems nine and ten of each session consisted of a missing wire that was also used during the warmup problems of session 1. Each of these four wires was assigned to a different problem. Consequently, sessions 2 and 3 are balanced for difficulty only through the first eight problems. Where appropriate, the cumulative results reported later in this chapter will separately list the results for the first eight problems and for all ten problems of a session.

7.3.3   Session 1 Procedure

The first 60 to 75 minutes consisted of training with the speech recognizer. Speech recognition training consisted of a brief orientation about the speech recognition process followed by training the system. System training involved speaking each word in the 125 word vocabulary at least two times followed by the speaking of 239 sentences one or more times according to the success of the recognizer with the sentences. These sentences were devised in order to balance the number of times each word was said and were not based on any particular set of sentences that were "grammatical" inputs to the dialog system.

After the initial speech recognition training, each subject would again practice on the speech recognizer for 30 sentences, and then be given the following general instructions which were pre-recorded on audio cassette tape.

1. The purpose of this experiment is to study the nature of task-oriented dialog between humans and computers.

2. Your task is to fix the electronic circuit which is in front of you. The identification number for this circuit is RS111. All the equipment necessary for completing the task is present. You are encouraged to use all the knowledge that you have and acquire in order to fix the circuit as quickly as possible and conclude the dialog.

3. The computer system has all the knowledge necessary to fix the circuit. This includes knowledge about the circuit as well as knowledge about any required tasks or knowledge on how to use any necessary equipment. You can receive assistance from the computer by engaging in dialog with it. Feel free to request the same type of assistance from the computer that you would from a friend who was assisting you. The computer is supposed to be your assistant, not vice-versa.

4. Communication with the computer is accomplished through a speech recognizer. This speech recognizer uses the voice patterns you have recorded

during training. As you know from your training, due to imperfections in this technology, it is very likely that some of your words will be "misunderstood" by the computer. The computer system is designed to overcome some confusion, but it is possible that it will misinterpret what you say. Please observe the following rules when speaking.

- All utterances you wish to send to the computer should start with the word "verbie" and end with the word "over"; if you start an utterance which you wish to change, say "cancel" and then after a momentary pause, begin again with "verbie" and say your desired utterance.

- When the speech recognizer "understands" what you have said, it will emit a beep, and then transmit your utterance for further processing. If you hear no beep after a brief interval (1-2 seconds), please try repeating your utterance. Be sure the first word is "verbie" and the last word is "over."

- To enhance the quality of the speech recognition process, use only the words in the vocabulary, speak in the natural tone of voice that you used when you trained the speech recognizer, and try to use utterances of 3 to 6 words in length, not counting "verbie" and "over."

- When uttering numbers, you must utter each digit individually as well as the decimal point when needed. For example, the number "127" would be uttered as "one two seven", and the number 34.8 would be uttered as "three four point eight."

- Restrict your utterances to one sentence/thought at a time. The following are examples of utterances which violate this restriction.

  Verbie, the switch is up. The LED is flashing, Over.
  Verbie, there is no wire. What should I do now? Over.
  Verbie, I need help. Where is connector one zero two?
  Over.

5. The computer will signify its readiness by an initial greeting. The speech synthesizer will enunciate the computer's utterances. If you cannot understand what it is saying, please signify by saying "Verbie, repeat. Over".

6. Each time the computer says something it expects a response; and each time you say something the computer will respond.

7. The task is complete when the dialog is terminated. The dialog is not necessarily terminated when the circuit appears to be functioning properly. When the dialog is successful, the computer will say good-bye and you will hear a bell ring.

8. The experimenter will remain in the room to oversee the interaction. Please do not direct any comments to the experimenter while working on the circuit unless you are experiencing physical discomfort or wish to terminate the session. You are free to speak with the experimenter between tasks, but the experimenter may defer answering some of your questions until the end of your participation. The experimenter may occasionally provide you with instruction depending on the progress of the task. For purposes of experimental control, the experimenter is greatly restricted in the type of instruction allowed.

Following the tape, the subjects were asked the following questions to ensure that they understood the instructions.

— What is your task?

— How can you receive assistance?

— How must your utterances be restricted?

— How do you know when the computer is ready to begin?

— Under what conditions may you direct comments to the experimenter?

— When is the task complete?

The remainder of the orientation proceeded as follows.

1. Subjects were shown the voltmeter and shown the appropriate scale from which to make readings.

2. Subjects were then given practice listening to the DECtalk by hearing the DECtalk speak the following four sentences

   • The LED is supposed to be displaying alternately flashing one and seven.

   • What is the switch at when the LED is displaying only a not flashing one on the left hand side?

   • Now, in the middle right of this green region is the control knob.

   • What is the voltage between connector one two one and connector eight three?

The sentences were repeated until the subject could understand all the words. Understanding was determined by their repeating of the utterance. These sample sentences were chosen on the basis of the different types of sentences the system might say to the user during an interaction.

3. The subjects were shown a picture on a 3x5 index card of the primary LED display showing the alternately flashing one and seven. They were not shown the location of the LED on the circuit board. In addition, they were shown on a separate index card a sample LED display that would not occur during the experiment and given the instruction to try to always describe the LED in terms of what is displaying as opposed to what is not displaying. For the sample display the contrasting sentences were:

> ```
> The LED is displaying the one and the bottom
>     part of the seven (Good).
> ```

> ```
> The LED is not displaying the top part of
>     the seven (Bad).
> ```

Subjects were given this instruction for two reasons. (1) Due to the ad hoc nature of the construction of the grammar, the coverage for sentences involving "not" for the LED display was rather sketchy, and (2) Preliminary testing showed that "not" was prone to misrecognition. It was felt that this instruction assisted in system performance without overly restricting the type of utterances people could say.

In addition, subjects were told that if the system asked about specific features of the LED display, that these features would be very distinctive and not subtle. This instruction was provided in order to avoid confusion caused by the user misreporting information on the LED display due to a misunderstanding over the degree of "brightness," "flashing", and "duration of displaying" that was being considered. In the domain processor model, all these characteristics were very distinctive.

4. The subjects were then provided with a sheet of paper listing the vocabulary words and shown a poster board with three sheets of paper attached that provided assistance in putting utterances together. Subjects were instructed to first decide on what they wished to talk about and to only use the vocabulary and utterance aids if they had trouble forming a response.

5. Subjects were then read the specific instructions about their interaction with the system for the session. For the first session these instructions were the following.

> You will now practice using the system by working on four problems. It is hoped that you will succeed in all of these problems, but do not be discouraged if you do not. The purpose of these practice problems is to get you accustomed to interacting with the system in the experimental environment.

During this session the computer will act as a teacher rather than assistant. Please listen carefully to the computer and follow its instructions as well as you can. Please do not become frustrated if you feel the computer is not allowing you enough freedom in fixing the circuit. Please do your best to fix the circuit as quickly as possible but remember to follow instructions. Remember that the computer cannot see or hear what you do.

6. Finally, the subject was asked if he/she had any final questions.

After the orientation, the subject then used the system to work on the warmup problems. An effort was made to allow the subject to complete each problem, but a dialog could be halted before completion if excessive time was being spent on a problem in order to allow the user exposure to the other problems.

7.3.4   Session 2 Procedure

The first 15 to 20 minutes consisted of reorientation. The subject would first practice on the speech recognizer for 60 sentences. Afterward, the subjects were again asked the review questions to ensure they remembered the general instructions. The remainder of the reorientation was the same as session 1 except for the specific instructions about the interaction with the system for the session. These instructions were a function of the mode in which the system would operate.

Directive Mode

In this session you will use the system to fix eight to ten problems. You are expected to complete all these problems, but the experimenter will stop you if an excessive amount of time is spent on a given problem to assure you the chance to successfully complete other problems. During this session the computer will again act as a teacher. Please listen carefully to the computer and follow its instructions as well as you can. Please do not become frustrated if you feel the computer is not allowing you enough freedom in fixing the circuit. Please do your best to fix the circuit as quickly as possible but remember to follow instructions. Remember that the computer cannot see or hear what you do.

Declarative Mode—As noted in the discussion of the preliminary results, it was difficult to get subjects to take control of the dialog by just telling them they had control of the dialog. This also occurred with two pilot subjects for which different forms of instruction were tried before settling on the following.

In this session you will use the system to fix eight to ten
problems. You are expected to complete all these problems, but the experimenter will stop you if an excessive
amount of time is spent on a given problem to assure you
the chance to successfully complete other problems. Unlike the previous session, the computer will now function
as an assistant rather than as a teacher. Consequently,
you will now have control of the dialog rather than the
computer. This will allow you more freedom to complete
the task by executing and reporting on the procedures
undertaken as you see fit. In particular, do not feel compelled to respond directly to the computer's utterance
if another response seems more helpful. Please use any
additional knowledge you acquired during the practice
problems to assist you in fixing the circuit more quickly.
For example, by now you have probably acquired enough
experience to be able to determine when the circuit is
working. The computer's role is to serve you.

To further emphasize the difference in the potential for the interaction from directive mode, an audio cassette tape was played
which was designed to illustrate the possibilities. The tape had the
following recorded dialog.

```
C: Hi, this is Radio Shack.  What can I do for you?
U: My rs83 circuit is not working.
C: It is supposed to display a flashing American flag.
U: It is displaying the stars but not the stripes.
C: Is transistor 2 connected?
U: I think the X27 pin on transistor 1 may be bent.
C: That could be a problem.
U: Can I just straighten it?
C: Sure.
U: I fixed it. Thanks.
C: You're welcome.
```

After the tape was played, the subject was told that its purpose
was to simply reinforce the notion that the subject now had control
of the dialog and that the subject should not feel compelled to respond directly to the computer's utterances. It was felt that these
instructions illustrated the potential differences for the interaction
without giving them a "recipe" or algorithm to follow. In particular, there were no additional constraints on what the subject chose
to say.

After reorientation, the subject then used the system on the test problems. In this session, the following rule was applied to determine if the interaction should be halted before completion.

> If the dialog exceeds 10 minutes without successful diagnosis or exceeds 15 minutes without completion, and there is no expectation that progress will occur within the next couple of minutes, stop the dialog.

7.3.5 Session 3 Procedure

This session was virtually identical to session 2, except for minor changes in the session-specific instructions as follows.

> Directive Mode—After the sentence ending "to assure you the chance to successfully complete other problems", the sentence "In order to test the effects of computer control of the dialog on expert users, the computer will again act as a teacher as it did during the practice problems in the first session." was inserted. The purpose of this instruction was to warn the users that they would not have the control they had in the previous session and to prepare them for the tediousness we expected them to feel.

> Declarative Mode—the phrase "Unlike the previous session" was changed to "Unlike the previous sessions," since subjects working in declarative mode in session 3 had used directive mode in both sessions 1 and 2.

In addition, after completing usage of the system the subject was asked to complete a form that measured subject response to usage of the system (see figure 7.1). The subject was also asked two additional questions for which the experimenter made notes on the back of the response form. These questions were: (1) To what extent did you use the vocabulary aids? and (2) What effect, if any, did the experimenter's comments have on your interaction with the computer?

7.4 Experimental Setup

Figure 7.2 provides a rough sketch of the room layout. The subject was seated facing the desk containing the circuit board, voltmeter, word list, tape recorder, and microphone. The charts providing assistance in structuring utterances were placed upright against the left edge of the desk. Communication with the speech recognizer was performed through a telephone handset. The experimenter was seated in front of the computer console from which the system was run. Thus, the subject's back was to the experimenter. The experimenter had a copy of the raw data form for the session, a copy of the word list (table 7.1), and a guide describing the allowed experimenter interaction with the subject (figure 7.3).

Subject Response to Use of Voice Dialog System

Rate your level of agreement with each of the following statements according to the scale given below:

	strongly disagree	disagree	do not know	agree	strongly agree
I found it easy to learn to use the system.	1	2	3	4	5
I enjoyed using the system.	1	2	3	4	5
I found the system easy to use.	1	2	3	4	5
I found the system tiring.	1	2	3	4	5
At the start of the experiment the system had too much control of the dialog.	1	2	3	4	5
At the end of the experiment the system had too much control of the dialog.	1	2	3	4	5

On any of the following, use the back for answers if needed.

What features, if any, about the system did you particularly like?

What features, if any, about the system did you particularly dislike?

Any other comments about usability of system.

Figure 7.1
Response Form

EXPERIMENTAL SETUP

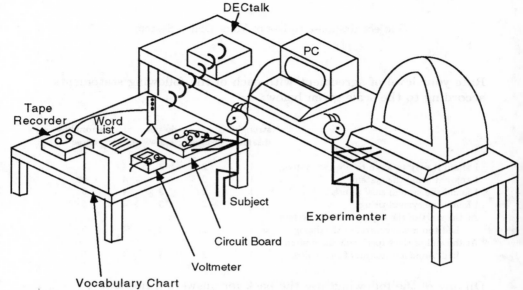

Figure 7.2
Room Setup

In all cases, the experimenter was myself (the first author, Smith) or Dania Egedi, another member of the project team. Egedi had assisted in the development of the experimental procedure. In order to facilitate consistency in experimenter interaction, She was present while I ran the pilot subjects, and I remained in the room to monitor her performance when she ran some of the pilot subjects as well as some of the "warmup" sessions (session 1) of our actual subjects. This allowed us to discuss how we applied our experimental interaction guide in practice. In all sessions 2 and 3 either she or I were alone in the room with the subject.

The steps which the experimenter followed for each problem were the following.

1. Prepare dialog system to be started.

2. Ensure tape recorder was ready.

3. Out of subject's visual range, induce the error into the circuit.

4. Place circuit board in front of the subject.

5. Start tape recorder.

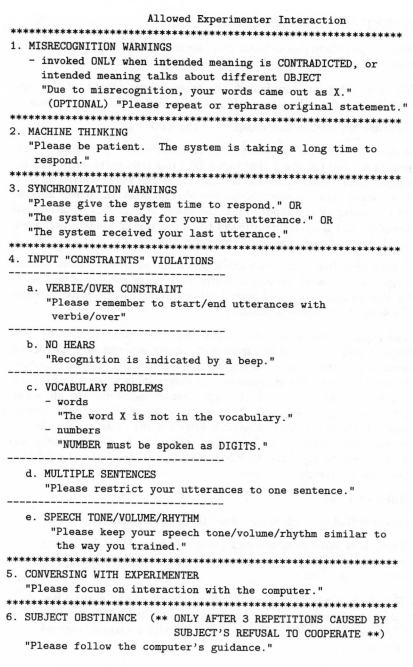

```
                    Allowed Experimenter Interaction
*******************************************************************
1. MISRECOGNITION WARNINGS
   - invoked ONLY when intended meaning is CONTRADICTED, or
     intended meaning talks about different OBJECT
     "Due to misrecognition, your words came out as X."
     (OPTIONAL) "Please repeat or rephrase original statement."
*******************************************************************
2. MACHINE THINKING
   "Please be patient.  The system is taking a long time to
   respond."
*******************************************************************
3. SYNCHRONIZATION WARNINGS
   "Please give the system time to respond." OR
   "The system is ready for your next utterance." OR
   "The system received your last utterance."
*******************************************************************
4. INPUT "CONSTRAINTS" VIOLATIONS
   -----------------------------------
   a. VERBIE/OVER CONSTRAINT
      "Please remember to start/end utterances with
      verbie/over"
   -----------------------------------
   b. NO HEARS
      "Recognition is indicated by a beep."
   -----------------------------------
   c. VOCABULARY PROBLEMS
      - words
        "The word X is not in the vocabulary."
      - numbers
        "NUMBER must be spoken as DIGITS."
   -----------------------------------
   d. MULTIPLE SENTENCES
      "Please restrict your utterances to one sentence."
   -----------------------------------
   e. SPEECH TONE/VOLUME/RHYTHM
      "Please keep your speech tone/volume/rhythm similar to
      the way you trained."
*******************************************************************
5. CONVERSING WITH EXPERIMENTER
   "Please focus on interaction with the computer."
*******************************************************************
6. SUBJECT OBSTINANCE  (** ONLY AFTER 3 REPETITIONS CAUSED BY
                           SUBJECT'S REFUSAL TO COOPERATE **)
   "Please follow the computer's guidance."
```

Figure 7.3
Experimenter Interaction Guide

6. Hit RETURN to start dialog system.

7. Start stopwatch to check the elapsed time in case of a need for premature termination of the dialog due to excessive elapsed time.

8. When a dialog was terminated, the experimenter turned off the tape recorder and reset the stopwatch and proceeded to the next problem.

Data collection mechanisms consisted of the following.

1. Automatic logging of the words received from the speech recognizer (subject input) and the words sent to the DECtalk (computer output). This logging information included the time the words were received or sent. In addition, time information was recorded for when the parser finished its processing of the input, when the usage of dialog expectation was complete and the interpretation of the input was computed, and when the dialog processor was ready to receive input.

2. A tape recording of the interaction was made in order to make a transcript that included the actual words used by the subject as well as to be able to note when and what kind of interactions occurred between the subject and the experimenter.

3. The experimenter made notes about the interaction on the raw data form as well as marked occurrences of subject-experimenter interaction according to the category into which the interaction could be classified. In order to assist the experimenter in determining when a misrecognition or "no hear" occurred, the experimenter monitored the file where automatic logging occurred. If there was no log of the words being recognized within a couple of seconds after the utterance was made, the experimenter knew a "no hear" had occurred. A misrecognition was noted when the log of the snf interpretation was observed to be different from what it should have been.

7.5 Subject Pool

It was decided that subjects should meet the following criteria:

- They must have demonstrated problem-solving skills by having successfully completed one computer science course and have taken or be taking another.

- They must not have excessive familiarity with AI and natural language processing. In particular, they should not have had a class in AI and they should not have interacted with a natural language system.

- They must not be an electrical engineering major. Such individuals could probably fix the circuit without any assistance.

7.6 Cumulative Results

This section will present the cumulative results based on the eight subjects run using the experimental procedure just described. Subjects were run during the period from mid-February to early April 1991. The subjects were all currently taking a second computer science course. The subjects consisted of six freshman and two sophomores at Duke University. Six of the subjects were male and two subjects were female.

7.6.1 Basic System Performance

In each of the problem-solving sessions a subject could work on up to ten different problems. A total of 141 problems were attempted of which 118 or 84% were successfully completed. Of the 23 that were not completed successfully, 22 were terminated prematurely due to excessive time being spent on the dialog. Misunderstandings due to misrecognition were the cause in 13 of these failures. Misunderstandings due to inadequate grammar coverage occurred in 3 of the failures. In 4 of the failures the subject misconnected a wire. The domain processor did not have sufficient knowledge to properly assist the user in this situation. In one failure there was confusion by the subject about when the circuit was working, and in another failure there were problems with the system software. A hardware failure caused termination of the final dialog. Thus, the cause of over two-thirds of the failures was due to miscommunication between the computer and user. The vast majority of these failures were due to misrecognition by the computer. In fact, out of 2840 utterances, only 50% were correctly recognized word for word by the speech recognizer. However, due to the development of the error-correcting parser (Chapter 5) in conjunction with using dialog expectations to select among equally likely parses, 81.5% were still interpreted correctly. Furthermore, the robustness that a goal-seeking dialog processor provides enabled the vast majority of dialogs to be completed successfully in spite of the recognition problems.

7.6.2 Parameter Definitions

Definitions for the values reported in this section are given below.

- # Attempted—the total number of separate dialogs attempted. In a few isolated cases, a given problem was attempted twice because no progress was made during the first attempt.

- # Diagnosed—the total number of dialogs in which a successful diagnosis was made. A successful diagnosis occurred when all the missing wires for the problem were mentioned in the dialog. In all situations, an attempt to add the missing wire was then made. In some cases, dialogs in which a diagnosis was made were not completed for various reasons.

- \# Completed—the total number of dialogs which were completed. Completion of a dialog occurred when the computer was satisfied that the dialog was complete by a response of "good-bye."

- Average diagnosis time (first eight)—the average time (in seconds) required to make a successful diagnosis. The average is computed for all dialogs concerning any of the first eight problems of a session for which diagnosis occurred. The time was measured based on the log entry of the first computer utterance and the computer utterance where the missing wire was mentioned. In some cases, the missing wire was never mentioned by the computer, but the user determined which wire was missing. In these cases, an approximation for the diagnosis time was made by the experimenter.

- Average completion time (first eight)—the average time (in seconds) required to complete a dialog. This average is computed for all successful dialogs concerning any of the first eight problems of a session. The time was measured based on the log entry of the first and last computer utterances of the dialog.

- Average diagnosis time (all)—the same value as "average diagnosis time (first eight)," but is computed for all dialogs in the session where a successful diagnosis was made.

- Average completion time (all)—the same value as "average completion time (first eight)," but is computed for all completed dialogs in the session. The purpose for separately computing these values for the first eight problems is that these were the "balanced" problems of a session (see section 7.3.2) where a more meaningful comparison between sessions can be made. The last two problems of a session were "extras."

- Average \# of utterances/dialog (first eight)—the average number of subject utterances per dialog for all completed dialogs concerning any of the first eight problems of a session.

- Average \# of utterances/dialog (all)—the average number of subject utterances per dialog for all completed dialogs of a session.

- Average subject response time—gives the average elapsed time (in seconds), from the computer's utterance to the subject's response. It is believed that this is a better indicator for the "speech rate" of a subject than average utterances/minute because the number of utterances per minute is dependent on the speed of the computer system as well, and long utterances by the subject required longer response time for the computer. Average subject response time ignores this factor. However, both values are reported.

- Average utterances/minute—gives the average number of utterances spoken by the subject per minute. This is computed for all dialogs in a session, completed or not.

- % Non-trivial utterances—the percentage of subject utterances in a session that were "non-trivial" (i.e. consisted of more than one word).

- Average length of a non-trivial utterance—the average number of words in a non-trivial utterance.

- # Different words used—the total number of different words used by all subjects.

- # Utterances—the total number of utterances spoken by all subjects.

- # Experimenter interactions—the total number of times the experimenter had to speak to a subject during the dialogs. This value is based on the notes marked by the experimenter on the raw data form for the session.

- # Misrecognition interactions—the total number of experimenter interactions caused by misrecognition of the user's words. The experimenter would say, "Due to misrecognition, your words came out as ...".

- Recognition rate (parser)—the percentage of subject utterances that were correctly interpreted by the parser after error-correction and expectation usage.

- Recognition rate (verbex)—the percentage of subject utterances that were correctly recognized by the speech recognizer. The match between spoken and recognized words had to be exact.

7.6.3   Aggregate Results

Results as a Function of Mode

The cumulative results for all subjects as a function of mode are presented in table 7.2. The main hypotheses for when a user gains experience and takes the initiative are restated below.

1. Average completion time will decrease.

2. The average number of utterances will decrease.

3. The rate of speech by the user will decrease.

4. The percentage of non-trivial utterances will increase.

Cumulative Data—All Subjects

	Declarative	Directive
# attempted	75	66
# diagnosed	66	61
# completed	60	58
avg. diagnosis time (1st 8)	225.0 (183.7)	277.3 (167.5)
avg. completion time (1st 8)	303.8 (211.3)	541.0 (247.2)
avg. diagnosis time (all)	199.9 (177.2)	258.9 (166.6)
avg. completion time (all)	270.6 (202.9)	511.3 (244.4)
avg. # utterances/dialog (1st 8)	12.0 (8.2)	28.8 (10.8)
avg. # utterances/dialog (all)	10.7 (7.9)	27.6 (10.7)
avg. subject response time (sec.)	17.0 (16.2)	11.8 (9.3)
avg. utterances/min.	2.3	3.1
% non-trivial utterances	62.9	39.7
avg. length of non-trivial	5.4	4.8
# different words used	100	84
# utterances	1011	1829
# experimenter interactions	174	100
# misrecognition interactions	118	69
recognition rate (parser)	75.3	85.0
recognition rate (verbex)	44.3	53.1
overall recognition rate (parser)	81.5	
overall recognition rate (verbex)	50.0	

Table 7.2
Cumulative Results for All Eight Subjects

5. The average length of a non-trivial utterance will increase.

All these hypotheses except the last seem to be supported by the results. Bar graphs of the four significant[2] results are shown in figure 7.4. The "-" level of computer initiative corresponds to declarative mode while the "+" level of computer initiative corresponds to directive mode. The values for average completion time and average number of utterances are for the first eight problems of a session. Other comments about the results follow.

- A possible cause for the small difference in average length of a non-trivial utterance is that the primary source for non-trivial utterances in directive mode was LED descriptions, whose length

---

[2]Although the trends appear significant, the results are not statistically significant. This is due to the large standard deviations shown in the data tables as the values in parentheses. See section 7.6.5 for a discussion of the results from a non-parametric statistical test.

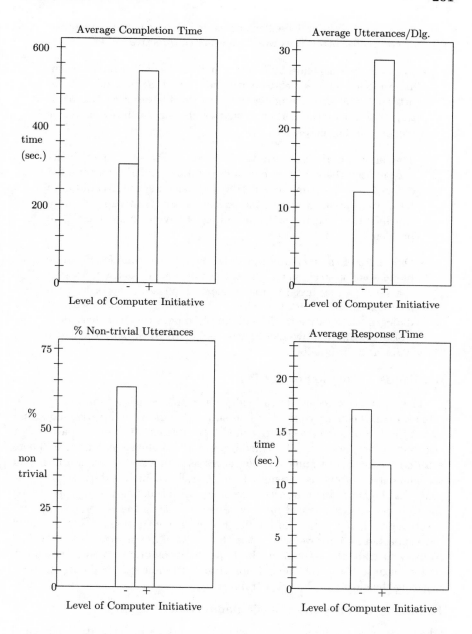

Figure 7.4
Main Results as a Function of Computer Initiative

would tend to be independent of mode. However, the percentage of non-trivial utterances was 23% lower in directive mode.

- Recognition was almost 10% better in directive mode than in declarative mode. This correlates with the result that over 60% of the utterances in directive mode were one-word utterances. Recognition is better by the Verbex in shorter utterances, implying better recognition by the parser.

- The number of dialogs successfully completed was not much different between the modes although the number of dialogs attempted differed by nine. A maximum of 80 problems per mode could have been attempted. Many of the sessions in declarative mode were concluded very early due to the subject's having completed the 10 problems.

- Only 22% of the increase in average completion time for directive mode was due to an increase in the average diagnosis time. Most of the slowdown occurred in the verification phase of the task, when a subject familiar with the steps could perform the checks without dialog in declarative mode and simply report that the "circuit is working." In directive mode subjects had to go through the entire verification subdialog.

Results as a Function of Session

The cumulative results for all subjects separated by session are given in table 7.3. Each column consists of four subjects working in directive mode and four subjects working in declarative mode. Bar graphs for the same parameters as shown before, but now subdivided by session, are shown in figure 7.5. There were no particularly significant differences as a function of session although the number of problems attempted and completed in the third session was somewhat higher than in the second session, which is not surprising considering the subjects would have had more experience in using the system. Somewhat surprisingly, there was not much difference in the recognition rates. One would have expected an improvement in the third session as subjects had extra time to use and train the recognizer. Perhaps the recognition rate was not much better because the percentage of non-trivial utterances rose slightly as well, negating the effects of the extra training.

Results as a Function of Session and Mode

The cumulative results for all subjects when working in declarative mode and separated by session are given in table 7.4. The analogous information for directive mode is given in table 7.5. Bar graphs for the previously reported parameters, but now subdivided by mode and session, are given in figure 7.6. The order for the bars in each graph from left to right are: (1) declarative

Cumulative Data—All Subjects

	Session 2	Session 3
# attempted	67	74
# diagnosed	61	66
# completed	53	65
avg. diagnosis time (1st 8)	265.0 (172.6)	237.0 (181.8)
avg. completion time (1st 8)	436.1 (234.8)	415.2 (278.6)
avg. diagnosis time (all)	240.1 (173.8)	217.2 (174.8)
avg. completion time (all)	400.6 (233.3)	379.3 (271.0)
avg. # utterances/dialog (1st 8)	21.9 (12.6)	19.5 (13.0)
avg. # utterances/dialog (all)	20.2 (12.5)	18.0 (12.8)
avg. subject response time (sec.)	13.9 (13.5)	13.4 (11.3)
avg. utterances/min.	2.8	2.8
% non-trivial utterances	44.4	51.6
avg. length of non-trivial	5.1	5.0
# different words used	104	80
# utterances	1432	1408
# experimenter interactions	162	112
# misrecognition interactions	107	80
recognition rate (parser)	81.1	82.0
recognition rate (verbex)	47.2	52.8
overall recognition rate (parser)	81.5	
overall recognition rate (verbex)	50.0	

Table 7.3
Cumulative Results for All Eight Subjects by Session

mode, second session, (2) declarative mode, third session, (3) directive mode, second session, and (4) directive mode, third session. Observations of interest include the following.

- There was a 28% reduction in average completion time from sessions 2 to 3 for subjects working in declarative mode, while there was a 15% increase for subjects working in directive mode. Clearly, subjects with an extra session of practice with the computer in charge were ready to take over when their time to control the dialog occurred. Conversely, subjects that had the opportunity to be in control of the dialogs during the second session had difficulty in giving control back to the computer, causing an increase in the time taken to complete the dialogs as the subjects attempted to retain some control of the dialog, a fruitless task. This is particularly reflected in the observation that average diagnosis time decreased in session 3 for directive mode subjects although average

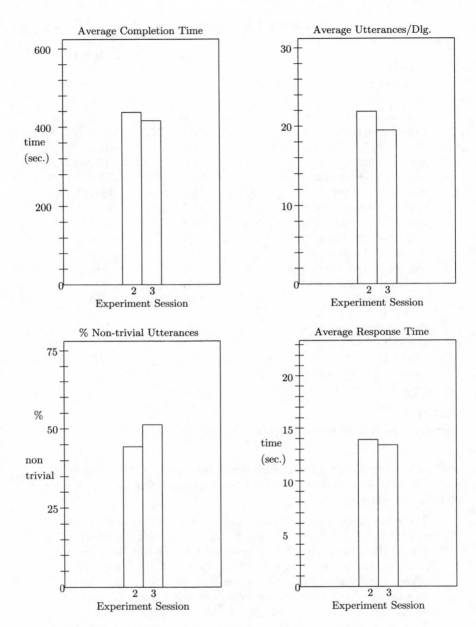

Figure 7.5
Main Results as a Function of Session

Cumulative Data—All Subjects
Declarative Mode

	Session 2	Session 3
# attempted	34	41
# diagnosed	30	36
# completed	25	35
avg. diagnosis time (1st 8)	236.1 (159.4)	214.7 (206.2)
avg. completion time (1st 8)	360.0 (189.3)	260.0 (220.5)
avg. diagnosis time (all)	213.9 (159.5)	188.2 (192.2)
avg. completion time (all)	326.3 (190.6)	230.7 (204.7)
avg. # utterances/dialog (1st 8)	13.6 (6.2)	10.9 (9.3)
avg. # utterances/dialog (all)	12.1 (6.7)	9.7 (8.7)
avg. subject response time (sec.)	19.2 (18.5)	14.8 (13.1)
avg. utterances/min.	2.0	2.6
% non-trivial utterances	61.2	64.6
avg. length of non-trivial	6.0	4.8
# different words used	93	69
# utterances	503	508
# experimenter interactions	111	63
# misrecognition interactions	76	42
recognition rate (parser)	74.4	76.2
recognition rate (verbex)	43.5	45.1
overall recognition rate (parser)	75.3	
overall recognition rate (verbex)	44.3	

Table 7.4
Cumulative Results for Declarative Mode

completion time increased. This correlates with the futile attempts of the subjects to complete the verification process without engaging in dialog with the computer, an unacceptable proposition for the computer when it was running in directive mode.

- Another discrepancy in the trends for declarative and directive mode was average length of a non-trivial utterance. It decreased by 1.2 words from sessions 2 to 3 for declarative mode subjects, but increased 0.8 words for directive mode subjects.

- When subdivided by session, the differences in overall performance as a function of mode were still observable.

Cumulative Data—All Subjects
Directive Mode

	Session 2	Session 3
# attempted	33	33
# diagnosed	31	30
# completed	28	30
avg. diagnosis time (1st 8)	292.9 (183.1)	261.1 (151.6)
avg. completion time (1st 8)	502.8 (253.7)	576.4 (240.6)
avg. diagnosis time (all)	265.5 (185.7)	252.0 (147.1)
avg. completion time (all)	467.0 (250.8)	552.7 (234.9)
avg. # utterances/dialog (1st 8)	29.2 (12.2)	28.5 (9.7)
avg. # utterances/dialog (all)	27.4 (12.1)	27.8 (9.5)
avg. subject response time (sec.)	11.0 (8.5)	12.5 (10.0)
avg. utterances/min.	3.4	3.4
% non-trivial utterances	35.3	44.3
avg. length of non-trivial	4.4	5.2
# different words used	70	63
# utterances	929	900
# experimenter interactions	51	49
# misrecognition interactions	31	38
recognition rate (parser)	84.7	85.3
recognition rate (verbex)	49.2	57.1
overall recognition rate (parser)	85.0	
overall recognition rate (verbex)	53.1	

Table 7.5
Cumulative Results for Directive Mode

7.6.4   Results as a Function of Problem

Another area of interest was an examination of the key parameters, average completion time and average number of utterances, as a function of the problem type. Recall that the first eight problems for sessions 2 and 3 were "balanced," that is, problem 1 of both sessions was of the same type, problem 2 of both sessions was of the same type, etc. Due to an error in the ordering on the raw data forms, there was one discrepancy in this balancing. Problem 7 of session 2 was balanced with problem 8 of session 3, and problem 8 of session 2 was balanced with problem 7 of session 3. We wanted to see if the trends that occurred in the aggregate results also occurred when examined on a problem by problem basis. The results of this investigation are reported in this section.

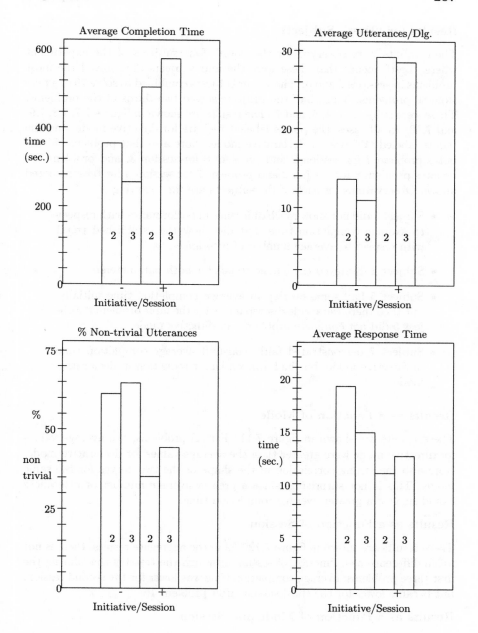

Figure 7.6
Main Results as a Function of Computer Initiative

Results for "Best" Subjects

These results were observed for the "best" four subjects of the experiment where "best" means that these were the four subjects that solved the most problems in sessions 2 and 3. These four subjects combined to solve 79 of a possible 80 problems. Thus, half the subjects solved two-thirds of the problems. These were subjects 1, 4, 5, and 7. The results are shown in figures 7.7, 7.8, 7.9, and 7.10. In all cases, the points labeled "+" are for directive mode, and the points labeled "□" are for declarative mode. Note also that problem "7" denotes problem 7 for session 2 and problem 8 for session 3, and problem "8" denotes problem 8 for session 2 and problem 7 for session 3 for reasons noted above. Observations for each of the subjects are the following.

- Subject 1 did not show much difference in performance with respect to average completion time, but did show the established trend with respect to average number of utterances.

- Subject 4 displayed the classic trends for both parameters.

- Subject 5 had some overlap in average completion time initially, but then there were wide discrepancies for the later problems. Subject 5 did not complete problem 5 in directive mode.

- Subject 7 demonstrated fairly constant average completion time in directive mode, but had a much larger reduction in declarative mode.

Results as a Function of Mode

These results are shown in figure 7.11. For all problems, the average values for directive mode were greater than the average values for declarative mode. Note also the strong correlation in the shape of the two curves for the same mode. This is not surprising, since a greater average number of utterances would suggest a greater average completion time.

Results as a Function of Session

These results are shown in figure 7.12. As in the aggregate results, there is not much difference as a function of session although the trend is that during the first three problems, average completion time was lower for the second session, but became lower for the third session after problem 4.

Results as a Function of Mode and Session

These results are shown in figure 7.13. Some interesting observations are the following.

- The average number of utterances is higher for directive mode in both sessions at all problems.

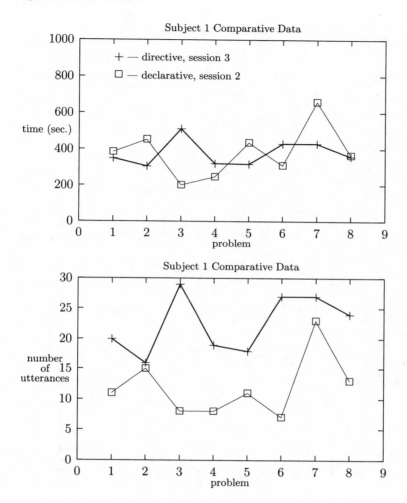

Figure 7.7
Subject 1 Results

- The average completion time for problem 1 was the least for directive mode users for session 2. It would seem that initially, subjects were most comfortable in the mode in which they had completed the warmup session. However, subjects quickly grasped the power they had in declarative mode and began to complete dialogs much quicker than subjects working in directive mode.

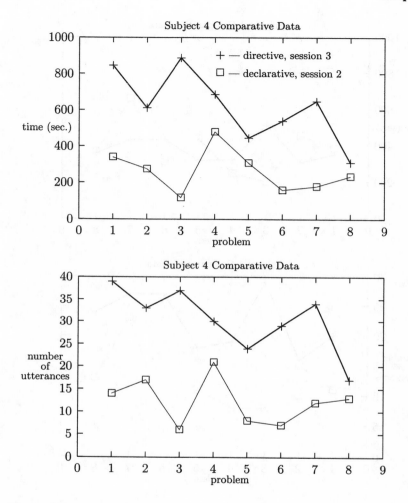

Figure 7.8
Subject 4 Results

7.6.5 Statistical Analysis of the Results

In terms of statistical tests, only four of the subjects completed a high enough percentage of the dialogs to enable a within-subject comparison of behavioral differences as a function of initiative. These four "best" subjects completed 79 of 80 possible dialogs. Table 7.6 shows comparative results for these subjects for each of the seven balanced problems that all subjects completed in both sessions (i.e. the one dialog not completed was one of the balanced problems so that particular problem was eliminated from consideration). As can be seen

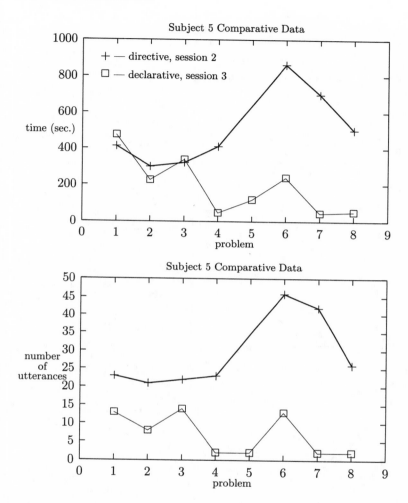

Figure 7.9
Subject 5 Results

from the table, for all these subjects the comparative values for the parameters under study all show the proper trend to support our hypotheses. That is, for each subject, average completion time and average number of utterances were less in declarative mode while % non-trivial utterances and average subject response time were greater in declarative mode. Consequently, for these subjects, a Wilcoxson signed rank test (see [LM81]) yields p = .125 (the lowest value possible for a sample size of four) for the reported parameters. Thus, we feel optimistic that these results indicate true dialog behavioral differences as

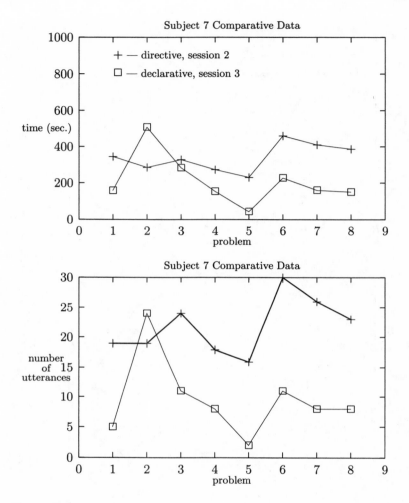

Figure 7.10
Subject 7 Results

a function of initiative although we were not quite able to run enough subjects to establish this mathematically.

7.7   Results from Subject Responses about System Usage

Recall that after finishing the experiment subjects completed the response form shown in figure 7.1. Table 7.7 provides a summary of the subject's ratings of agreement and disagreement with the first set of questions given on the form. Recall that 1 denoted "strongly disagree" and 5 denoted "strongly agree."

Interestingly, subjects tended to agree with both "I enjoyed using the sys-

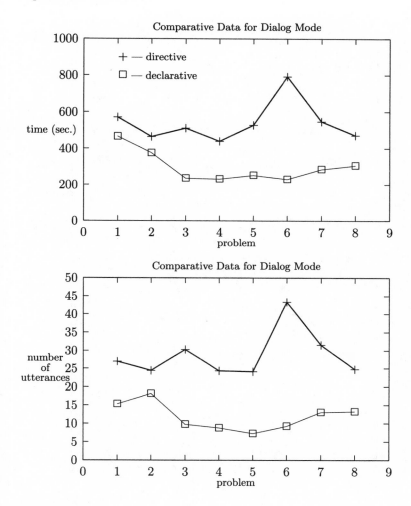

Figure 7.11
Comparative Results as a Function of Mode

tem," and "I found the system tiring." Apparently, the novelty of talking to a computer was a source of enjoyment. It should also be noted that the four "least successful" subjects agreed much more strongly with the statement, "I found the system tiring," than the most successful subjects. The only other noticeable discrepancy between contrasting groups of subjects concerned the level of agreement with, "At the end of the experiment the system had too much control of the dialog." Subjects that worked in directive mode in the final session tended to agree with that statement while subjects that worked in declarative mode in the final session tended to disagree with that statement.

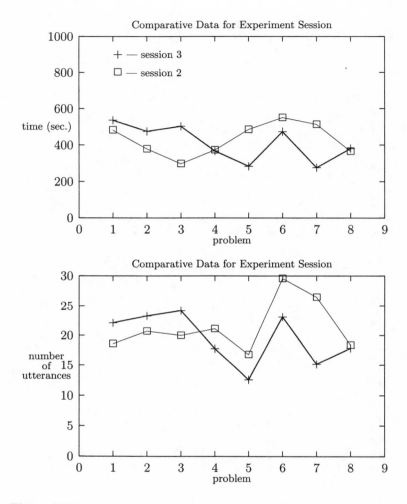

Figure 7.12
Comparative Results as a Function of Session

7.8   Conclusions

- There appear to be differences in the interaction between computer
  and human as a function of dialog mode. The values for the parameters average completion time, average number of utterances
  per dialog, percentage of non-trivial utterances, and speech rate
  provide indications of this.

- The warmup session was very effective in making subjects comfortable with interacting with the computer.

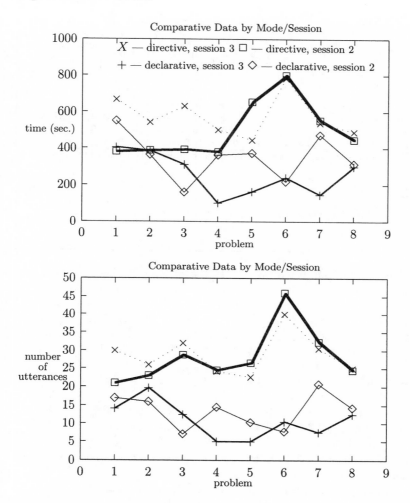

Figure 7.13
Comparative Results as a Function of Mode and Session

- Any future experiments involving restricted vocabulary should use a "bidirectional" vocabulary to the extent possible. That is, all the words used by the computer in producing responses should be available for usage by the human.

- Improved reliability in speech recognition is crucial. The use of error-correction and expectation improved performance, but there is no substitute for better input. Experimenter interaction was crucial to subject success, particularly when misrecognitions

Comparative Data—Best Subjects							
Parameter	Subject 1 Decl. Dir.		Subject 4 Decl. Dir.		Subject 5 Decl. Dir.		Subject 7 Decl. Dir.
Session Number	2	3	2	3	3	2	3	2
avg. completion time	375.0	387.0	255.6	647.1	203.7	502.6	235.1	356.6
avg. # utterances/dialog	12.1	23.1	12.9	31.3	7.7	29.0	10.7	22.7
% non-trivial utterances	75.3	34.0	53.3	43.4	64.8	35.0	60.0	22.0
avg. subject response time (sec.)	20.8	9.8	13.0	11.8	17.1	9.9	16.5	10.5

NOTE: These results are based on seven problems attempted and completed by each subject per session.

Table 7.6
Comparative Data for Best Four Subjects

Summary of Subject Responses to Use of Voice Dialog System

	Easy to Learn to Use	Enjoyed Using	Easy to Use	Tiring	(System Had) Too Much Control Initially	Too Much Control at End
All Subjects	4.4	4.1	3.9	3.9	2.8	3.3
Decl. Mode Last	4.5	4.2	3.8	3.8	3.0	2.5
Dir. Mode Last	4.2	3.9	4.0	4.0	2.6	4.1
Most Successful	4.2	3.9	3.9	3.2	2.8	3.5
Least Successful	4.5	3.9	4.0	4.5	2.9	3.1

NOTE: "Most successful" were the four subjects that completed the most problems.

Table 7.7
Subject Response to System Usage

occurred. Without a description of the nature of the misrecognition, it would have appeared at times that the computer was engaging in arbitrary behavior rather than coherent dialog. Of the number of times that experimenter interaction was required in sessions 2 and 3, 68% involved reporting computer misrecognitions. Although speech recognition technology will continue to improve, it is highly unlikely that 100% reliable input will ever be achieved. Consequently, there is a need for "metadialog" for verification of human inputs. An example of such a metadialog follows.

```
U: The switch is off. (Recognized as "which yes knob.")
C: Did I understand you to say "which knob?"
U: No, the switch is off.
```

Two key parameters for deciding when to engage in a verification subdialog follow.

1. The error score for the parse. A higher error score would indicate a greater likelihood of misrecognition.

2. An estimation of the cost of a misrecognition. When undetected, certain misrecognitions will not extend the length of a dialog very much. However, other misrecognitions could cause the length of the dialog to be extended greatly or even to cause failure. This cost estimate must be balanced against the time cost of verification to determine if verification should be performed.

Chapter 9 presents some preliminary work on verification. The sample dialogs of the first chapter were obtained from usage of our augmented system that contained a verification capability. This system was not available during the initial experiment.

- It should be noted that although subjects were being asked to solve a restricted set of problems, the capability of the system was completely general. For example, we removed every wire from the circuit board, interacted with the system in directive mode, and rebuilt the circuit in 26 minutes while speaking 93 utterances.

Chapter 8

Performance of the Speech Recognizer and Parser

The results of the experiments reported in the previous chapter were independently analyzed[1] in order to measure the accuracy of the speech recognizer and parser. A summary of the key results of this analysis follows.

- On average, one out of every three words emitted by the speech recognizer was in error.

- On average, three out of every four sentences contained one or more speech recognition errors.

- In spite of the high speech recognition error rate, the meanings of the spoken utterances were correctly deduced 83% of the time.

- Finally, and perhaps most surprisingly, it was found that dialog expectation was helpful only as a tie-breaker in deducing the correct meaning of spoken utterances.

The remainder of this chapter describes the analysis in detail.

8.1 Preparation of the Data

The performance measurements of the speech recognizer and parser were computed from transcripts of 2804 individual utterances[2] taken from the second and third sessions of the 8 experimental subjects. No information from the pilot subjects or from the first session with each subject was used in this analysis. Information about each utterance was collected and converted to a standardized, machine-readable format. The information that was collected follows.

- The sequence of words actually spoken by the user. These were manually entered by the experimenters based on the audio recordings of the experiment.

---

[1] By "independent analysis" it is meant that the same raw data were studied separately by different people without significant communication between them. Specifically, the results reported in the previous chapter are by the first author (Smith), while the results reported in this chapter are by the second author (Hipp), and the two authors did not compare their analysis methods until their analyses were both complete. Because both analyses involve subjective judgements concerning the correctness of the parser, and because the two authors may make some judgements differently, the results reported in this chapter differ slightly from the results reported in the previous chapter. The reader should not view these differences as contradictions or inconsistencies, but rather as independent confirmations of the correctness of the two analyses.

[2] The value 2804 is not a transcription error of the total number of utterances reported in the first chapter, 2840. The results in this chapter are based on 2804 of the 2840 utterances.

- The sequence of words recognized by the speech recognizer. This information was recorded automatically during the experiments.

- The set of up to K minimum matching strings between elements of the hypothesis set and dialog expectations, together with an utterance cost and an expectation cost for each. (See section 5.8.5).

- The final output of the parser.

- The text spoken by the dialog controller immediately prior to the user's utterance, and notes concerning the user's utterance which were entered by the person who transcribed the utterance from the audio tapes. This information was used to assist in manually judging the correctness of each parse.

After the above information was collected and carefully audited to remove errors, the following additional features of each utterance were computed through a combination of automatic and manual processing.

- A notation was made on each record to indicate whether or not the output of the parser was the meaning intended by the user.

- A second notation was made on each record to indicate whether or not the parser would have found the user's intended meaning if the speech recognizer had made no errors.

The judgement of whether or not the parser found the user's intended meaning is often very subjective. For example, suppose the user says "the LED is alternately flashing a one and a seven," but due to misrecognition of one or more words of the utterance, the parser determines the meaning to be the equivalent of "the LED is displaying a one and a seven and the one is flashing." In this example (which occurred in the actual data), the information that the seven is flashing has been lost. Nevertheless, the parser clearly had the right idea about what the user meant, even thought it was wrong in one minor detail. In a case such as this, does one judge the parse to be correct or incorrect? Uncertainty about the parser's correctness can arise due to reasons other than misrecognitions. What does one do, for example, if the user's intended meaning is not clear even to another person? Should the parser be faulted for failing where even a human expert is puzzled? Suppose, as another example, the user speaks a phrase whose meaning cannot possibly be expressed in the mathematical language of the dialog controller. Any attempt to parse such an utterance is doomed to fail even before it begins. Should the parser be faulted for failing to perform the impossible?

For the purposes of this chapter, the following decision criteria were used to judge the correctness of a parsed utterance.

1. If the parser finds exactly the intended meaning, mark the parse as "correct."

2. If the meaning found by the parser matches most of the meaning of the spoken utterance, and nothing in the parser's result contradicts the user's intended meaning, then mark the parse "correct."

3. If the parser's output contains any information which contradicts information which the user intended to communicate, mark the parse as "wrong."

4. If the user's meaning cannot be represented in the dialog controller's language, then mark the parse "wrong."

5. If the parser's result and the spoken utterance do not contradict, but less than half of the meaning of the spoken utterance is preserved in the parser's output, then mark the parse as "wrong."

6. If the user's meaning is ambiguous, then mark the parse "correct" if the meaning found by the parser matches any possible interpretation of what the user said.

8.2 Speech Recognizer Performance

Even though the speech recognizer used in the experiments is a commercial system, and is not itself part of our research, its performance has been carefully measured. This was done because performance of the speech recognizer has a significant effect on the performance of the parser.

The first measure of the speech recognizer's performance is called the percent of words correct, or *PWC*. The PWC is the number of words spoken by the user that were correctly recognized by the speech recognizer divided by the total number of correct words and multiplied by 100.

$$\text{PWC} = 100 \cdot \frac{\text{number of correctly recognized words}}{\text{number of words actually spoken}} \tag{8.1}$$

When a spoken word is misrecognized, or is not recognized at all, the PWC is reduced. On the other hand, when extra words are inserted by the speech recognizer the PWC remains unchanged.

The PWC for the Verbex 6000 speech recognizer as used in the experiments described in the previous chapter is reported by the line of numbers below. Each number in the normal font is the PWC for one experimental subject. The large bold-face number is the PWC for all subjects combined. This manner of presentation is intended to give the reader an intuitive feel for how much the PWC varied among the experimental subjects. A similar presentation format will be used for statistics throughout this chapter.

Percent Words Correct (PWC)								
89	88	88	79	**75**	72	68	65	63

A second measure of the speech recognizer's accuracy will be called modified PWC. As with ordinary PWC, modified PWC is computed by taking the number of words correctly recognized, multiplying by 100, and then dividing. The difference is that in ordinary PWC, the divisor is the number of words actually spoken, but in modified PWC the divisor is the number of words output by the speech recognizer. We have:

$$\text{Modified PWC} = 100 \cdot \frac{\text{number of correctly recognized words}}{\text{total number of words recognized}} \qquad (8.2)$$

With modified PWC, insertion errors do make a difference, since they increase the divisor and thus lower the score. Another view of modified PWC is that it is the percentage of words seen by the parser that were actually spoken by the user. The modified PWC for the experiments was:

Modified PWC								
85	84	80	74	**67**	63	54	54	51

A third measure of speech recognition accuracy is called the error rate. The error rate is the number of errors in an utterance divided by the correct length of the utterance, and multiplied by 100.

$$\text{Error Rate} = 100 \cdot \frac{\text{number of errors}}{\text{number of spoken words}} \qquad (8.3)$$

The number of errors in an utterance is the minimum number of insertions, deletions, and substitutions needed to transform what was spoken into what was output from the speech recognizer.[3] The error rate for the speech recognizer in the experiments was:

Error Rate								
71	67	57	43	**41**	35	23	17	16

The speech recognizer could understand a vocabulary of only 125 words. A list of the 125-word vocabulary is shown in table 7.1. Occasionally, the user will speak some word that is not in this vocabulary. The percent of utterances that contain one or more words not found in the 125-word vocabulary is shown by the following values.

Percent of utterances containing a word that is not in the vocabulary								
3.3	2.8	1.8	**1.6**	1.3	1.0	0.9	0.9	0.7

[3]An efficient algorithm for computing the number of errors is described in [WF74].

System Name	Perplexity	Error rate
ARM [RPP+90]	497	13%
BBN SLS [CR89]	700	13%
SPHINX [LHR90]	997	29%
SPICOS [PN89]	124	9%
SUMMIT [ZGG+90]	1000	56%
Verbex 6000	124	41%
Human	122	3%

Table 8.1

Error rates of several speech recognizers

The fact that very few utterances contained any words that were not in the speech recognizer's vocabulary suggests that the limited vocabulary was not a serious detriment to the overall performance of the system.

The percent of utterances recognized without error is reported next. This value allows one to compute an upper bound on the performance of a parser that can not handle recognition errors. Trivial utterances and utterances that contain words not in the speech recognizer's vocabulary were not considered when computing the following numbers.

Percent of utterances recognized perfectly

| 58 | 47 | 40 | **23** | 16 | 13 | 10 | 9 | 3 |

8.2.1 Comparison to Other Speech Recognizers

Table 8.1 shows error rates for several research speech recognition systems. The *perplexity* value is a measure of how many words the speech recognizer must choose from at any given moment. Larger perplexity values tend to increase the error rate, since having more words to choose from increases the chance of choosing the wrong word. For purposes of comparison, table 8.1 also shows the error rate measured on the Verbex 6000 during the experiments, and the error rate of a human listener from an experiment described in section 8.2.2.

8.2.2 Comparison to Humans

The following simple experiment was conducted in an effort to measure the speech recognition performance of humans under conditions similar to those experienced by mechanical speech recognizers. A list of 100 random utterances was read by one of the authors (Hipp) to the other author (Smith) over a telephone. The listener typed what he heard into a computer for later analysis. Each utterance had a length that was uniformly distributed between 2 and 7 words. The words were selected at random[4] from a 122-word vocabulary, which was really the 125-word vocabulary shown in table 7.1 with the three special words "verbie", "over", and "cancel" removed. The utterances were randomized in order to prevent the hearer's expert knowledge of English grammar from assisting in his word recognition. The telephone was used for two reasons. First, the telephone blocked all non-verbal communication, such as facial expressions or hand gestures, which might have subconsciously aided in word recognition. Second, the telephone limited the speech signal bandwidth and thus prevented the hearer from using sound information which is not normally available to mechanical speech recognizers. The style of speaking used in this experiment was connected speech.

Out of 462 words spoken in this experiment, there were 13 errors—11 substitutions and 2 deletions. The PWC was 97.2, and the error rate was 2.8%.

8.3 Parser Performance

The percentage of all utterances for which the parser was able to find the correct meaning was:

Percent correct parses								
97	91	90	88	83	**83**	80	73	64

Slightly more than half (52%) of the utterances are trivial one-word responses to questions from the computer. If these trivial utterances are removed from consideration, the percentage of utterances for which the parser found the correct meaning becomes:

Percent correct parses of non-trivial utterances								
99	85	83	78	**69**	65	63	56	46

Most of the parsing errors were a result of speech recognition errors. If the text of what was actually spoken were input to the parser instead of the text which the speech recognizer produced, the percentage of all utterances that would have been parsed correctly becomes:

Percent correct parses assuming no recognition errors								
100	99	99	98	98	98	**97**	96	89

---

[4]The `drand48` function in the C library on UNIX was used to select both the length of each utterance and the words contained within the utterance.

The performance of the parser assuming perfect speech recognition is not significantly degraded when only non-trivial (multi-word) utterances are considered.

It is interesting to consider what percentage of inputs to the system were ungrammatical.[5] In [EM81], Eastman and McLean report that about a third of the inputs to a natural language database query system were not syntactically well formed. On the other hand, Fineman argues in [Fin83] that ungrammatical input is not normally a problem since only about 2% of natural language inputs are ungrammatical. Our experimental data supports the findings of Eastman and McLean. Even without speech recognition errors, the percentage of non-trivial utterances that were ungrammatical was more than a third, specifically:

Percent of ungrammatical inputs assuming no recognition errors								
49	46	43	41	**37**	35	28	28	25

When speech recognition errors are considered, the percentage of ungrammatical inputs was even higher.

Percent of ungrammatical inputs taking recognition errors into account								
98	92	90	88	84	**82**	78	67	56

In interpreting these results, the reader should remember that the developer of the translation grammar for use by our system knew from the beginning that the system was capable of handling ungrammatical inputs, and so little effort was made to give the translation grammar complete language coverage. Nevertheless, we believe that our system would have never achieved a parsing accuracy as high as it did had it not been able to guess the meaning of highly ungrammatical inputs.

Figures 8.1, 8.2, and 8.3 are diagrams of the relationship between the number of non-trivial utterances that were parsed correctly and measures of the speech recognizer's accuracy. Each point in these diagrams represents the results from a single experimental subject. The ordinate of each point is the percent of correct parses and the abscissa is the speech recognizer accuracy. Let the variable C represent the percent of non-trivial utterances that were correctly parsed, let P be the PWC, M is the modified PWC, and let R be the speech recognizer's error rate. The linear equations that predict the value of C with minimum squared error as a function of P, M, or R, respectively, are equations 8.4, 8.5, and 8.6 given next.

---

[5]We consider an ungrammatical input to be any input which is not in the input language of the translation grammar.

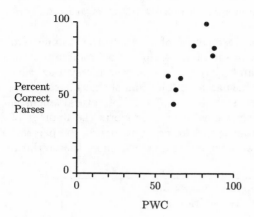

Figure 8.1
The parser accuracy on non-trivial utterances plotted against the percent of correctly recognized words for each experimental subject.

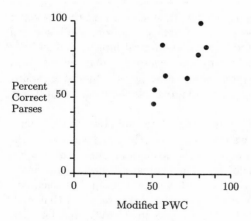

Figure 8.2
The parser accuracy on non-trivial utterances plotted against the *modified* PWC for each experimental subject.

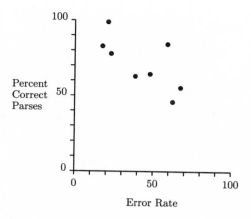

Figure 8.3
The parser accuracy on non-trivial utterances plotted against the speech recognizer error rate for each experimental subject.

$$C = 1.15983P - 12.5233 \qquad (8.4)$$
$$C = 0.880417M + 13.2553 \qquad (8.5)$$
$$C = 97.2912 - 0.601699R \qquad (8.6)$$

Figure 8.4 shows the percentage of non-trivial utterances that were correctly parsed plotted against the percentage of non-trivial spoken utterances that were not in the input language of the translation grammar. Notice that the two subjects with the lowest rate of extragrammatical utterances have the worst and the best parser performance, respectively. This suggests that the accuracy of the parser and the percentage of spoken utterances that are extragrammatical are not linearly related.

8.4   Optimal Expectation Functions

In section 5.8.6, three tunable expectation functions were described by equations 5.2, 5.3, and 5.4. For the sequence of experiments described in the previous chapter, equation 5.2 with $\beta = 0.98$ was used as the expectation function. This choice of expectation function and β was based largely on intuition and our preconceived notions of what ought to work. However, now that extensive experimental data is available, we can recompute the parser's hypothesis selection using different expectation functions and parameters, and thereby experimentally determine the optimal expectation function and parameter for our system.

Assume that equation 5.2 had been used as the expectation function. Figure 8.5 shows the percentage of utterances that would have been parsed correctly as a function of the parameter β. When β is exactly 1.0, the expectation

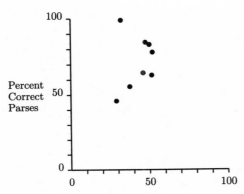

Figure 8.4
The parser accuracy on non-trivial utterances plotted against the percentage of extragrammatical spoken utterances for each experimental subject.

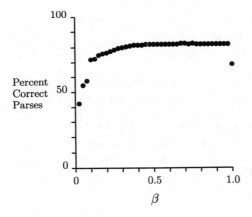

Figure 8.5
The parser's accuracy as a function of the β parameter to the expectation function of equation 5.2

is effectively ignored and the final parser output is determined by selecting an hypothesis at random from among the hypotheses with the minimum utterance cost. This strategy gives an overall parser accuracy of only 69%. For all other values of β greater than 0.5, however, the parser produces the much better accuracy of 83%. Furthermore, the accuracy seems not to be influenced at all by which value between 0.5 and 1.0 is chosen for β.

Figure 8.6 shows what happens when equation 5.3 is used as the expectation

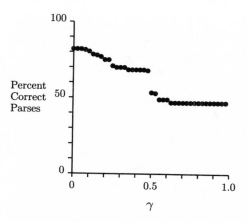

Figure 8.6
The parser's accuracy as a function of the γ parameter to the expectation function of equation 5.3

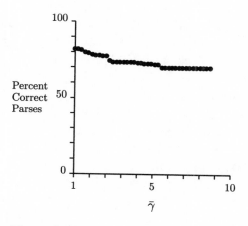

Figure 8.7
The parser's accuracy as a function of the $\bar{\gamma}$ parameter to the expectation function of equation 5.4

function and the parameter γ is varied between 0.0 and 0.97. The peak parser accuracy of 83% is obtained when γ is set to exactly 0.0. Even values for γ as small as 0.005 do not perform as well as when γ is exactly 0.0. It seems that expectation is only helpful in deciding between two hypotheses when both have exactly the same utterance cost.

Figure 8.7 shows the parser's accuracy when equation 5.4 is used and the parameter $\bar{\gamma}$ is varied between 1.0 and 8.8. The parser accuracy is maximized at 83% correct when $\bar{\gamma}$ is set to exactly 1.0. Even a $\bar{\gamma}$ of 1.01 did not do as well. This is consistent with the observation above that expectation is only helpful when it is called upon to break an exact tie in utterance cost.

Chapter 9

Enhanced Dialog Processing: Verifying Doubtful Inputs

9.1 Handling Misunderstandings

Every natural language parser will sometimes misunderstand its input. Misunderstandings can arise from speech recognition errors or inadequacies in the language grammar, or they may result from an input that is ungrammatical or ambiguous. Whatever their cause, misunderstandings can jeopardize the success of the larger system of which the parser is a component. For this reason, it is important to reduce the number of misunderstandings to a minimum.

In a dialog system, it is possible to reduce the number of misunderstandings by requiring the user to verify each utterance. Some speech dialog systems implement verification by requiring the user to speak every utterance twice, or to confirm a word-by-word readback of every utterance. Such verification is effective at reducing errors that result from word misrecognitions, but does nothing to abate misunderstandings that result from other causes. Furthermore, verification of all utterances can be needlessly wearisome to the user, especially if the system is working well.

A superior approach is to have the spoken language system verify the deduced meaning of an input only under circumstances where the accuracy of the deduced meaning is seriously in doubt, or correct understanding is essential to the success of the dialog. The verification is accomplished through the use of a *verification subdialog*—a short sequence of conversational exchanges intended to confirm or reject the hypothesized meaning. The following example of a verification subdialog will suffice to illustrate the idea.

> computer: What is the LED displaying?
> user: The same thing.
> computer: Did you mean to say that the LED is displaying the same thing?
> user: Yes.

As will be further seen below, selective verification via a subdialog results in an unintrusive, human-like exchange between user and machine.

A recent enhancement to the Circuit Fix-it Shop dialog system is a subsystem that uses a verification subdialog to verify the meaning of the user's utterance only when the meaning is in doubt or when accuracy is critical for the success of the dialog. Notable features of this new verification subsystem include the following.

- Verification is *selective*. A verification subdialog is initiated only if there is reason to suspect that the overall performance and accuracy of the dialog system will be improved. In this way, the verification subsystem responds much as a person would.

- Verification is *tunable*. The propensity of the system to verify can be adjusted so as to provide any required level of speech understanding accuracy.

- Verification *operates at the semantic level*. The system verifies an utterance's meaning, not its syntax. This helps overcome misunderstandings that result from inadequacies in the language model, or ungrammatical or ambiguous inputs.

The most important aspect in the development of a verification subdialog system is the decision of whether or not a particular input should be verified. In our system, we accomplish this task by computing for each meaning a *confidence* (a measure of how plausible the parser's output is) and a *verification threshold* (a measure of how important the meaning is toward the success of the dialog). A verification subdialog is undertaken if the confidence drops below the verification threshold.

The performance of the implemented verification system is aesthetically pleasing. The verification subdialogs are fluid and natural, so much so that some observers fail to notice that a verification has taken place. As an example, look back at Dialog 1 in the first chapter. It contains three verification subdialogs. Furthermore, the net accuracy of the parser is greatly improved. The percentage of utterances that are correctly understood can be raised from 83% to about 97% with only a small verification overhead.

9.2 Deciding When to Verify

The decision to verify a particular input is governed by two factors.

1. The likelihood that the meaning deduced by the parser is what the user intended to communicate.

2. The importance of the meaning to the success of the overall dialog.

A simple method of incorporating both of these factors into the verification decision follows. Assign to each meaning a *confidence* (an estimate of the chance that the meaning was correctly deduced from the user's original speech), and a *verification threshold* (a measure of the importance of the deduced meaning to the success of the dialog). Initiate a verification if and only if the confidence is less than the verification threshold. Methods for estimating the confidence and verification threshold are described in the following two subsections.

9.2.1 Confidence Estimates

Several algorithms for estimating the confidence of a particular meaning have been developed and compared in an effort to find one general method that provides consistently good results. All of the algorithms tested compute the confidence as a linear function of four measurements.

Total Error The *total error* of a particular utterance is the amount of deviation between the user's speech and the most similar speech template. The deviation can be measured at both the speech recognition level (how closely does the user's speech match internal speech templates) and at the grammatical level (how closely does the sequence of words output by the speech recognizer match a well-formed phrase in the grammatical model of the input language).

In the implementation, the total error is taken to be the total cost computed by the expectation function. (See section 5.8.6.) Deviation at the speech recognition level could not be used because requisite information is not available from the commercial speech recognizer used in the implementation.

Normalized Error The *normalized error* is the amount of deviation per fixed unit of input. The normalized error is therefore just the total error divided by the size of the user's input. The size of an input might be its temporal length, or the number of words in the phrase, or some other appropriate measure. In this implementation, the size of an utterance is the number of words output by the speech recognizer.

Expectation Cost The *expectation cost* is the value obtained from the dialog controller that attempts to predict how strongly the utterance was anticipated in the current dialog context.

Distinctness The *distinctness* is a measure of ambiguity in an utterance. A high distinctness shows that the meaning deduced by the speech understander is the only reasonable interpretation of the input. A low distinctness indicates that there are several competing interpretations of the user's speech, and that the meaning output by the speech understander is only one of these interpretations.

In this paper, distinctness is computed as the difference between the total error of the meaning and the total error of that meaning that was the parser's second choice.

Over- and Under-verifications Here are two important definitions: An *under-verification* is defined as the event where the parser generates a meaning that is incorrect but not verified. An *over-verification*, on the other hand, occurs when a correct meaning is verified. An under-verification results in a misunderstanding, but an over-verification is only a vexation to the user. The goal of any confidence estimating function is to simultaneously minimize the number of both under- and over-verifications. It is usually the case, however, that under- and over-verifications trade off against one another, so that one may decrease the number of under-verifications only by increasing the

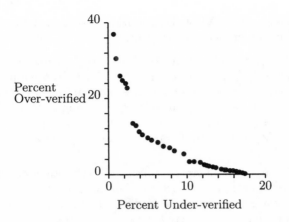

Figure 9.1
Performance curve for the confidence estimating function named α

number of over-verifications, and vice versa. Hence, it is instructive to think of over-verifications as the price one pays for reducing the number of under-verifications.

The performance or, "goodness", of a particular confidence estimating function can be visualized by plotting the number of under-verifications versus the number of over-verifications that occur using the given confidence estimator, for various thresholds, over a fixed set of meanings. Figure 9.1 shows the performance curve for a particular confidence estimating function named α. The function α computes the confidence as a linear combination of normalized error and dialog expectation, weighted so that a single level change in context is approximately equal to inserting or deleting a single content word in a twenty-word long utterance. Each point in figure 9.1 represents the number of over- and under-verifications that would result if a single threshold value were used in conjunction with confidence estimator α in order to decide whether or not to verify each of a standard set of meanings. The over- and under-verifications are expressed as a percentage of the total number of meanings analyzed. The data used to generate figure 9.1 is the 2804 utterances and their meanings recorded during the experiments described in chapter 7.

Comparison of various confidence estimating functions Two confidence estimators may be compared by plotting their performance curves on the same graph. A confidence estimator is normally judged to be better if it consistently has a smaller over-verification rate for any given under-verification rate. Figures 9.2 through 9.5 compare α to confidence estimators based on the four fundamental confidence measurements mentioned above. The α function is used in these comparisons since it has been found to provide the best results under most circumstances. Other confidence estimating functions compared

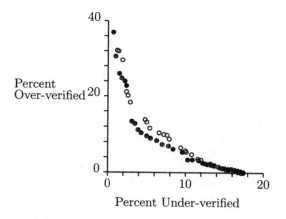

Figure 9.2
Performance curve for the confidence estimator based on total error alone (o) versus the confidence estimator α (•).

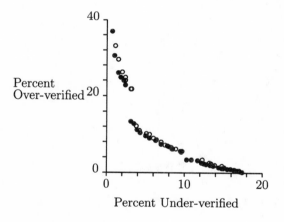

Figure 9.3
Performance curve for the confidence estimator based on normalized error (o) versus the confidence estimator α (•).

to α and that were found to be inferior follow.

- Functions built from a linear combination of normalized error and total error.

- Functions built from a linear combination of total error and the sum of normalized error and dialog expectation.

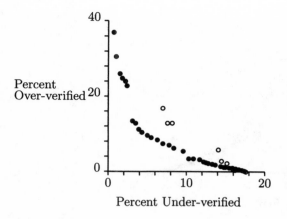

Figure 9.4
Performance curve for the confidence estimator based on only dialog expectation (○)
versus the confidence estimator α (•).

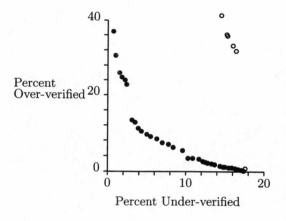

Figure 9.5
Performance curve for the confidence estimator based on only distinctness (○) versus
the confidence estimator α (•).

- Functions that select the greater of normalized error and weighted total
  error.

- Functions that select the lesser of normalized error and weighted total
  error.

All the performance curve plots displayed in this these are derived from the
2804 utterances collected from the experiments described in chapter 7. How-

ever, this was not the only dataset used in the actual analysis. Other datasets include the following.

- The 2804 utterances in the experiments, but with duplicate occurrences of the same input removed. This reduced the number of utterances to 1134.

- The 2804 utterances in the experiments, but processed using the second implementation of the parser, and using a heavily revised version of the grammar.

- The data specified in the previous bullet but with duplicate entries removed.

- Subsets of the data specified in all of the previous bullets consisting of only utterances spoken by one of the eight experimental subjects.

In every case, the performance plots were scaled differently to reflect the differing speech recognition and parsing accuracy of the various data sets, but the basic shape of the performance curves was preserved. Though in some cases other confidence estimating functions did just as well, none were better than the function α.

9.2.2 Selecting a Verification Threshold

The second concern in deciding whether or not to verify a given meaning is the selection of a verification threshold against which to compare the confidence estimate. The verification threshold is the quantity used to tune the propensity of the system to verify. A low verification threshold means that verifications will be frequent, to the point of being bothersome, but that the effective misunderstanding rate will be low. A high verification threshold will result in infrequent verifications, but a higher misunderstanding rate.

It is important to note that the verification threshold need not be a constant; it may depend on the meaning deduced by the speech understander. Meanings that are critical to the success of the dialog may be given a high threshold, thus requiring that there be high confidence in the accuracy of the meaning to avoid verification, whereas superficial or unimportant meanings may be given a low threshold, so that the system will not waste the user's time verifying unimportant details.

The selection of an appropriate verification threshold is highly dependent upon the requirements of the dialog system. As a result, it is difficult to make general statements about which verification thresholds are appropriate and which are not. In many cases, however, the selection of a verification threshold might be aided by a *dialog work* analysis. Dialog work is an intuitive concept that can be thought of as roughly the number of user-machine interactions or the amount of time needed to complete a dialog. The analysis that uses dialog work to select a verification threshold follows.

A particular meaning, m, is computed by the speech understander, and a verification threshold is wanted for this meaning. Let V be the amount of dialog work needed to verify m, and let E be the amount of extra dialog work needed to recover if m is a misunderstanding and is not verified. Let u be the probability of under-verification, and let $f(u)$ be the corresponding over-verification probability. Assume that u and $f(u)$ can be computed from historical under- and over-verification rates, so that $f(u)$ is actually the performance curve for the chosen confidence estimator. Let the dialog work required after m is processed be K. If we assume that a verification subdialog will always find the correct meaning, then the total dialog work required for a given under-verification rate u is $W(u)$ in the following equation:

$$W(u) = uE + f(u)V + K. \qquad (9.1)$$

If we could compute the value of u in equation 9.1 that minimized the dialog work, then this u could be used in conjunction with the confidence estimator's performance curve to find the corresponding verification threshold. The desired u can be found by solving the equation

$$\frac{d}{du}W(u) = 0. \qquad (9.2)$$

The solution is

$$\frac{d}{du}f(u) = -\frac{E}{V}. \qquad (9.3)$$

Equation 9.3 says that the under-verification rate that minimizes the dialog work is the ordinate of the point on the performance plot of the confidence estimator function that has a slope of $-E/V$. Here is the key observation: the performance plots of many confidence estimators contain a small region that has a large second derivative. Call such a region a *knee* of the graph. For example, there is a knee in α in the vicinity of $u = 0.03$. For many values of $-E/V$, the point on the performance graph that has a slope of $-E/V$ will be on the knee of the graph. Hence, the under-verification rate that minimizes the dialog work will likely be in the knee of the performance graph.

It is not difficult to find objections to the above analysis. Perhaps the most serious are that V is not constant but rather depends on u, and that a verification subdialog does not guarantee that the intended meaning will eventually be found. Nevertheless, the above analysis is a reasonable first-order approximation.

9.3 Experimental Results

The verification subsystem was not implemented in time to be used in the experiments described in chapter 7. Nevertheless, the data gathered in these experiments can be used to estimate how well the verification subsystem would have improved the parser's performance had the subsystem been operational.

Before presenting the performance results of the system with the verification subsystem working, first recall how the system performed without verification. The following table is a duplicate of the one at the beginning of section 8.3 that shows the percent of all input utterance for which the correct meaning was deduced by the parser.

Percent correct parses (without verification)								
97	91	90	88	83	**83**	80	73	64

When the verification subsystem was activated and the verification threshold was adjusted so as not to burden the user with too many over-verifications, the performance of the system improved dramatically—the parsing accuracy went from 83% to 97%.

Percent correct parses (with verification)								
99.4	99.4	98.5	97.3	**96.9**	96.5	96.2	95.8	92.0

The above performance was obtained with the following over-verification rate.

Percent of utterances over-verified								
63	36	23	**22**	15	15	11	9	7

Even when only non-trivial (multi-word) utterances are considered, the performance of the parser remains high.

Percent of non-trivial utterances correctly parsed (with verification)								
99.0	98.9	98.6	96.8	**95.0**	94.2	93.0	92.1	88.2

Percent of non-trivial utterances over-verified								
44	40	29	28	**25**	18	16	16	14

9.4   Summary of Verification Subdialogs

Our experiments with verification subdialogs indicate that it can be a powerful mechanism for improving the reliability and accuracy of a spoken language dialog system. Nevertheless, we feel that more research is necessary in order to better determine when to initiate a verification subdialog, and on how to incorporate verification subdialogs into the more general dialog control mechanism.

Chapter 10

Extending the State of the Art

This book has presented a computational model for integrated dialog processing. The primary contributions of this research follow.

- A mechanism (the Missing Axiom Theory) for integrating subtheories that each address an independently studied subproblem of dialog processing (i.e. interactive task processing, the role of language, user modeling, and exploiting dialog expectation for contextual interpretation and plan recognition).

- A computational theory for variable initiative behavior that enables a system to vary its responses at any given moment according to its level of initiative.

- Detailed experimental results from the usage of a spoken natural language dialog system that illustrate the viability of the theory and identify behavioral differences of users as a function of their experience and initiative level.

This chapter provides a concluding critique, which identifies areas of ongoing work and offers some advice for readers interested in developing their own spoken natural language dialog systems.

10.1 Continuing Work

This section describes important issues we did not successfully address in this research because either (1) we studied the problem but do not as yet have a satisfactory answer; or (2) it was not necessary to investigate the problem for the current system. Regardless of the reason, incorporating solutions to these problems is needed to strengthen the overall model.

10.1.1 Automatic Switching of Initiative

In section 4.7.3 we have already discussed the difficulties in determining when and how to change the level of initiative during a dialog as well as the problems in maintaining coherence when such a change occurs. Ongoing work in this area is being conducted by Guinn [Gui93]. His model for setting the initiative is based on the idea of "evaluating which participant is better capable of directing the solution of a goal by an examination of the user models of the two participants." He provides a formula for estimating the competence of a dialog participant based on a probabilistic model of the participant's knowledge about the domain. Using this formula, Guinn has conducted extensive experimental simulations testing four different methods of selecting initiative.

- Random Selection—at the start randomly choose the participant that will be in control throughout the dialog. If the participant is unable to prove the overall goal by any solution path, it will pass the initiative to the other participant.

- Single Selection—as with Random Selection choose the controlling participant at the start except that now the selected participant is the one considered most competent rather than simply a random choice.

- Continuous Selection—after each failure by the controlling participant to prove a goal via a selected solution path, the selection process is repeated. Note that this differs from Random Selection where control is passed only when the controlling participant cannot prove the goal after trying *all* its known possible solution paths.

- Optimal Selection—an oracle selects the participant that has the correct solution path highest in its list of possible paths.

The results of the simulations indicate that Single and Continuous mode selection tend to perform much better than Random Selection. In addition, Continuous is more efficient than Single Selection when the participants have about the same amount of knowledge. While this work provides added insight into changing the initiative during a dialog, it does not address the problem of maintaining dialog coherence when a change occurs. It is hoped that this work can be integrated into the overall model at some future time.

10.1.2 Exploiting Dialog Context in Response Generation

No attempt has been made to incorporate a sophisticated model of response generation that relates discourse goals to utterances. The Missing Axiom Theory provides a basic connection—that the purpose of an utterance is to obtain a missing axiom—but no general strategies have been used other than to apply a few rules of thumb for exploiting dialog context to modify the final utterance specification sent to the linguistic generator (sections 4.4.1 and 4.4.2). The work conducted by Moore and Paris [MP93], Cawsey [Caw92], and Zukerman and McConachy [ZM93] offers possible solutions to this problem.

Moore and Paris describe a text planner in the advisory dialog domain that maintains information about its past utterances in order to plan future responses. Their planner extends previous work by considering both the intentions of utterances and the possible rhetorical strategies for communicating the utterances. Once the planner is notified of a communicative goal to be achieved, it begins decomposing the goal into various subgoals down to the level of speech acts. These speech acts can then be formulated into a specification that can be used by an actual generator to produce the utterance. The planning operators are based on general principles of advisory dialogs and thus are applicable to any advisory domain. Furthermore, the operators consider the effects on a user's knowledge and goals as well, thus enabling specific clarification subdialogs to be handled. The general nature of the representation makes it portable to many different systems.

Cawsey describes a model for generating multisentential explanations that permits clarifying questions while the explanation is produced. The explanation is modified as needed if topics are discussed "out of order" with respect to the initial plan for generating the explanation. This system was developed in a tutorial environment where long textual explanations may be given. While it lacks the general knowledge about why certain dialog actions were selected (a feature of the system of Moore and Paris), it does deal more directly with important dialog issues such as turn-taking and, to a limited extent, initiative, although it only uses a menu interface for user inputs.

Zukerman and McConachy describe a content planning mechanism in the student tutorial domain that considers the possible inferences of a user in selecting the most concise discourse that achieves a given communicative goal. Their mechanism applies backward reasoning from the communicative goal to determine appropriate rhetorical actions for achieving the goal. After this is completed, forward reasoning is applied to see what the effects of a selected rhetorical action will be on the user's beliefs. If it is believed the user will make improper inferences, then additional rhetorical actions may be needed. If inferences are expected that were to be explicitly mentioned, then rhetorical actions may be eliminated. This process may produce several possible sets of rhetorical actions that are adequate to achieve the communicative goal, and an optimization process must be performed to minimize the number of rhetorical actions used in producing the actual response.

While it would seem that some type of synthesis of these approaches could provide a better model for response generation in dialog, one must realize that the type of dialog for which these models were developed is different from normal spoken natural language dialog. All of these models are for planning multisentential text that may not be appropriate in spoken interaction, especially if the system is producing voice output. Normal two-way spoken interaction consists of rapid interactions where utterances are not multisentential. Cognitive overload will occur if the system tries to communicate too much information in one spoken utterance. In such an environment, there is no need for detailed planning of a multisentential response, especially if there are constraints for maintaining quick response times. For our domain the experimental results indicate that the simple response algorithm was adequate, but it was a domain where only simple utterances were needed most of the time. If the dialog is of an advisory or tutorial nature, a multisentential response may be appropriate. However, the response should be communicated in pieces where the system waits for an acknowledgment, question, comment, or command from the user before proceeding to the next piece. In such situations, a more sophisticated model of response generation may be quite useful.

10.1.3 Miscommunication and Metadialog

Discussed at length in chapter 9 was one approach for handling misunderstandings—verification of inputs where the accuracy of the deduced meaning is in doubt. While preliminary experimental results indicate potential benefits from such an approach, it does not appear that 100% accuracy is ever likely, even with the rapidly improving speech recognition technologies appearing at the present time. Complementary intelligent strategies for detecting and recovering from miscommunication are needed.

Integrating Expectation with Signal Processing

One such strategy already in use is to exploit dialog expectation directly in the processing of the speech input signal. The utility of this has been demonstrated in the MINDS [YHW+89] and VODIS [YP89] systems discussed in section 2.7.4. This approach can greatly improve the accuracy of the initial input of words to the parsing component of the overall system. We were unable to utilize such an approach in our system due to the limitations of the commercial speech recognition hardware used. It only returned one hypothesis for the input signal instead of the multiple hypotheses required for such an approach.

Higher-Level Detection of Misunderstanding

A more recent higher-level approach to detecting misunderstanding has been proposed by McRoy and Hirst [MH93]. Their approach uses abduction for interpreting utterances—the hearer tries to identify the reasons why an utterance was produced based on the observed utterance itself. The hearer uses expectations based on social conventions of language use (e.g. if a question is asked, expect an answer) as well as expectations based on linguistic intentions (e.g. speaker intends that the hearer will know the location of connector 104). When the current utterance violates the hearer's expectations, the hearer may conclude that his model of the dialog is inaccurate due to a misunderstanding of a previous utterance. McRoy and Hirst provide an explicit formalization of the social conventions and linguistic intentions as well as the rules for determining that a misunderstanding has occurred. Their formalization is domain-independent and can provide a complementary approach for detecting misunderstandings as it enables detection after an incorrect interpretation was previously made.

Negotiating Understanding via Metadialog

When misunderstandings are conjectured or identified, there must be a means of removing the misunderstanding so that the dialog can continue to progress. One such means involves negotiation of what are the actual facts in the current dialog situation. Lambert and Carberry [LC92] propose a plan based model of negotiation subdialogs. This model was developed within the framework of their tripartite plan-based model of dialog [LC91] that differentiates between domain actions (e.g. connect a wire), problem solving actions (e.g. construct a plan for connecting a wire), and discourse actions (e.g. inform someone that a wire needs connecting). They have observed that listeners assimilate their understanding of each utterance by the following series of steps.

1. Basic understanding of the utterance.

2. Determining if the utterance is consistent with the listener's beliefs.

3. Determining the appropriateness of the utterance within the current context.

Their model recognizes when an utterance is initiating a negotiation subdialog by determining when the listener's beliefs indicate the speaker is expressing doubt about the validity of a claim expressed earlier in the dialog. The strength of their model is the integration of both linguistic and pragmatic knowledge sources in the recognition process. The model could be incorporated into an overall dialog processing model to assist in recognizing when the user is claiming the existence of a misunderstanding.

In general, resolving misunderstandings and providing for smooth transition during initiative changes requires *metadialog*, or dialog about the dialog. Metadialog was briefly mentioned in section 7.8. Developing an appropriate model of metadialog that can be easily integrated into the Missing Axiom model of problem solving dialog remains an important unsolved research issue. One feasible architectural possibility is an addition to the dialog controller of a metadialog decision making algorithm that will analyze the dialog situation before every computer utterance to determine whether metadialog is needed. However, we have no concrete suggestions about what the decision making algorithm should be.

10.1.4 Less Restricted Vocabulary

At the time the experiment was conducted, we needed to use a small vocabulary due to hardware and processing time constraints. As expected, subjects adapted well to using a restricted vocabulary, but further study is required in domains where larger vocabularies are needed. Fortunately, the performance of speech recognizers is improving, making such studies feasible. One important issue that we did not address due to the restricted vocabulary environment is the use of expectations based on the linguistic content of previous utterances. As initially described in section 3.5.2, we categorized semantic expectations that were independent of the linguistic form used to initiate the current dialog topic. Linguistic expectations are needed for handling various types of elliptical responses as well as questions like the following.

```
C: Take the free ends of the wire.
U: The three ends?
```

```
C: Add a wire between connectors 102 and 104?
U: From 102 to where?
```

During the Wizard of Oz studies (section 1.3) very few of these kinds of responses were made so we chose not to address this issue directly. We chose instead to provide "repeat" in the vocabulary and implemented it in such a way as to cause the DecTalk to slow its rate of speaking whenever the user uttered "repeat." In addition, experimental subject training included practice at understanding the DecTalk's output (section 7.3.3). As a result of this training, only 23 of the 2840 utterances were requests for the DecTalk to repeat its previous utterance. If detailed clarification was needed, the model provides for such dialog behavior (section 4.7.1). However, it is believed that linguistic-based expectations must be modeled in a domain allowing a larger vocabulary. Conversely, if a system designer has a restricted problem domain where a restricted vocabulary can be used, it can provide the following benefits: (1) reduce grammar complexity, thus increasing parser efficiency; and (2) reduce the number of linguistic phenomena to be considered. If a restricted vocabulary is used, then the following guidelines should be considered.

1. Make the vocabulary as small as possible, but do not omit important synonyms.

2. Be sure your vocabulary is bidirectional (i.e. don't let the computer use any words it cannot recognize).

3. Do not totally eliminate pronouns (we allowed "it").

4. Try to make each word as phonetically distinct as possible to improve recognition performance.

10.1.5 Evaluating Model Applicability

The model presented in this book is most appropriate for task-oriented domains where there is a task being conducted concurrently with the dialog. It was this dialog environment that provided the framework for the research. The most important environmental feature exploited in the model is the close coupling between task actions and dialog actions. This coupling tightly constrains the expectations for user responses and greatly enhances the processing efficiency of the system.

Other important environments where spoken natural language dialog may be applicable include advisory dialogs and tutorial dialogs. In an advisory dialog the system is providing advice about some task the user will perform but there is no restriction that the task is ongoing with the dialog. In such a system the coupling between task and dialog is looser. Consequently, expectation usage may be less helpful. In order to better assess this hypothesis, the model should be applied to an actual advisory system.

In a tutorial environment the system is trying to teach the user about some domain. In such an environment it is highly likely that other communicative interfaces may also be used, such as multimedia displays by the computer and pointing and clicking commands by users. In contrast to the advisory domain, there should be a tighter coupling between the dialog and the domain material currently under study. There is much work ongoing in the area of multimedia presentations of information (e.g [AHvM93]), but there still needs to be an overall model of the dialog. It is an open question as to whether the dialog model presented in this book can be applied to tutorial dialogs where "utterances" may be either linguistic or non-linguistic. It would seem to be adequate, but again, an actual application of the model to such a system is needed.

10.2   Where Do We Go Next?

As speech recognition technology improves, study of spoken natural language dialog should proceed in both theoretical and empirical directions. These should not be mutually exclusive, but a given endeavor will tend to emphasize one over the other. It is hoped that this book offers a bridge between theory and practice, enabling efforts in both areas to benefit from the other's results. As continuing theoretical advancements are made, there is a need to investigate how these advancements integrate into an overall practical model. The construction and testing of working systems is necessary to uncover the limits of the theories as well as to observe the dynamics of actual human-computer natural language dialog—dynamics that are likely to be different from human-human dialog. Furthermore, testing can provide valuable samples of actual human-computer dialog that can then be used as data in further theoretical studies. The ultimate goal would be testing that does not require an experimenter to remain in the room, but is instead a completely independent dialog between user and machine that can use the full expressive power of natural language to describe the problem situation, detect and resolve misunderstandings, and successfully complete the dialog. A continuing cycle of theoretical study in conjunction with empirical testing that provides the basis for further theoretical study is a promising paradigm for continuing advancement in the development of practical spoken natural language dialog systems.

Appendix A

The Goal and Action Description Language

The Goal and Action Description Language (GADL) is a domain-independent notation for representing the major entities of task processing—goals, actions, and states. A description of the notation is given below.

GADL Notation

Goals

> **goal(Agent,ActionDescription)**—**Agent** wants the action described by **ActionDescription** accomplished

Action Descriptions

> **obs(phys_state(StateDescription,Certainty))**—"sense" a physical state
>
> **ach(phys_state(StateDescription,Certainty))**—manually achieve a physical state
>
> **perf(PrimitiveActionDescription)**—perform a specific physical or sensory action
>
> **learn(KnowledgeDescription)**—learn some item of knowledge

State Descriptions

> **phys_state(StateDescription,Certainty)**—defines a physical state description; **Certainty** gives the level of certainty for which belief about the state's existence is held; **State-Description** provides the description about the state information; the possible forms for this are given below.
>
> (i) prop(Obj,PName,PValue)—qualitative description
>> Obj—describes the portion of the object that has the property. More specifically,
>>
>> if Obj = X(ObjName) then the description is for only part of the object where X tells what part
>>
>> if Obj = ObjName then the description is for the whole object;
>>
>> if ObjName = [Name,Type] then type information is given in Type; else ObjName = Name

PName—property name

PValue—a descriptor that provides property information; PValue may be uninstantiated (i.e. represent an unknown value);

Examples:

prop(switch,position,up)—"the position of the switch is up."

prop(perf(ident(Obj)),action_attribute,doable)— "the primitive action of identifying Obj is doable."

prop(perf(ident(Obj)),action_attribute,done)— "the primitive action of identifying Obj has been done."

prop(top_half(box),color,green)—"the color of the top half of the box is green."

prop(red_lead,att_to,value(obj('-com'),deg(secure)))— "the red_lead is securely attached to the object '-com'."

(ii) meas(Des,Val)—quantitative description

Des—Name(List)

Name—name of measure

List—ordered list of items for which measure is a relation

e.g. voltage—list the two terminals
      distance—list the two objects
      frequency—list the one behavior

Val—the value of the measurement

(iii) behav(Behaviors,Conditions)—conditional property or measure

Behaviors—List of properties and measures that define the conditional property or measure

Conditions—List of properties and measures that must exist when Behaviors are observed (i.e. defining conditions of the event)

Example:

behav(B,C) where B = [phys_state(prop(LED, display,X),true)], and C = [phys_state(prop(switch, position,up),true)]— "the display of the LED is X when the position of the switch is up.".

mental_state(Agent,KnowledgeDescription,Certainty)

Agent—possessor of mental state

KnowledgeDescription—denotes the knowledge to which this mental state refers; has one of the following forms.

ext_know(StateDescription)—denotes extensional knowledge of the physical or mental state given by StateDescription

int_know(phys_state(_,_))—denotes intensional knowledge about a physical state (i.e. knowledge about the defining characteristics)

has_goal(Action)—denotes that a goal of **Agent** is the accomplishment of Action

int_know_action(ActionKnowledge)—denotes intensional knowledge about actions; each possible form of ActionKnowledge represents a type of knowledge; these forms are:

effects_of(Action)—denotes knowledge about the effects of an action on the world state

is_substep_of(ActionChild,ActionParent)—denotes knowledge of the fact that ActionChild is a substep of ActionParent

how_to_do(Action)—denotes knowledge about how to do Action

decomp_of(Action)—denotes knowledge about the decomposition of Action into subactions; closely related to how_to_do

Certainty—gives the level of certainty for which belief about the state's existence is held.

Knowledge Descriptions about Actions

action_decomp(Action,SubActionList)—SubActionList defines the decomposition of **Action** into subactions; it is a list of the action descriptions of the subactions.

action_effects(Action,Agent,EffectList)—EffectList is the list of effects on physical and mental states that result from **Agent** performing **Action**.

Some special comments about GADL follow.

- There has been no attempt to represent more formally the state value definitions (e.g. the object names, property names, property values, etc.). Keywords are currently used for most of these values although more complicated representations could be and are used as needed.

- The notation for primitive action descriptions is not formalized.

- Some of the representations are not currently used in the implemented system. They have been included for the sake of completeness and with the hope of future use.

Appendix B

User's Guide for the Interruptible Prolog SIMulator (IPSIM)

B.1 Introduction

This appendix presents the user's guide for IPSIM, a theorem prover that simulates the methodology of Prolog for proving theorems, but that also allows outside interaction for any of the following purposes: (1) to acquire missing axioms; (2) to alter the proof process; and (3) to inquire about the proof status. The motivation for the development of IPSIM is the development of a natural language dialog system for task-oriented dialogs. Task step completion is viewed as a theorem to be proved. The interactive features allow natural language dialog to be used to facilitate completion of the task (or analogously proof of the theorem). To be able to allow outside interaction requires the ability to interrupt or suspend the proof process. This is done by special markers that indicate the need for axioms that may be acquired by outside interaction (such as dialog) at various points in the proof.

If a program can be run in Prolog, it can also be run using IPSIM. However, IPSIM may place some restrictions on the form of the program written. It is not clear if the operations available with IPSIM allow for more programming power, or if they simply provide a more convenient way for performing operations necessary in an interactive environment where the outside world may require arbitrarily complicated computations. This appendix assumes that the user is familiar with Prolog (see Clocksin and Mellish [CM87]) and the concept of proof trees.

The organization of this appendix is as follows: Section B.2 describes the method for specifying rules and axioms for use by IPSIM; Section B.3 provides information on how to use IPSIM; and Section B.4 tells how the user may replace a default predicate of IPSIM to provide additional semantic capabilities for dynamically producing information when acquiring axioms via outside interaction.

B.2 Specifying Rules and Axioms for IPSIM

Meeting the design goals for IPSIM requires that there be a representation of the rules and axioms in special clauses that IPSIM can access to carry out the proof process. In order to facilitate the usage of IPSIM, a means has been provided whereby the user can describe their rules and axioms using a method that is very similar to a regular Prolog description. The conventions and restrictions of this specification method are described in this section.

B.2.1 Sample Specification and Description

A partial Prolog specification of a theorem:

```
start :- talk('is the light on').

talk('is the light on') :-
  axiom_need('is the light on',[yes,no,'where is the light']),
  thm_branch('is the light on').
talk('is the light on') :- talk('is the light on').

thm_branch('is the light on') :- know(yes),talk('thank you').
thm_branch('is the light on') :- know(no),talk('turn it on').
thm_branch('is the light on') :-
  know('where is the light'), talk('below the switch').
```

could be described to IPSIM as:

```
begin_rule(start).
start :- talk('is the light on').

begin_rule(talk('is the light on')).
talk('is the light on') :-
  axiom_need('is the light on',[yes,no,'where is the light']),
  thm_branch('is the light on').
talk('is the light on') :- talk('is the light on').


begin_rule(thm_branch('is the light on')).
thm_branch('is the light on') :- know(yes),talk('thank you').
thm_branch('is the light on') :- know(no),talk('turn it on').
thm_branch('is the light on') :-
  know('where is the light'), talk('below the switch').
```

Thus, the only major addition to a regular Prolog specification are the
begin_rule clauses. A set of Prolog predicate descriptions with a common
left hand side (**Consequent**) should be preceded by a clause of the form **begin_rule(ConsequentTemplate)** where **ConsequentTemplate** is a most
general unifier for the set of descriptions. The purpose of the **begin_rule**
clause is to allow IPSIM to determine if a specification for the proof of a given
predicate has been provided, and if it has, to delimit the set of clauses that
may be used to prove the predicate.

B.2.2 Additional Requirements for the Specification

1. Disjunctions must be represented in separate predicates (i.e. no
   use of ';' allowed). If it is desired that disjunction be represented

in one predicate, then all the predicates involved must be defined directly in Prolog (see step 5 below).

2. The ordering for the predicates should be the same as they would be in a Prolog specification.

3. Cuts may be specified by inserting **cut** as a part of the antecedent at the point where the cut is to occur. For example,

```
can_assist_with(fix_circuit) :-
   learn_circ_num(CircNum), !,
   has_knowledge_of(circuit(CircNum)).
```

would be specified as:

```
can_assist_with(fix_circuit) :-
   learn_circ_num(CircNum), cut,
   has_knowledge_of(circuit(CircNum)).
```

4. The user should not name any predicates **root** or **null**. **root** is used as the global root of proof trees, and **null** represents its pseudo-parent.

5. For the sake of efficiency, a user may define some rules and axioms directly in Prolog subject to the following restriction: When backtracking occurs, these rules and axioms cannot be resatisfied by IPSIM because IPSIM uses its special clauses to determine the status of the proof for each rule. If these are not available, IPSIM cannot attempt to resatisfy the rule, and backtracking will pass over the rule. This restriction also applies to any routines already defined by the Prolog system that the user may wish to use. The only exception is **repeat**. IPSIM will properly handle resatisfaction of **repeat**. Prolog-defined rules and axioms may be used in IPSIM-defined rules by simply specifying them as part of the antecedent of the appropriate clause as would be done for a regular IPSIM-specified rule. *A rule cannot be defined partially for IPSIM and partially in regular Prolog.*

6. Also for the sake of efficiency when uninstantiating variables during backtracking, the specification is restricted as follows. Within a set of antecedent clauses, it is assumed that if a variable is instantiated, it was instantiated by the consequent or by the first clause in the antecedent where the variable appeared. Thus, in the following specification,

```
fact(X,Y,Z) :- learn(X),son(X,Y),is_true(Y,Z).
```

assuming that everything was uninstantiated when fact(X,Y,Z) was called, then it is assumed that X was instantiated in learn and Y was instantiated in son. Any specification that violates this restriction may not work properly on backtracking. However, it is believed that any specification that violates this restriction can be rewritten such that it does not violate this restriction.

7. One of the key goals in the design of IPSIM is to be able to suspend the proof process to engage in outside interaction to obtain a missing axiom. However, there must be a way of distinguishing between this situation and one in which a missing axiom indicates failure in the proof and that backtracking, the normal Prolog response, should be performed. To specify the use of outside interaction requires a special clause, **axiom_need(Description,AxiomList)**, where **Description** should provide information on the missing axiom and **AxiomList** is a list of the expected possible axioms which satisfy the requirements for the missing axiom. This clause should be inserted at the appropriate point in the specification. Note that the **axiom_need** marker may be defined to dynamically produce a list of expected possible axioms instead of just **AxiomList**. This is described in section B.4.

B.2.3 The Special Clauses of IPSIM

As mentioned at the beginning of this section, IPSIM uses special clauses to carry out the proof process. These special clauses are derivable from the specification provided by the user. An IPSIM command is available that converts the specification into these special clauses. It will be described in the next section. The exact format of these clauses is not important to know, for it is not intended that the user should be allowed free access to them, but should only access them via IPSIM commands. However, one feature is important to know. It is that IPSIM assigns a different ID number to each different predicate in a proof tree. This number distinguishes between predicates with the same left hand side. Thus, within the proof tree constructed by IPSIM where each node on the tree corresponds to a predicate to be proven, each node is defined by a **[PredicateName,PredicateNum]** pair, where the **PredicateName** is a description of the left hand side of the predicate, and **PredicateNum** is the corresponding unique ID number that gives the specific predicate. The user may learn the unique ID number of a predicate either by using a dynamic definition of the **axiom_need** marker, (see section B.4), or by using one of the IPSIM commands that accesses the proof tree. In addition, some of the commands of IPSIM use the predicate ID number as an input in order to access a node on the proof tree. If the ID number is left uninstantiated, the search for a node will be based on the **PredicateName** only and the ID number will be instantiated upon successful search of the tree. This predicate ID number is a feature of the special clauses that may be useful to the user in accessing a particular node in the proof tree.

B.3   Using IPSIM

The purpose of IPSIM is to be able to interactively simulate the Prolog theorem proving process. Interactive simulation allows the opportunity to supply new axioms to a proof, alter the proof order, alter the proof status, to suspend and resume proofs, and to even have multiple proofs active simultaneously. This section discusses how to use IPSIM in order to fully utilize its capabilities.

B.3.1   The IPSIM Command Language

Once IPSIM is loaded, the user may use the commands in the IPSIM command language. These commands are in standard Prolog syntax and can be used inside any Prolog program. The commands are divided into two categories (1) initialization commands and (2) operational commands. Once a theorem specification has been loaded and a command for initializing a proof is issued, any of the operational commands may be invoked according to the user's desires and the IPSIM restrictions on commands. Descriptions of the commands are given in the following few pages.

Initialization Commands

> **load_theorems(InputFile,_)** where **InputFile** is the name of a file containing the specification of a set of theorems to be transformed into the special clauses needed by IPSIM. This command takes the file as input and converts the theorem specifications to the required special clauses and loads them. The second argument is currently unused and should be specified by the anonymous variable as shown.

> **remove_theorems** removes all theorem information. After this command is issued, another **load_theorems** command is required before IPSIM can be used in theorem proving.

The remaining initialization commands are used for initializing or reinitializing proofs. Their general form is:

$$\text{init\_ipsim(OpCode,TopGoal,ProofNum)}$$

where **OpCode** is the code that describes the type of initialization to be performed, **TopGoal** is the name of the theorem to be proven, and **ProofNum** will be the ID number for the proof of **TopGoal**. IPSIM will assign each new proof a unique ID number that is to be used in specifying all other operational commands for this proof. Thus, **ProofNum** would be passed uninstantiated when an **OpCode** of **start** or **erase_all** is issued and should be supplied when an **OpCode** of **restart** or **erase_one** is used. Each of these commands is described below.

- **init_ipsim(start,TopGoal,ProofNum)** initializes a new proof with **TopGoal** as the theorem to be proven. **ProofNum** will be instantiated to the ID number for the proof. This ID number must be used in all other commands to specify this particular proof.

- **init_ipsim(erase_all,TopGoal,ProofNum)** causes all proofs to be deleted and initializes a new proof with **TopGoal** as the theorem to be proven. **ProofNum** will be instantiated to the ID number for the new proof.

- **init_ipsim(restart,TopGoal,ProofNum)** causes the proof with ID number **ProofNum** to be reinitialized with **TopGoal** as the theorem to be proven. All other proofs are left unchanged.

- **init_ipsim(erase_one,_,ProofNum)** causes the proof with ID number, **ProofNum** to be deleted.

- **init_ipsim(proof_duplicate,[ProofNum,PredicateName,PredicateNum], NewProofNum)** causes the proof with ID number, **ProofNum** to be duplicated, making the node [**PredicateName,PredicateNum**] the current subtheorem to be proven with its **axiom_need** marker the next child to be proven. **NewProofNum** will be the ID number of the duplicated theorem. In the duplication process, all nodes to the left of the special node (**PredicateName**) will be copied as they were in the original proof. All of the direct ancestors of the special node will be instantiated according to the values in the subtrees to the left of their link to the special node. All subtrees to the right will not be duplicated with any instantiations that occurred in **ProofNum**. **NewProofNum** will be set equal to *error* if the operation is unsuccessful.

Operational Commands

The general form of operational commands is:

call_ipsim(ProofNum,OpCode,Input,Message,ExtraOutput)

where **ProofNum** is the ID number for the proof, **OpCode** is the code that describes the type of operation IPSIM is to perform, **Input** is any additional input the user must provide IPSIM in order for IPSIM to perform the operation, **Message** is the output IPSIM returns to the user that describes the result of the operation, and **ExtraOutput** will be an additional output provided in certain situations described below. The possible values for OpCode are: **next_goal**, **try_other**, **fail_rule**, **input**, **set_id**, **get_id**, **add_child**, **skip**, **get_parent**, **get_root**, and **get_children**. These commands are divided into two types: (1) process commands that control the proof flow, and (2) structural commands that either access or alter the proof structure. The effects of each command are described below. When one of the arguments to **call_ipsim** is not needed, the argument will be specified by the anonymous variable. First are described the process commands.

call_ipsim(ProofNum,next_goal,_,Message,ExtraOutput) causes IPSIM to continue (or start after an initialization command) the proving process for the theorem with ID **ProofNum** (set in an initialization command). IPSIM will return *halt* in **Message** if it successfully proves the theorem, and it will return the fully instantiated description of **TopGoal** based on the completed proof in **ExtraOutput**. It will return *fail* in **Message** if it cannot prove the theorem. Otherwise, it will suspend processing when it reaches a step in the proof where there is a missing axiom that may be obtainable from outside interaction. Such a step is marked by a clause of the form **axiom_need(Message,ExtraOutput)** as described in item 7 in section B.2.2. Either **AxiomList** or some dynamically computed list of expected possible axioms will be returned in **ExtraOutput**. The step in the proof at which IPSIM suspends operation may be a step in proving **TopGoal** or some descendant of it. Note that it is possible for the user to define other possible values for **Message** if the user creates a procedural definition of **axiom_need** instead of merely using the declarative marker approach provided as a default in IPSIM. See section B.4 for more details.

call_ipsim(ProofNum,try_other,_,Message,ExtraOutput) causes IPSIM to continue the proving process by trying to find another way to prove the current node where the current node is the predicate which IPSIM was trying to prove when it was suspended because of a missing axiom. This current node may be **TopGoal** from the initialization command or it may be a child of **TopGoal** or some other descendant. This command should be invoked only after issuing an **input** command. **Message** and **ExtraOutput** will return the same values as in the **next_goal** command.

call_ipsim(ProofNum,fail_rule,_,Message,ExtraOutput) causes IPSIM to continue the proving process by failing the current node and initiating backtracking in the parent of the current node (i.e. the consequent of the rule for which the current node is a part of the antecedent). Current node is the same as defined above. **Message** and **ExtraOutput** are also the same as defined above.

call_ipsim(ProofNum,input,Input,Message,_) determines if the input, specified in **Input** and assumed to be a description of a missing axiom, is one of the expected possible axioms for the missing axiom which originally caused suspension of IPSIM. IPSIM will return *expected_axiom* in **Message** if the input was one of the expected possible axioms. In addition, unification between the input, the expected possible axiom with which the input unifies, and the description of the missing axiom specified in the **axiom_need** clause will occur, and it will mark this **axiom_need** clause as having succeeded. If the input was not one of the expected possible axioms, it will return *not_expected* in **Message**, and the **axiom_need** clause will not have succeeded yet. This operation uses the **axiom_need** clause of the current rule, and assumes that it is the next child of this rule.

To illustrate the different effects of **next_goal**, **try_other**, **fail_rule**, and **input** consider the following example (definitions of c, d, e, and f omitted):

```
a(X) :- b(X), c(X).              /* clause 1 */
a(X) :- f(X).                    /* clause 2 */
b(X) :- axiom_need(X,Y), d(X).   /* clause 3 */
b(X) :- e(X).                    /* clause 4 */
```

Suppose **init_ipsim(start,a(X),ProofNum)** had been issued and then a **next_goal** command issued. IPSIM would first try to prove a(X) by proving clause 1. This would cause an attempt to prove b(X) by proving clause 3, just as Prolog would attempt the proof. axiom_need(X,Y) denotes a point where there is a missing axiom, so IPSIM would be suspended with the current node being b(X). If, after receiving the input and issuing the **input** command a **try_other** command was issued, IPSIM would resume the proof by trying to prove clause 4 instead (i.e. it would try to find another way to prove the current node b(X)). If instead, a **fail_rule** command was given, IPSIM would resume the proof by trying to prove clause 2 instead (i.e. it would fail b(X) and initiate backtracking in clause 1; since there is no left sibling of b(X) in clause 1, IPSIM would then look for an alternative method for proving a(x) – clause 2). If a **next_goal** command was given, the result would depend on whether or not the input had been one of the expected possible axioms. If it was, then axiom_need(X,Y) succeeded, and IPSIM would resume the proof with d(X). Otherwise, it would again suspend itself on axiom_need(X,Y).

Next, the structural commands are described.

call_ipsim(ProofNum,set_id,_,_,_) sets the value for "current proof ID" to ProofNum. This value is retrievable via the **get_id** command.

call_ipsim(ProofNum,get_id,_,Message,_) gets the value for "current proof ID" and returns it in ProofNum. This command should not be issued until after a **set_id** command has initialized a value for "current proof ID." **Message** will be set equal to *error* if this value is undefined. These two commands may be useful when the user has active multiple proofs, each of which may use different sets of axioms. They allow the user to keep track of the ID number for each proof. A further discussion on the use of knowledge is given in section B.3.2.

call_ipsim(ProofNum,add_child,Input,Message,_) where **Input** is of the form **[PredicateName,PredicateNum,Child]**, where **PredicateName** and **PredicateNum** specify a node on the proof tree as described in section B.2.3, causes IPSIM to add **Child** to the antecedent list of the specified node in the proof tree as the next predicate to be proven. In addition, this node is made the current node to be proven. This allows the user to dynamically modify the proof structure. *ok* will be returned in Message if the command succeeds; otherwise, *error* is returned. *error* will be returned if **[PredicateName,PredicateNum]** is not a node in the proof tree.

call_ipsim(ProofNum,skip,Input,Message,_) also causes IPSIM to modify the proof structure. **Input** should be of the form **[PredicateName,PredicateNum]** where **PredicateName** and **PredicateNum** are defined as above. The command makes **Input** the current node to be proven and skips over unproven children of **Input** (i.e moves them from the list of children to be proven to the list of children already proven) so that the **axiom_need** marker, which is a child of this rule, is the next child to be proven. *ok* is returned in **Message** if the command succeeds. Otherwise, *error* is returned. *error* will be returned if the input node is not in the proof tree or if it does not have an **axiom_need** marker.

call_ipsim(ProofNum,get_parent,Input,Message,_) where **Input** is of the form **[PredicateName,PredicateNum]** as above causes IPSIM to return in **Message** the name of this node's parent in the proof tree, **[ParentName,ParentNum]**. *error* will be returned in **Message** if the input node is not in the proof tree.

call_ipsim(ProofNum,get_root,_,Message,_) returns in **Message** the root of the proof tree associated with ID **ProofNum**. This value will be the corresponding value of **TopGoal** from the associated **init_ipsim** command that initialized theorem **ProofNum**.

call_ipsim(ProofNum,get_children,Input,Message,_) where **Input** is of the form **[PredicateName,PredicateNum]** as above causes IPSIM to return in **Message** a list of the children of this node in the proof tree. The form of this list is **[Done,ToDo]** where **Done** is the list of children already proven and **ToDo** is the list of children to be proven. *error* will be returned in **Message** if the input node is not in the proof tree.

B.3.2   The Use of Knowledge

IPSIM is a theorem prover, and theorem proving uses axioms. Knowledge acquired during the course of processing may be usable as axioms that can be used in the proofs of IPSIM. However, some of this knowledge may only be relevant to a specific proof, while other knowledge may be relevant to all proofs. To distinguish the two cases, the user may elect to associate a proof number with each item of knowledge acquired in order to specify when the knowledge is relevant. Because different executions may result in the system assigning different ID numbers to the same proof, the **set_id** and **get_id** commands may be useful in keeping track of the ID number of a particular proof at different times in order to associate a knowledge item with the corresponding proof.

B.3.3   A Sample Control Scheme

Figure B.1 illustrates a simple Prolog program that uses IPSIM for interactive theorem-proving. This simple example does not take advantage of many of the available commands of IPSIM for altering the proof flow and/or proof structure in different ways. These commands may facilitate the ability to perform general natural language dialog complete with interrupts and dynamically created and deleted subgoals. In this simple example no altering of proof structure is performed, and the proof flow follows that of regular Prolog. The backtracking scheme of **try_other** just tries to find another way to prove the same theorem. It does not jump back to the parent of the current node immediately as a **fail_rule** command would.

B.4   Creating Dynamic Lists of Missing Axioms

The declarative **axiom_need** marker allows only for static definition of missing axioms and expected possible axioms. A procedural definition is needed to use dynamic aspects of the domain. How can this be defined to be used with IPSIM? This section provides some answers.

B.4.1   The Defaults

For the user who does not need dynamic computation for **axiom_need** markers, use the following default definition:

```
axiom_need(_,_,_,Message,Expectation,Message,Expectation).
```

If the user does not wish to use this definition, then the user must provide appropriate definitions in another file and load that file when using IPSIM.

B.4.2   Redefining axiom_need

To redefine **axiom_need** requires replacing the default predicate with one's own predicate or predicates. For a marker of the form

$$\text{axiom\_need(Description, AxiomList)}$$

```
/*  Sample controller */

/* load IPSIM code and defaults */
:- consult('thm-prover/IPSIM').
:- consult('thm-prover/DEFAULTS').

run_program(InputFile,GoalTheorem) :-
  load_theorems(InputFile,_),   /* map spec. to IPSIM clauses. */
  init_ipsim(start,GoalTheorem,ProofNum), /* initialize proof */
  proving_loop(ProofNum,next_goal,GoalTheorem).

proving_loop(ProofNum,OpCode,GoalTheorem) :-
  call_ipsim(ProofNum,OpCode,_,Message,ExtraOutput),
  (
   ( Message = halt,           /* proved theorem */
     ExtraOutput=GoalTheorem
   )
   ;
   ( Message = fail )          /* proof failed */
   ;

/* otherwise, received a description of a needed axiom.  Engage
   in dialog to receive.  */

   ( do_output(Message),               /* NL Generation */
     receive_input(Input),             /* NL Understanding */
     call_ipsim(ProofNum,input,Input,Result,_), /* check input */
     (
      ( Result = expected_axiom,       /* got needed axiom */
        processing_loop(ProofNum,next_goal,Theorem)
      )
      ;
      ( Result = not_expected,         /* got different axiom */
        processing_loop(ProofNum,try_other,Theorem)
      )
     )
   )
  )
 ).
```

Figure B.1: Simple Example of Interactive Theorem-Proving in IPSIM

the predicate defined should be in the following form:

axiom_need(ProofNum,PredicateName,PredicateNum,Description,
AxiomList,Message,Expectation)

where **PredicateName** and **PredicateNum** provide the description of the
node in the proof tree that represents the current node and is where the missing
axiom has been detected. **Message** will unify with the **Message** argument
of the **call_ipsim** command that led to this **axiom_need** call, and **Expectation** will be unified with the **ExtraOutput** argument of the **call_ipsim**
command. The default predicate simply returns the two arguments from the
axiom_need marker back to the user in **Message** and **ExtraOutput**, respectively, without computing anything. However, the usage of a predicate
allows the user to define one's own predicates for dynamically computing the
message and expectation as desired.

B.5   Using IPSIM Calls within Theorem Specifications

It is possible to define calls to IPSIM within theorem specifications used by
IPSIM, but this should be done only under very controlled circumstances. The
most likely circumstance is when proof dependent knowledge is being maintained, and some of the theorems require the altering of knowledge structures.
In such a case, the **get_id** operation can be used to obtain the proof ID. Regardless, the only IPSIM calls that should be used are the structural commands
where knowledge about the structure is changed, but no altering of the structure occurs. This includes **get_id**, **get_parent**, **get_root**, and **get_children**.
Attempting to use the other commands will involve "self-modifying" theorems,
and the results are undefined.

Appendix C

Obtaining the System Software Via Anonymous FTP

To obtain the software for the spoken natural language dialog system described in this book, carry out the following steps.

1. Make your current directory on your machine the one which will be the root directory of the system software

2. Ftp to the host machine duke.cs.duke.edu

3. Use anonymous as your login name with your email address as password

4. cd to pub/rws/system.

5. set the transfer mode to binary

6. get the file dlgsys.sh.Z

7. Uncompress dlgsys.sh.Z with the UNIX uncompress program

8. Extract the files from dlgsys.sh via the command `/bin/sh dlgsys.sh`

9. Setup the files into the correct directories via the command `/bin/sh setup.sh`

To run the software requires Quintus Prolog (current version 3.1.4) and the gcc compiler for C (current version 2.5.2). There is a hierarchical structure to the system files. Detailed information is presented in the README file that should be in the root directory of the system software. In addition, transcripts of the 141 experimental dialogs are available from the subdirectory pub/rws/stats. There are a total of 16 files of transcripts, one per subject per session. The naming convention is subXsesY.dat where X is the subject number and Y is the session number. Thus, the transcript for session 3 with subject 5 is named sub5ses3.dat. These files are also in compressed form. In addition, there is a small file called transcript.format that describes the format of the lines contained in the transcript file. A sample interaction for obtaining the system software is given on the next page ("sysprompt%" represents your system's machine prompt):

```
sysprompt% ftp duke.cs.duke.edu
Connected to duke.cs.duke.edu.
220 duke FTP server (SunOS 4.1) ready.
Name (duke.cs.duke.edu:rws): anonymous
331 Guest login ok, send ident as password.
Password:
230 Guest login ok, access restrictions apply.
ftp> cd pub/rws/system
250 CWD command successful.
ftp> binary
200 Type set to I.
ftp> get dlgsys.sh.Z
200 PORT command successful.
150 Binary data connection for dlgsys.sh.Z (150.216.1.237,1466)
    (367119 bytes).
226 Binary Transfer complete.
local: dlgsys.sh.Z remote: dlgsys.sh.Z
367119 bytes received in 29 seconds (12 Kbytes/s)
ftp> quit
221 Goodbye.
sysprompt% uncompress dlgsys.sh
sysprompt% /bin/sh dlgsys.sh
extracting README
 .
 . (a listing of all files extracted from the archive will be)
 . (printed, one file per line)
 .
extracting sysarchive.sh
sysprompt% /bin/sh setup.sh
    ( shellscript will run silently except when the gcc
      compiler builds the parser and when prolog runs
      to translate some notation files into syntactically
      legal Prolog )
```

Questions, comments or problems can be addressed via Internet email to
rws@cs.duke.edu or masmith@ecuvax.cis.ecu.edu.

Bibliography

[Adv93]   Advanced Research Projects Agency. *ARPA Human Language Technology Workshop*. Morgan Kaufmann Publishers, Inc., 1993.

[AFL82]   J.F. Allen, A.M. Frisch, and D.J. Litman. ARGOT: The Rochester dialogue system. In *Proceedings of the 2nd National Conference on Artificial Intelligence*, pages 66–70, 1982.

[AGH+89]   J. Allen, S. Guez, L. Hoebel, E. Hinkelman, K. Jackson, A. Kyburg, and D. Traum. The discourse system project. Technical Report 317, University of Rochester, November 1989.

[AHvM93]   Y. Arens, E. Hovy, and S. van Mulken. Structure and rules in automated multimedia presentation planning. In *Proceedings, Thirteenth International Joint Conference on Artificial Intelligence*, pages 1253–1259, 1993.

[All83]   J.F. Allen. Recognizing intentions from natural language utterances. In M. Brady and R.C. Berwick, editors, *Computational Models of Discourse*, pages 107–166. MIT Press, Cambridge, Mass., 1983.

[All87]   J.F. Allen. *Natural Language Understanding*. The Benjamin/Cummings Publishing Company, Inc., Menlo Park, California, 1987.

[AP72]   A.V. Aho and T.G. Peterson. A minimum distance error-correcting parser for context-free languages. *SIAM Journal on Computation*, 1(4):305–312, 1972.

[AP80]   J.F. Allen and C.R. Perrault. Analyzing intention in utterances. *Artificial Intelligence*, 15(3):143–178, 1980.

[AU69]   A.V. Aho and J.D. Ullman. Properties of syntax directed translations. *Journal of Computer and System Sciences*, 3(3):319–334, 1969.

[Aus62]   J.L. Austin. *How to Do Things with Words*. Harvard University Press, Cambridge, Mass., 2nd edition, 1962. Edited by J.O. Urmson and M. Sabisà.

[BBS83]   A.W. Biermann, B.W. Ballard, and A.H. Sigmon. An experimental study of natural language programming. *Intl. J. Man-Machine Studies*, 18:71–87, 1983.

[BD89]   M. Boddy and T. Dean. Solving time-dependent planning problems. In *Proceedings, Eleventh International Joint Conference on Artificial Intelligence*, pages 979–984, 1989.

[Bil91]   E. Bilange. A task independent oral dialogue model. In *Proceedings of the Fifth Conference of the European Chapter of the Association for Computational Linguistics*, pages 83–88, 1991.

[BKK+77]   D.G. Bobrow, R.M. Kaplan, M. Kay, D.A. Norman, H. Thompson, and T. Winograd. GUS, a frame driven dialog system. *Artificial Intelligence*, 8:155–173, 1977.

[BKKS85]   L. Bolc, A. Kowalski, M. Kozlowski, and T. Strzalkowski. A natural language information retrieval system with extensions towards fuzzy reasoning. *Intl. J. Man-Machine Studies*, pages 335–367, October 1985.

[Car88]   S. Carberry. Modeling the user's plans and goals. *Computational Linguistics*, 14(3):23–37, 1988.

[Car90]   S. Carberry. *Plan Recognition in Natural Language Dialogue*. MIT Press, Cambridge, Mass., 1990.

[Caw92]   A. Cawsey. *Explanation and Interaction: The Computer Generation of Explanatory Dialogues*. MIT Press, Cambridge, Mass., 1992.

[CBM83]   J.G. Carbonell, W.M. Boggs, and M.L. Mauldin. The XCALIBUR PROJECT: A natural language interface to expert systems. In *Proceedings of the 8th International Joint Conference on Artificial Intelligence*, pages 653–656, 1983.

[Chi89]   D.N. Chin. KNOME: Modeling what the user knows in UC. In A. Kobsa and W. Wahlster, editors, *User Models in Dialog Systems*, pages 74–107. Springer-Verlag, New York, 1989.

[CJ89]   R. Cohen and M. Jones. Incorporating user models into expert systems for educational diagnosis. In A. Kobsa and W. Wahlster, editors, *User Models in Dialog Systems*, pages 313–333. Springer-Verlag, New York, 1989.

[CL90]   P.R. Cohen and H.J. Levesque. Rational interaction as the basis for communication. In P.R. Cohen, J. Morgan, and M.E. Pollack, editors, *Intentions in Communication*, pages 221–255. MIT Press, Cambridge, Mass., 1990.

[Cla79]   W.J. Clancey. Dialogue management for rule-based tutorials. In *Proceedings of the 6th International Joint Conference on Artificial Intelligence*, pages 155–161, 1979.

[CM87]   W.F. Clocksin and C.H. Mellish. *Programming in Prolog.*
            Springer-Verlag, Berlin, third edition, 1987.

[CMP90]   P.R. Cohen, J. Morgan, and M.E. Pollack, editors. *Intentions in
            Communication.* MIT Press, Cambridge, Mass., 1990.

[CP79]   P.R. Cohen and C.R. Perrault. Elements of a plan-based theory
            of speech acts. *Cognitive Science*, 3(3):177–212, 1979.

[CP88]   N. Carbonell and J.M. Pierrel. Task-oriented dialogue process-
            ing in human-computer voice communication. In H. Niemann,
            M. Lang, and G. Sagerer, editors, *Recent Advances in Speech Un-
            derstanding and Dialog Systems*, pages 491–496. Springer-Verlag,
            New York, 1988.

[CR89]   Y. Chow and S. Roukos. Speech understanding using a unification
            grammar. In *ICASSP-89*, pages 727–730, 1989.

[CWG90]   H.H. Clark and D. Wilkes-Gibbs. Referring as a collaborative
            process. In P.R. Cohen, J. Morgan, and M.E. Pollack, editors,
            Intentions in Communication, pages 463–493. MIT Press, Cam-
            bridge, Mass., 1990.

[Dam81]   F.J. Damerau. Operating statistics for the transformational ques-
            tion answering system. *Computational Linguistics*, 7(1):30–42,
            1981.

[DGA⁺93]   J. Dowding, J.M. Gawron, D. Appelt, J. Bear, L. Cherny,
            R. Moore, and D. Moran. Gemini: A natural language system for
            spoken-language understanding. In *Proceedings of the 31st An-
            nual Meeting of the Association for Computational Linguistics*,
            pages 54–61, 1993.

[EHRLR80]   L.D. Erman, F. Hayes-Roth, V.R. Lesser, and D.R. Reddy. The
            Hearsay-II speech-understanding system: Integrating knowledge
            to resolve uncertainty. *ACM Computing Surveys*, pages 213–253,
            June 1980.

[EM81]   C.M. Eastman and D.S. McLean. On the need for parsing ill-
            formed input. *American Journal of Computational Linguistics*,
            7(4):257, 1981.

[FB86]   P.E. Fink and A.W. Biermann. The correction of ill-formed in-
            put using history-based expectation with applications to speech
            understanding. *Computational Linguistics*, 12(1):13–36, 1986.

[Fin83]   L. Fineman. Questioning the need for parsing ill-formed inputs.
            American Journal of Computational Linguistics, 9(1):22, 1983.

[Fin89]   T.W. Finin. GUMS: A general user modeling shell. In A. Kobsa
             and W. Wahlster, editors, *User Models in Dialog Systems*, pages
             411–430. Springer-Verlag, New York, 1989.

[Fre88]   R.E. Frederking. *Integrated Natural Language Dialogue: A Com-
             putational Model.* Kluwer Academic Publishers, Boston, 1988.

[GAMP87]   B.J. Grosz, D.E. Appelt, P.A. Martin, and F.C.N. Pereira.
             TEAM: An experiment in the design of transportable natural-
             language interfaces. *Artificial Intelligence*, 32:173–243, 1987.

[GH89]   M. Gerlach and H. Horacek. Dialog control in a natural language
             system. In *Proceedings of the Fourth Conference of the European
             Chapter of the Association for Computational Linguistics*, pages
             27–34, 1989.

[Gri75]   H.P. Grice. Logic and conversation. In P. Cole and J.L. Morgan,
             editors, *Syntax and Semantics, Vol. 3: Speech Acts*, pages 41–58.
             Academic Press, New York, 1975.

[Gro78]   B.J. Grosz. Discourse analysis. In D.E. Walker, editor, *Under-
             standing Spoken Language*, pages 235–268. North-Holland, New
             York, 1978.

[Gro81]   B.J. Grosz. Focusing and description in natural language dia-
             logues. In A. Joshi, B. Webber, and I. Sag, editors, *Elements of
             Discourse Understanding*, pages 84–105. Cambridge University
             Press, New York, 1981.

[GS86]   B.J. Grosz and C.L. Sidner. Attentions, intentions, and the
             structure of discourse. *Computational Linguistics*, 12(3):175–204,
             1986.

[GS90]   B.J. Grosz and C.L. Sidner. Plans for discourse. In P. R. Cohen,
             J. Morgan, and M.E. Pollack, editors, *Intentions in Communica-
             tion*, pages 417–444. MIT Press, Cambridge, Mass., 1990.

[Gui93]   C.I. Guinn. A computational model of dialogue initiative in
             collaborative discourse. In *Proceedings of the Fall 1993 AAAI
             Fall Symposium on Human-Computer Collaboration: Reconciling
             Theory, Synthesizing Practice*, 1993.

[HCM+83]   W. Hoeppner, T. Christaller, H. Marburger, K. Morik, B. Nebel,
             M. O'Leary, and W. Wahlster. Beyond domain-independence:
             Experience with the development of a German language access
             system to highly diverse background systems. In *Proceedings of
             the 8th International Joint Conference on Artificial Intelligence*,
             pages 588–594, 1983.

[HG85]   C.D. Hafner and K. Godden. Portability of syntax and semantics in Datalog. *ACM Transactions on Office Information Systems*, pages 141–164, April 1985.

[HHCT86]   P.J. Hayes, A.G. Hauptmann, J.G. Carbonell, and M. Tomita. Parsing spoken language: A semantic caseframe approach. In *COLING-86: Proceedings of the 11th International Conference on Computational Linguistics*, pages 587–592, Bonn, August 1986.

[HJ79]   J.E. Hopcroft and J.D. Ullman. *Introduction to Automata Theory, Languages, and Computation*. Addison-Wesley Publishing Company, 1979.

[HM81]   P.J. Hayes and G.V. Mourandian. Flexible parsing. *American Journal of Computational Linguistics*, 7(4):232–242, 1981.

[HR83]   P.J. Hayes and D.R. Reddy. Steps toward graceful interaction in spoken and written man-machine communication. *Intl. J. Man-Machine Studies*, 19:231–284, 1983.

[HS91]   D.R. Hipp and R.W. Smith. A demonstration of the "circuit fix-it shoppe". A 12 minute videotape available from Dr. Alan W. Biermann at Duke University, Durham, NC 27708-0129, August 1991.

[HSSS78]   G.G. Hendrix, E.D. Sacerdoti, D. Sagalowicz, and J. Slocum. Developing a natural language interface to complex data. *ACM Transactions on Database Systems*, pages 105–147, June 1978.

[J91]   A. Jönsson. A dialogue manager using initiative-response units and distributed control. In *Proceedings of the Fifth Conference of the European Chapter of the Association for Computational Linguistics*, pages 233–238, 1991.

[JLM90]   F. Jelinek, J. D. Lafferty, and R. L. Mercer. Basic methods of probabilistic context free grammars. In P. Laface and R. De-Mori, editors, *Speech Recognition and Understanding—Recent Advances, Trends and Applications*. Springer-Verlag, Berlin, 1990.

[JM89]   C. Jullien and J. Marty. Plan revision in person-machine dialogue. In *Proceedings of the Fourth Conference of the European Chapter of the Association for Computational Linguistics*, pages 153–160, 1989.

[Kap82]   S.J. Kaplan. Cooperative responses from a portable natural language query system. *Artificial Intelligence*, 19(2):165–187, 1982.

[KF87]   R. Kass and T. Finin. Rules for the implicit acquisition of knowl-
          edge about the user. In *Proceedings of the Sixth National Con-
          ference on Artificial Intelligence*, pages 295–300, 1987.

[KF88]   R. Kass and T. Finin. Modeling the user in natural language
          systems. *Computational Linguistics*, 14(3):5–22, 1988.

[Kor87]   R.E. Korf. Planning as search: A quantitative approach. *Artificial
          Intelligence*, 33:65–88, September 1987.

[KVED91] H. Kitano and C. Van Ess-Dykema. Toward a plan-based un-
          derstanding model for mixed-initiative dialogues. In *Proceedings
          of the 29th Annual Meeting of the Association for Computational
          Linguistics*, pages 25–32, 1991.

[KW88]   A. Kobsa and W. Wahlster, editors. *Special Issue on User Mod-
          eling*. MIT Press, Cambridge, Mass., September 1988. A special
          issue of *Computational Linguistics*.

[KW89]   A. Kobsa and W. Wahlster, editors. *User Models in Dialog Sys-
          tems*. Springer-Verlag, New York, 1989.

[LA87]   D.J. Litman and J.F. Allen. A plan recognition model for subdi-
          alogues in conversations. *Cognitive Science*, 11(2):163–200, 1987.

[LA90]   D.J. Litman and J.F. Allen. Discourse processing and common-
          sense plans. In P.R. Cohen, J. Morgan, and M.E. Pollack, editors,
          Intentions in Communication, pages 365–388. MIT Press, Cam-
          bridge, Mass., 1990.

[LC89]   J.F. Lehman and J.G. Carbonell. Learning the user's language:
          A step towards automated creation of user models. In A. Kobsa
          and W. Wahlster, editors, *User Models in Dialog Systems*, pages
          163–194. Springer-Verlag, New York, 1989.

[LC91]   L. Lambert and S. Carberry. A tripartite plan-based model of
          dialogue. In *Proceedings of the 29th Annual Meeting of the Asso-
          ciation for Computational Linguistics*, pages 47–54, 1991.

[LC92]   L. Lambert and S. Carberry. Modeling negotiation subdialogues.
          In *Proceedings of the 30th Annual Meeting of the Association for
          Computational Linguistics*, pages 193–200, 1992.

[Leh92]   J.F. Lehman. *Adaptive Parsing: Self-Extending Natural Language
          Interfaces*. Kluwer Academic Publishers, Boston, 1992.

[Lev85]   S.E. Levinson. Structural methods in automatic speech recogni-
          tion. *Proceeding of the IEEE*, 73(11):1625–1650, 1985.

[Lev90]   J.M. Levine. PRAGMA—a flexible bidirectional dialogue system. In *Proceedings of the 8th National Conference on Artificial Intelligence*, pages 964–969, 1990.

[LGK+90]   D.B. Lenat, R.V. Guha, K. Pittman, D. Pratt, and M. Shepherd. CYC: Toward programs with common sense. *Communications of the ACM*, pages 30–49, August 1990.

[LHR90]   K.F. Lee, H.W. Hon, and R. Reddy. An overview of the SPHINX speech recognition system. In A. Waibel and K.F. Lee, editors, *Readings in Speech Recognition*, pages 600–610. Morgan Kaufman, San Mateo, CA, 1990.

[LM81]   R.J. Larsen and M.L. Marx. *An Introduction to Mathematical Statistics and Its Applications*. Prentice Hall, Inc., Englewood Cliffs, New Jersey, 1981.

[Loc91]   K.E. Lochbaum. An algorithm for plan recognition in collaborative discourse. In *Proceedings of the 29th Annual Meeting of the Association for Computational Linguistics*, pages 33–38, 1991.

[LS68]   P.M. Lewis II and R.E. Stearns. Syntax directed transduction. *Journal of the Association for Computing Machinery*, 15(3):465–488, 1968.

[Lyo74]   G. Lyon. Syntax-directed least errors analysis for context-free languages. *Communications of the ACM*, 17(1):3–14, 1974.

[McC87]   M. McCord. Natural language processing in prolog. In A. Walker, editor, *Knowledge Systems and Prolog*. Addison Wesley, Reading, Mass., 1987.

[McC88]   K.F. McCoy. Reasoning on a highlighted user model to respond to misconceptions. *Computational Linguistics*, 14(3):52–63, 1988.

[McK85]   K.R. McKeown. *Text Generation*. Cambridge University Press, New York, 1985.

[MH93]   S. McRoy and G. Hirst. Abductive explanation of dialog misunderstandings. In *Proceedings of the Sixth Conference of the European Chapter of the Association for Computational Linguistics*, pages 277–286, 1993.

[MHK78]   H.G. Miller, R.L. Hershman, and R.J. Kelly. Performance of a natural language query system in a simulated command control environment. Technical Report NOSC ACCAT, United States Navy, 1978.

[Moo88]   T.S. Moody. *The Effects of Restricted Vocabulary Size on Voice Interactive Discourse Structure.* PhD thesis, North Carolina State University, 1988.

[Mor89]   K. Morik. User models and conversational settings: Modeling the user's wants. In A. Kobsa and W. Wahlster, editors, *User Models in Dialog Systems*, pages 364–385. Springer-Verlag, New York, 1989.

[MP88]   J. Mudler and E. Paulus. Expectation-based speech recognition. In H. Niemann, M. Lang, and G. Sagerer, editors, *Recent Advances in Speech Understanding and Dialog Systems*, pages 473–477. Springer-Verlag, New York, 1988.

[MP93]   J.D. Moore and C.L. Paris. Planning text for advisory dialogues: Capturing intentional and rhetorical information. *Computational Linguistics*, 19(4):651–694, 1993.

[MS88]   M. Moens and M. Steedman. Temporal ontology and temporal reference. *Computational Linguistics*, 14(2):15–28, 1988.

[MTT88]   C.A. McCann, M.N. Taylor, and M.I. Tuori. ISIS: The interactive spatial information system. *Intl. J. Man-Machine Studies*, 28:101–138, 1988.

[Nag93]   K. Nagao. Abduction and dynamic preference in plan-based dialogue understanding. In *Proceedings, Thirteenth International Joint Conference on Artificial Intelligence*, pages 1186–1192, 1993.

[Ney91]   H. Ney. Dynamic programming parsing for context-free grammars in continuous speech recognition. *IEEE Transactions on Signal Processing*, 39(2):336–340, 1991.

[Nie90]   J. Nielsen. Traditional dialogue design applied to modern user interfaces. *Communications of the ACM*, pages 109–118, October 1990.

[Nil80]   N.J. Nilsson. *Principles of Artificial Intelligence.* Tioga Publishing Co., Palo Alto, CA, 1980.

[OC74]   R.B. Ochsman and A. Chapanis. The effects of 10 communication modes on the behavior of teams during co-operative problem-solving. *Intl. J. Man-Machine Studies*, 6:579–619, 1974.

[Par88]   C.L. Paris. Tailoring object descriptions to a user's level of expertise. *Computational Linguistics*, 14(3):64–78, 1988.

[Pec91]   J. Peckham. Speech understanding and dialogue over the tele-
            phone: An overview of progress in the SUNDIAL project. In
            *Proceedings of the 2nd European Conference on Speech Commu-
            nication and Technology*, pages 1469–1472, 1991.

[Per90]   C.R. Perrault. An application of default logic to speech act theory.
            In P.R. Cohen, J. Morgan, and M.E. Pollack, editors, *Intentions
            in Communication*, pages 161–185. MIT Press, Cambridge, Mass.,
            1990.

[PN89]   A. Paeseler and H. Ney. Continuous-speech recognition using a
            stochastic language model. In *ICASSP-89*, pages 719–722, 1989.

[Pol86]   M.E. Pollack. A model of plan inference that distinguishes be-
            tween the beliefs of actors and observers. In *Proceedings of the
            24th Annual Meeting of the Association for Computational Lin-
            guistics*, pages 207–214, 1986.

[Pol90]   M.E. Pollack. Plans as complex mental attitudes. In P.R. Cohen,
            J. Morgan, and M.E. Pollack, editors, *Intentions in Communica-
            tion*, pages 77–103. MIT Press, Cambridge, Mass., 1990.

[Pow79]   R. Power. The organisation of purposeful dialogues. *Linguistics*,
            17:107–151, 1979.

[PR90]   M.E. Pollack and M. Ringuette. Introducing the Tileworld:
            Experimentally evaluating agent architectures. In *Proceedings,
            Eighth National Conference on Artificial Intelligence*, pages 183–
            189, 1990.

[PS87]   F.C.N. Pereira and S.M. Shieber. *Prolog and Natural Language
            Analysis*. CSLI, Stanford, CA, 1987.

[QDF88]   A. Quilici, M. Dyer, and M. Flowers. Recognizing and respond-
            ing to plan-oriented misconceptions. *Computational Linguistics*,
            14(3):38–51, 1988.

[Ram89]   L. Ramshaw. A metaplan model for problem-solving discourse.
            In *Proceedings of the Fourth Conference of the European Chapter
            of the Association for Computational Linguistics*, pages 35–42,
            1989.

[Ram91]   L. Ramshaw. A three-level model for plan exploration. In *Pro-
            ceedings of the 29th Annual Meeting of the Association for Com-
            putational Linguistics*, pages 39–46, 1991.

[Rei80]   R. Reiter. A logic for default reasoning. *Artificial Intelligence*,
            13:81–132, 1980.

[Rei85]   R. Reichman. *Getting Computers to Talk Like You and Me*. MIT Press, Cambridge, Mass., 1985.

[RPP+90]   M.J. Russell, K.M. Ponting, S.M. Peeling, S.R. Browning, J.S. Bridle, and R.K. Moore. The ARM continuous speech recognition system. In *ICASSP-90*, pages 69–72, 1990.

[Sad90]   J.M. Sadock. Comments on Vanderveken and on Cohen and Levesque. In P.R. Cohen, J. Morgan, and M.E. Pollack, editors, *Intentions in Communication*, pages 257–270. MIT Press, Cambridge, Mass., 1990.

[SC88]   M.H. Sarner and S. Carberry. A new strategy for providing definitions in task-oriented dialogues. In *Proceedings of the International Conference on Computational Linguistics*, pages 567–572, 1988.

[Sea75]   J.R. Searle. Indirect speech acts. In P. Cole and J.L. Morgan, editors, *Syntax and Semantics, Vol. 3: Speech Acts*, pages 59–82. Academic Press, New York, 1975.

[Sea90]   J.R. Searle. Collective intentions and actions. In P.R. Cohen, J. Morgan, and M.E. Pollack, editors, *Intentions in Communication*, pages 401–415. MIT Press, Cambridge, Mass., 1990.

[Sen92]   S. Seneff. TINA: A natural language system for spoken language applications. *Computational Linguistics*, pages 61–86, March 1992.

[SHB92]   R.W. Smith, D.R. Hipp, and A.W. Biermann. A dialog control algorithm and its performance. In *Proceedings of the 3rd Conference on Applied Natural Language Processing*, pages 9–16, 1992.

[SI81]   C.L. Sidner and D.J. Israel. Recognizing intended meaning and speakers' plans. In *Proceedings, International Joint Conference on Artificial Intelligence*, pages 203–208, 1981.

[Smi87]   R.W. Smith. The use of physical and mental information by a natural language generator in assisting users with locating objects. Master's thesis, Duke University, 1987.

[Smi88]   R.W. Smith. Providing natural language assistance in locating objects: A general model for information selection and generation. In *Proceedings of the First International Conference on Industrial & Engineering Applications of Artificial Intelligence & Expert Systems*, pages 922–930. ACM Press, 1988.

[Smi91]   R.W. Smith. *A Computational Model of Expectation-Driven Mixed-Initiative Dialog Processing*. PhD thesis, Duke University, 1991.

[Sow84]   J.F. Sowa. *Conceptual Structures: Information Processing in Mind and Machine*. Addison Wesley, Reading, Mass., 1984.

[TBD89]   H. Trost, E. Buchberger, and G. Dorffner. An expert advising system with acoustic output. *SIGART*, (109):33–35, July 1989.

[TH92]   D.R. Traum and E.A. Hinkelman. Conversation acts in task-oriented spoken dialogue. *Computational Intelligence*, 8(3):575–599, 1992.

[Tho90]   R.H. Thomason. Accomodation, meaning, and implicature: Interdisciplinary foundations for pragmatics. In P.R. Cohen, J. Morgan, and M.E. Pollack, editors, *Intentions in Communication*, pages 325–363. MIT Press, Cambridge, Mass., 1990.

[Wal78]   D.E. Walker, editor. *Understanding Spoken Language*. North-Holland, New York, 1978.

[War91]   W. Ward. Understanding spontaneous speech: The phoenix system. In *ICASSP-91*, pages 365–367, 1991.

[WCL+88]   R. Wilensky, D.N. Chin, M. Luria, J. Martin, J. Mayfield, and D. Wu. The Berkeley UNIX consultant project. *Computational Linguistics*, 14(4):35–84, 1988.

[Web88]   B.L. Webber. Tense as discourse anaphor. *Computational Linguistics*, 14(2):61–73, 1988.

[WF74]   R.A. Wagner and M.J. Fischer. The string-to-string correction problem. *Journal of the Association for Computing Machinery*, 21:168–173, 1974.

[Wil84]   D.E. Wilkins. Domain-independent planning: Representation and plan generation. *Artificial Intelligence*, 12:269–301, April 1984.

[Woo70]   W.A. Woods. Transition network grammars for natural language analysis. *Communications of the ACM*, pages 591–606, 1970.

[WS81]   R.M. Weischedel and N.K. Sondheimer. Meta-rules as a basis for processing ill-formed input. *American Journal of Computational Linguistics*, 9(3–4):161–177, 1981.

[WS88]   S. Whittaker and P. Stenton. Cues and control in expert-client dialogues. In *Proceedings of the 26th Annual Meeting of the Association for Computational Linguistics*, pages 123–130, 1988.

[WW90]   M. Walker and S Whittaker. Mixed initiative in dialogue: An investigation into discourse segmentation. In *Proceedings of the 28th Annual Meeting of the Association for Computational Linguistics*, pages 70–78, 1990.

[YHW+89]   S.R. Young, A.G. Hauptmann, W.H. Ward, E.T. Smith, and P. Werner. High level knowledge sources in usable speech recognition systems. *Communications of the ACM*, pages 183–194, February 1989. See also [YHW+90].

[YHW+90]   S.R. Young, A.G. Hauptmann, W.H. Wood, E.T. Smith, and P. Werner. High level knowledge sources in usable speech recognition systems. In A. Waibel and K.F. Lee, editors, *Readings in Speech Recognition*, pages 538–549. Morgan Kaufman, San Mateo, CA, 1990. See also [YHW+89].

[YP89]   S.J. Young and C.E. Proctor. The design and implementation of dialogue control in voice operated database inquiry systems. *Computer Speech and Language*, 3:329–353, 1989.

[ZGG+90]   V. Zue, J. Glass, D. Goodine, M. Phillips, and S. Seneff. The SUMMIT speech recognition system: Phonological modelling and lexical access. In *ICASSP-90*, pages 49–52, 1990.

[ZM93]   I. Zukerman and R. McConachy. Generating concise discourse that addresses a user's inferences. In *Proceedings, Thirteenth International Joint Conference on Artificial Intelligence*, pages 1202–1207, 1993.

Index